WITHDRAWN

The Early Masters
of
English Fiction

The Early Masters
of
English Fiction

by

Alan Dugald McKillop

UNIVERSITY OF KANSAS PRESS - - LAWRENCE, 1956

TO BETTY'S CHILDREN

ALAN AND PAMELA

Preface

The present work has been planned as a brief critical and historical survey of the major works of the principal British novelists in the half century extending from the publication of *Robinson Crusoe* to the publication of *Humphry Clinker*. We are here on familiar ground, but perhaps we can still gain something by considering the contributions of Defoe, Richardson, Fielding, Smollett, and Sterne in perspective. Eighteenth century studies have progressed to a point where these writers no longer require rediscovery or apology; they are unquestionably *les cinq grands* of their field and time, yet we may readjust views, redistribute emphasis, and attain a more complete understanding. We are in a position to read these novelists in the light of their age, and also in the light of the heightened consciousness of the theory of prose fiction which is characteristic of our own time. Far from inviting condescension or mere tolerance, these five masters stand up well under such scrutiny and represent a great tradition which may too easily be taken for granted.

The past generation has gone far toward providing the essential biographical studies for all these men. I have drawn on Cross for Fielding and Sterne, on Knapp, Kahrl, and Martz for Smollett, on Sale, Downs, and Dottin, together with my own previous work, for Richardson, on Moore's numerous contributions for Defoe, together with those of Dottin, Secord, and Sutherland. This brief list falls far short of adequacy, nor can I frame even an approximate statement of the use I have made of other biographical and critical contributions.

Gladly and gratefully I make other acknowledgments. My profound thanks are due to certain libraries—the Fondren Library of the Rice Institute, where I have worked from year to year, the Widener Library at Harvard, the British Museum, and, for the final stage of the project, the Newberry Library. The Editor of the University of Kansas Press has been unstinting in his helpful suggestions for revision and his incessant attention to all the details of publication. Professor George Sherburn may not agree with everything I say, but his *obiter dicta* have helped me more than he realizes. During my visits to Cambridge I have enjoyed the friendly counsel of Professor H. E. Rollins, though he has never tried to indoctrinate me about these novelists. For the inestimable aid of my wife from first to last, no sentence or paragraph in a preface could possibly suffice.

It is a pleasure to make specific acknowledgments of permission to use certain materials—to the Committee on Publications of the Rice Institute for allowing me to incorporate part of my essay on Richardson's epistolary technique from the *Rice Institute Pamphlet*, XXXVIII (1951), to the *Comité de Rédaction* of *Études Anglaises* for authorizing similar use of my essay on Sterne from that periodical, VII (1954), to the Huntington Library for an extract from one of Richardson's letters, and to the *Yale Review* for a long passage from Fielding's important letter to Richardson, copyright by the Yale University Press. The portraits of Richardson, Smollett, and Sterne are reproduced by permission of the National Portrait Gallery, London.

Alan Dugald McKillop

The Rice Institute
August 5, 1955

Contents

Illustrations

I

Daniel Defoe

I

DEFOE'S CONTRIBUTION to fiction has never been fully analyzed, interpreted, or even identified. Deceptively simple though it may appear at first sight, it must be construed in terms of his own experiences, interests, and activities, and also in terms of current forms of popular writing and the state of the literary market. Views of Defoe as a man and as a representative of a social group can both help and hinder a just view of Defoe as a novelist.

We never tire of calling Defoe middle-class, meaning that he was committed to the attitudes of Protestant dissent and to the utilitarian morality of the tradesman. Such attitudes appear to many modern readers oppressive to the free spirit, and we must reckon with this antagonism in trying to get a just estimate of Defoe and Richardson. If middle-class fiction looks toward the upper classes it may be accused of being either servile or excessively critical of the aristocratic way of life; if it looks toward crime and sexual offence or error, it may be accused of taking a hypocritical interest in such themes; and if it centers on the approved standards of the bourgeoisie it may be accused of being excessively conventional and complacent. The advice by Robinson Crusoe's father to his wayward son will be remembered:

Peace and plenty were the handmaids of a middle fortune; . . . temperance, moderation, quietness, health, society, all agreeable diversions, and all desirable pleasures, were the blessings attending the middle station of life; . . . this way men went silently and smoothly through the world, and comfortably out of it, not embarrassed with the labours of the hands or of the head, not sold to the life of slavery for daily bread, or harassed with perplexed circumstances, which rob the soul of peace, and the body of rest; not enraged with the passion of envy, or secret burning lust of ambition for great things; but in easy circumstances sliding gently through the world, and sensibly tasting the sweets of living, without the bitter, feeling that they are happy, and learning by every day's experience to know it more sensibly.[1]

In somewhat similar vein, Benjamin Hoadly once remarked, "It may be truly said of this *middle* State, That it doth not, by its natural Tendency, so much endanger Virtue, as either of the Two Extremes, of *Riches,* or *Poverty.*"[2]

Though this is a common eighteenth century choice of life, it befits a solid citizen in a suburban retreat rather than a man with his way to make. In the actual world peace and security are unattainable and indeed unnatural. "The Tradesman that is a thriving, managing, diligent Man, is full of Vigour, full of Vivacity, always stirring and bustling, never idle, never sottish; his Head and his Heart are employ'd; he moves with a kind of Velocity, unknown to other Men."[3] Or as the English merchant says to Robinson Crusoe in Bengal: "The whole world is in motion, rolling round and round; all the creatures of God, heavenly bodies and earthly, are busy and diligent; why should we be idle?" (II, 211) Here we come close to Daniel Defoe the businessman, projector, bankrupt, economist, social reformer, traveler, pamphleteeer, journalist, and novelist. He might have had his portrait painted with a hive of bees in the background to symbolize industry. He reserves special scorn for a "Nothing-Doing Wretch" like Roxana's first husband, an incompetent brewer, and assumes that the real option is between idleness and overt activity for immediate gain.

Defoe thus limits his field by leaving out of consideration the manifold varieties and uses of leisure. *The Life and Adventures of Mr. Duncan Campbell* (1720), though not entirely Defoe's own work, makes an interesting distinction here: "But there are two very distinct sorts of idleness, and two very different kinds of recreations; there is a shameful idleness which is no better than downright sloth; and there is a splendid kind of indolence, where a man, having taken an aversion to the wearisomeness of a business which properly belongs to him, neglects not, however, to employ his thoughts, when they are vacant from what they ought more chiefly to be about, in other

THE EARLY MASTERS OF ENGLISH FICTION

matters not entirely unprofitable in life, the exercise of which he finds he can follow with more abundant ease and satisfaction" (IV, 146). This "splendid kind of indolence" is further described thus: "His genius led him to a very gallant way of life; in his lodgings, in his entertainments, in paying and receiving visits, in coffee-houses, in taverns, in fencing-schools, in balls, and other public assemblies, in all ways, in fine, both at home and abroad, Duncan Campbell was a well-comported and civil gentleman; he was a man of pleasure, and nothing of the man of business appeared about him" (IV, 147). The life of the man of pleasure is a standard theme for eighteenth century drama and novel and conduct literature; Defoe avoids it almost entirely in his prose fiction. Even within the field of gainful activity, he does not concentrate on what we may call the eighteenth century success story, the sequence from apprentice to tradesman to great merchant to country gentleman. He accepted the pattern, as did Samuel Richardson after him, but neither novelist stays with the tradesman in his shop, in what we may call the middle stratum of the middle class. A close treatment of the urban middle class is less common in eighteenth century fiction than one might expect. Attention is usually concentrated on the lower or the upper levels, on those who are struggling to maintain a foothold of respectability, or on those near the top who can vie with the gentry. As to the upper levels, when Defoe's adventuress in high life, Roxana, is getting advice from Sir Robert Clayton, she reports: "Sir Robert and I agreed exactly in our notions of a merchant; Sir Robert said, and I found it to be true, that a true-bred merchant is the best gentleman in the nation; that in knowledge, in manners, in judgment of things, the merchant outdid many of the nobility; that having once mastered the world, and being above the demand of business, though no real estate, they were then superior to most gentlemen, even in estate" (XII, 193).

But "the dignity of trade in England" is not the subject of Defoe's fiction, though he discusses it at length, as we might expect, in *The Complete English Tradesman* and *The Com-*

pleat English Gentleman. He emphasizes the hazards rather than the sure gains, and starts with the man who has his fortune to make or to retrieve. "Will any Man say a Tradesman is safe from Disaster?" "Trade is like a Rolling Sea, that sometimes one Wave washes a Man over Board, the next returning Surge washes him on Board again."[4] Defoe's favorite figure of the dangerous ocean of trade reminds us that the tradesman or projector has something in common with the adventurer or outcast who is the central figure of the novels. We see the themes converging in Defoe's account of the bankrupt tradesman who is trying to retrieve his fortunes: "He may be truly said to walk after he is (civilly) dead; for he revives when the very Name of him is, as it were, buried and forgotten; if he is in this Part of the Globe or in another, 'Tis all one; his Hand or Head is always at Work, or perhaps both; he rolls about the World like a Snowball, always gathering more, always increasing, till he comes to a Magnitude sufficient to exist of himself."[5] Though Defoe goes on to say that recovery by fraud or knavery is like resorting to rapine and piracy, we can see how fortune and necessity may force a man into a twilight zone between right and wrong.

The projects of the enterpriser or adventurer will almost necessarily violate a strict moral and religious code which the commentator must nevertheless apply as best he can. It was impossible to stretch the code to cover the projects. An archetypal middle-class Protestant has been described by Weber, Tawney, and others, as a tradesman who believes that a Christian man of business is by virtue of his very Christianity not only diligent in but exclusively devoted to economic gain. In real life this view was not held in a stark and simple form unmodified by traditional Christian scruples, and in any case it applied to a "calling," a settled way of life, rather than to wildcat "projects." Mandeville, on the other hand, proclaimed a basic conflict between the profit motive and Christian ethics; there is an absolute standard of disinterested virtue, and nothing else deserves the name of virtue; but this standard can never

THE EARLY MASTERS OF ENGLISH FICTION

be maintained in the rough-and-tumble business of making a living, nor could the social and economic world in which we move continue to exist on such terms. Defoe accepts to a certain extent the Mandevillian opposition between self-interest and virtue, but in some of his more important works of fiction he softens the "paradox of trade and morality" by substituting for it a "paradox of adventure and morality," and this is one of the keys, though not the only key, to the careers of some of his fictional characters, Crusoe, Singleton, Moll Flanders, and Colonel Jacque.[6]

The modern student, who likes to begin with the author's own views and intentions, feels handicapped here by the absence of professed literary purpose. At best there is in Defoe's comments on fiction a grudging admission that feigned narrative may both teach and delight. It is startling to find a master of prose fiction, after he has done great work in that kind, discussing the subject in such a way as this:

> The Dispute began about the Reading or not Reading Romances, or fictitious Stories: They were both, as well Brother as Sister, against the reading them as a Diversion, there being no possible Pleasure in reading a Story which we know to be false, but related as if it were a Truth: But the Sister would have it to be, that it was not fit they should be read at all; nay, that it was a Sin; and that, as the making and writing them was criminal in itself, being, as she explained it, what the Scripture meant by *making a Lye;* so no pretended Use that might be made of it, could justify the Action: And that, if the writing or publishing a Romance, was a Lye; so, of Consequence, the reading it, that is to say, the reading it as a Diversion, or with Delight, must be the same.

> The Brother argued, That, as the End and Use of every Fable was in the Moral; so a Fiction, or what they call'd a Romance, told only with Design to deceive the Reader, bring him to believe, that the Fact related was true, and so to please and delight him with a Falshood instead of a History, must be what she had call'd it, criminal and wicked, and *making a Lye;* being done with a Design to deceive, and was made still more so, by how much it was more or less design'd to deceive prejudicially, and to the Hurt of the Person, as particularly when it was calculated to recommend Vice, discourage Virtue, debauch the Ears and Minds of Youth, raise loose and vain Conceptions of Things in the Thoughts, and the like.

> But on the contrary, when the Moral of the Tale is duly annex'd, and the End directed right, wherein it evidently accords; the enforcing sound Truths, making just and solid Impressions on the Mind; recommending great and good Actions, raising Sentiments of Virtue in the Soul, and filling the Mind with Just Resentments against wicked Actions

of all Kinds: He insisted then, and in such Cases, Fables, feigned Histories, invented Tales, and even such as we call *Romances,* have always been allow'd as the most pungent Way of writing or speaking; the most apt to make Impressions upon the Mind, and open the Door to the just Inferences and Improvement which was to be made of them. . . .

The Brother went a great Way farther in that Part of his Discourse, but lest they should seem too large in his Allowance of Romances in General; he forget [*sic*] not, however, to make a kind of Proviso at the End of his Discourse, against approving of such Fables and Romances as are usually the Product of the present Age, having no such moral or justifiable End attending them; and to recommend to his Sister the bringing her Taste of Things to such a Perfection, that she might be apt to judge of Truth, and receive due Impressions of Wisdom and Knowledge, tho' not dress'd up with far-fetch'd Allusions, Allegories, and invented Stories to enforce them; and to this Purpose, he gave her the just Characters of several fabulous Writings, which were much in Vogue in the Town, and also of their Writers.[7]

This of course is not Defoe's actual opinion of feigned narrative, but the severe attitude which it was deemed proper for the moralist to assume. From first to last didactic emphasis and the claim to literal truth were fixed upon Defoe. "And indeed, I cannot but own 'tis just, that if I tell a Story in Print for a Truth which proves otherwise, unless I, at the same time, give proper Caution to the Reader, by owning the Uncertainty of my Knowledge in the matter of fact, 'tis I impose upon the World; my Relater is innocent, and the Lye is my own. . . . I am sensible, that the want of this Caution is the Foundation of that great Misfortune we have in matters of ancient History; in which the Impudence, the Ribaldry, the empty Flourishes, the little Regard to Truth, and the Fondness of telling a strange Story, has dwindled a great many valuable Pieces of ancient History into meer Romance."[8]

As a writer of fictitious narrative he gets into the predicament of one of his own characters; it is difficult to reconcile natural self-interested action with the moral law. This austere view drives free invention and manipulation under cover and is intolerant of diversion and playfulness. It separates Defoe from that part of the picaresque tradition which admits of roguery as a diverting spectacle. Thus he introduces his pamphlet on Jonathan Wild (1725) by saying: "The following tract does not indeed make a jest of his story as [other accounts] do, or present

THE EARLY MASTERS OF ENGLISH FICTION

his history, which indeed is a tragedy of itself, in a style of mockery and ridicule, but in a method agreeable to the fact. They that had rather have a falsehood to laugh at than a true account of things to inform them, had best buy the fiction, and leave the history to those who know how to distinguish good from evil" (XVI, 236). A professed interest in practical moral reform and literal truth carried with it a professed hostility to elegance of style and lightness of touch:

The *Tattler* and *Spectator,* that happy Favourite of the Times, has pleas'd you all; indeed you were asham'd not to be pleas'd with so much Beauty, Strength, and Clearness; so much Wit, so Gentlemanly Reproofs, and such neat Touches at the vulgar Errors of the Times: But alas! Are we to be laugh'd out of our Follies? Will we be rally'd out of our dear Brutallity? Our Vices are too deep Rooted to be Weeded out with a light Hand; the soft Touches, the fineness of a clean Turn, nay, the keenest Satyr dress'd up in, and couch'd under gentle and genteel Expressions, has no effect here; that Gentleman that has all the Art of pleasing, may yet complain of the few Converts he has made, considering the Expence of Wit that he has laid out upon them. Experience tells us, this is not the Way the Temper of this rough and unpolish'd Nation is to be dealt with.[9]

Although the "Advice from the Scandalous Club" or "Little Review" is an important step in the development of the essay-periodical, Defoe considers the provision of entertainment a diversion from his main purpose. When the *British Apollo,* a question-and-answer periodical intended for polite amusement, began to appear, he commented: "The Answering of Questions, and particularly the wild Fancies of our amorous mad Men, is a Thing I have declin'd of late, and it seems a new Oracle for those Delusions is erected; I am sure, I do not at all envy them the Employment."[10] The essayist-observer has too serious a job to sport with human follies; he should set directly about improving morals or at least purveying useful information. In recommending historical and geographical studies he later remarked, "No romances, playes, or diverting storyes can be equally entertaining to a man of sence."[11] Thus Defoe consistently slights fiction as entertainment, nor is he from the first disposed, as Bunyan was, to undertake a long feigned narrative even when pointed to didactic ends.

This limitation of literary purpose goes with a professed unpretentiousness of style. As a "plain dealer" Defoe will have it that he avoids studied language. "As to language, I have been rather careful to make it speak English suitable to the manner of the story than to dress it up with exactness of style, choosing rather to have it free and familiar, according to the nature of essays, than to strain at a perfection of language which I rather wish for than pretend to be master of."[12] Of his journalistic style he remarks a little later: "When I am upon the Subject of Trade, and the Variety of Casual Story, I think my self a little loose from the Bonds of Cadence and Perfections of Stile, and satisfie my self in my Study to be explicit, easie, free, and very plain; and for all the rest, *Nec Careo, nec Curo*."[13] For this plain style he claims moral superiority, "since honesty shows the most beautiful, when artifice is dismissed, and she is honestly seen by her own light only,"[14] a superiority which is at the same time practical and aesthetic: "Easy, plain, and familiar language is the beauty of speech in general, and is the excellency of all writing, on whatever subject, or to whatever persons they are we write or speak."[15]

It will be noticed that in the first two references given above Defoe uses the word "story" to mean not "narrative" but "discussion," "account," or "report," somewhat as the word is now used in American journalism. He does not share our interest in the isolation and exact analysis of narrative intent. His way is to cite detail in support of an argument or moral, and it is hard to say when the detail becomes feigned narrative. Of the years before *Crusoe,* Professor Trent remarks, "The elements of which good fiction is composed had been, as it were, assembling themselves in his work."[16] And to somewhat the same effect, Professor John Robert Moore: "There is in Defoe no clear line of demarcation of literary methods or forms; history, fiction, moral tract, and economic treatise often run into the same mold."[17] Thus there is not much point in sorting out Defoe's narrative details mechanically as true or "invented." If we talk too much about Defoe as a fabricator of detail we simply

THE EARLY MASTERS OF ENGLISH FICTION

continue the critical discussion in the inadequate terms used by his contemporaries, as in the familiar remark in *Read's Journal* about the "little Art he is truly master of, of forging a Story, and imposing it on the World for Truth, . . . with all the little embellishments of Lies that are contriv'd to set it off."[18] As far as fiction is concerned, the congruity of details with respect to the larger end is more important than the origin, even more important than the interesting fact that many a naïve reader has taken *Robinson Crusoe* to be a true story. Elsewhere Professor Moore writes: "Defoe slipped into [historical fiction] imperceptibly by his imaginative insight into situations and events. He could not discuss an abstract subject for long without illustrating it by anecdotes and specific examples; he could not fairly complete a narrative without dramatizing part of it. sometimes assigning the speeches and even supplying stage directions as for a play."[19] Defoe's use of his material is so independent that we cannot claim exclusive and decisive influence of literary models, though we may say that he follows travel books, treatises on topography and trade, military memoirs, sociological tracts, domestic conduct-books, criminal biographies, collections of remarkable providences and other supernatural events. Professor Moore rightly adds Defoe's own observation and wide range of experience as an essential part of the great mass of material which he used for his various purposes.[20] Secord's important findings are in general accordance with these views in tending to put the entire content of Defoe's fictions on the same footing: the novelist's usual method is not to put invented incident into settings drawn from reading and observation, but to derive both setting and incident largely from his sources.[21] The process might be called compilation and recombination rather than fabrication.

A decisive step marking the difference between compilation and fiction is taken when the accumulated detail is related to the intention, interest, and point of view of a character impersonated by the author. But impersonation in Defoe is frequently connected with editorial writing or argument rather than with circumstantial narrative; the Highflying Tory from whose assumed point of view *The Shortest Way with the Dissenters* was written is an impersonation and so to some extent a character-creation, though the ironical intention makes this a special case. The simplest or minimum form of impersonation consists in providing a reporter or narrator who may appropriately give the details in his own way. This is a natural mode of journalism, and admits considerable variety of intention: Trent notes that during the second decade of the century Defoe wrote on various occasions like a Quaker, a Turk, a second-sighted Highlander, and "a Scots gentleman in the Swedish service."[22] We then proceed in the great fictions to the stage at which the impersonated reporter tells how he was forced to deal with pressing circumstances affecting his own survival or success; the interplay between the impersonated character and the circumstances gets us into a kind of circle, with each giving significance to the other. Even at this advanced stage of Defoe's art, the deliberating and discussing of policies and plans by the characters, the elaborate weighing of pros and cons, as in conference or committee, carries over into the long narratives a method typical of the pamphlets, in which we hear the writer asking incessantly and persistently, "In the light of these considerations and circumstances, what shall we do?"

Defoe always liked to present an instance, a circumstance, a situation, and to call for appropriate action. In the novels the reader is asked to participate in the narrator's call for action. In simple reporting the required action may be no more than belief, but it may be added that in the literature of edification in which Defoe's youth was nurtured simple belief could be very important. A classic case is *A True Relation of the Apparition of One Mrs. Veal* (1706). It has long been known that this famous narrative is not a fabrication of Defoe's, but his report of a story already in circulation about people well known in Canterbury and Dover. Moreover, though a good ghost story may well be its own excuse for being, Professor Coleman Parsons has recently pointed out that "apparition evidence" was

THE EARLY MASTERS OF ENGLISH FICTION

an important part of the Christian's arsenal against infidelity, and that collections of such stories were already in vogue.[23] More generally, *Mrs. Veal* represents a familiar type of anecdote or *exemplum*, with names, dates, and places given, used to enforce religious teachings and serving at the same time as scientific instance and as sensational episode. Bunyan's *Mr. Badman* and other less notable books are studded with such anecdotes. John Dunton a little later tried to make such material the staple content of a periodical called the *Christian's Magazine* (1713). Writers in this tradition naturally use strong examples or extreme cases and profess an invincible regard for truth. Defoe's own *Storm* (1704) cites "remarkable Deliverances" and "great Preservations." This concern with Providence and notable judgments is particularly prominent in the earlier of the famous novels, and dominates *Robinson Crusoe* and *A Journal of the Plague Year*. The primitive use of the illustrative anecdote or instance in the religious treatise persists in later works such as Defoe's *Essay on the History and Reality of Apparitions* (1727). *Mrs. Veal* is unique in restraint of presentation; we do not have here a melodramatic ghost, as in so many pieces of spectral evidence. The reports of the witnesses largely speak for themselves, reënforced by the unpretentious colloquial style which helps to attest their honesty. The narrator as reporter of testimony, not yet isolated and individualized, attains a credibility which will later stand the adventurer as narrator in good stead.

The collections of *exempla* may be assigned a special place in the immediate background of Defoe's narratives; they gave him a license to gather curious matter of widely varied interest, and, in the name of morals and religion, to indulge a natural bent for compilation. The *exempla* were used for edification by clergymen and devout laymen, and they also provided interesting and sensational matter for the general reader. At the end of the seventeenth century such works as the following would be within easy reach:

Samuel Clarke, A Mirrour or Looking-Glasse both for Saints, and Sinners, Held forth in about two thousand Examples: Wherein is presented, as Gods wonderful Mercies to the one, so his severe Judgments against the other. 1646. Fourth edition, 1671. (Title taken from second edition, 1654.)

"Richard Burton" [Nathaniel Crouch], Wonderful Prodigies of Judgment and Mercy, Discovered in Above Three Hundred Memorable Histories. 1681. Many later editions. (Title taken from 1685 edition.)

Increase Mather, An Essay for the Recording of Illustrious Providences. Wherein an Account is given of many Remarkable and very Memorable Events, which have happened in this last Age; especially in *New-England*. Boston, 1684.

William Turner, A Compleat History of the Most Remarkable Providences, both of Judgment and Mercy, Which have Hapned in this Present Age. 1697.

In this group, Mather's work has received most attention, especially in connection with the themes of science and witchcraft.[24] The whole group deserves consideration. Turner's compilation, published by John Dunton, shows how the "Judgment and Mercy" formula could be applied to a great variety of matter. The work is "recommended as useful to Ministers in Furnishing Topicks of Reproof and Exhortation, and to Private Christians for their Closets and Families." The range of material is comparable to Defoe's—judgments on evildoers, spectral evidence and witchcraft, sea-dangers and deliverances, "Prediction by Impulse" or "inward Motion"—the last a theme which assumes great importance for Defoe. It may be remarked that even Henry Fielding at the height of his career as novelist and magistrate was capable of relatively crude work of this kind, *Examples of the Interposition of Providence in the Detection and Punishment of Murder* (1752). Although the *exempla* do not contribute full impersonation, they affect both the content and the attitude of the narrator in the biographical record that constitutes the form of Defoe's longer works of fiction. It is not that a single instance is expanded by Defoe, as a relatively simple situation is expanded in the fiction of Richardson; it is rather that Defoe builds up a sequence of instances of the same general tone and kind.

To sum up in general terms, then, we may derive Defoe's fiction from the fact, circumstance, or episode, interesting in its own right and connected with a larger end. This larger end is (1) the illustration of moral and religious truth as stated in the relatively crude style of popular homiletics; (2) the self-interest, survival, or success, of the impersonated central character. Both (1) and (2) give rise to reflection and comment, moral and practical, and also to a conflict between these two veins of reflection. But elaboration of this comment is limited in Defoe's best work by his resolute attachment to specific circumstance and situation, set forth on the simple plan of having some one tell of his own "life and errors."

During the period of the *Review* (1705-13) Defoe treated political, social, and economic themes in which his mastery of detail was used for exposition, argument, and propaganda rather than for the presentation of the individual whose point of view is dramatized. Mr. Review and the members of the Scandalous Club are not made into characters like the Bickerstaff family in the *Tatler* and the Club in the *Spectator*. The impersonations are not notable. Although dialogue had become a standard form for political journalism, the use of dialogue in the *Review* does not show a marked increase of vitality. We have already noted that Defoe turned aside from the possibilities offered by the lighter aspects of the essay-periodical. Of his work in the last years of the *Review* and immediately thereafter, Trent writes: "In some of the tracts written between 1710 and 1714, notably in the two parts of *The Secret History of the October Club*, he had shown great ability in satiric portraiture and considerable skill in reporting speeches and dialogue."[25] Yet there is little narrative in the *Review* itself.

More directly important for Defoe's approach to the novel is *The Family Instructor* (1715, 1718). In extended dialogue with interspersed commentary, Defoe dwells on the obligations of masters to look after the religious welfare of servants and apprentices, and the obligations of parents to look after the religious welfare of their children, that is, to make them follow a rigorous program of religious observance. At this point Richardson was to start twenty years later, with the middle class London world of trade and family life, and with a particular concern for the morals of apprentices and servant-girls. But such matters as the "relative duties," even when presented in dialogue form, do not lend themselves to Defoe's absorbing interest in "variety of casual story," and the fairly complicated social relationships do not lead him naturally to center the story about a single point of view. The central situations would be good for three or four volumes of Richardson. For example, the father who has determined to put his family on a strict religious regimen appears to his children to be a tyrant, and the daughter in particular opposes him with some justification. The sullen and dogged spirit of Richardson's Harlowe family is foreshadowed. *The Family Instructor* is in two parts: "Relating I. To Family Breaches, and their Obstructing Religious Duties. II. To the great Mistake of Mixing the Passions in the Managing and Correcting of Children. With a great Variety of Cases, relating to setting ill Examples to Children and Servants." Richardson's *Clarissa* is described on the title-page as a history "comprehending the most Important Concerns of Private Life. And particularly shewing, the Distresses that may attend the Misconduct both of Parents and Children, in Relation to Marriage." "Family breaches" lead to a conflict of wills and a deadlock which is argued out, but not in Defoe to the intricate emotional dialectic of Richardson. Defoe had already shown in *An Essay on Projects* that he was concerned with the position of women in society: "I cannot think that God Almighty ever made them so delicate, so glorious creatures, and furnished them with such charms, so agreeable and so delightful to mankind, with souls capable of the same accomplishments with men, and all to be only stewards of our houses, cooks, and slaves."[26] Such feminism could lead Richardson from the heavy moralizing of the conduct-book to the heroines and drawing rooms of *Grandison*, but Defoe does not move in this direction. Like Richardson, however, he professed to be setting forth moral lessons by a new method, making concessions to the popular desire for entertainment:

The way I have taken for this, is entirely new, and at first perhaps it may appear something odd, and the method may be contemned; but let such blame their own more irregular tempers; that must have everything

14   THE EARLY MASTERS OF ENGLISH FICTION

turned into new models; must be touched with novelty, and have their fancies humoured with the dress of a thing; so that if it be what has been said over and over a thousand times, yet if it has but a different coloured coat, or a new feather in its cap, it pleases and wins upon them; whereas the same truths written in the divinest style in the world, would be flat, stale, and unpleasant without it.

If then, after all the pains which have been taken by ministerial labour and instruction, and by the pressing exhortations and moving arguments of eminent divines, even of all opinions, in their writings on this subject, this mean and familiar method should by its novelty prevail, this will be a happy undertaking, and at the same time be no reproach at all to the labours of others.[27]

The Family Instructor was highly successful in its century, and Defoe continued this kind of work with *Religious Courtship* (1722) and *A New Family Instructor* (1727). *Religious Courtship* comes closer to Richardson by connecting the question of religious principles with the choice of a husband, and by centering more exclusively on a single group of characters. Defoe calls these works "Historical Discourses" or "Historical Dialogues," which, he goes on to say, "have a very taking Elegancy in them, and the Story being handed forward in short Periods, and quick Returns, makes the retaining it in the Mind the easier, and the Impression the more lasting as well as delightful."[28] The first edition and two other issues of *A New Family Instructor* and the first edition of *Religious Courtship* (in part) have now been traced to Richardson's press, so that, as Professor Sale comments, "speculation about [Richardson's] possible knowledge of Puritan family literature need not remain so highly conjectural."[29]

The employment of dialogue among members of a family for the religious, ethical, and social discussions of the conduct-books was already well established; in these works Defoe, like Richardson in his volume of familiar letters, adopts and extends a device already in use. But the letter-form meant more to Richardson than the dialogue-form meant to Defoe. The total impact of his themes and interests kept him from concentrating intensively on dialogue put to the larger uses of expressing character and conveying a complex social situation. His dialogues, whether in set dramatic form or woven into the text, are colloquial, repetitious, sometimes extensive, but are kept subordinate to a policy or a moral. The dialogue, like the graphic anecdote, continues to crop up in many of his later works, whether narrative or not. An anthologist could exhibit excellent dialogues of various lengths from works published in the single year 1727—*The Complete English Tradesman, A System of Magick, An Essay on the History and Reality of Apparitions, A Treatise Concerning the Use and Abuse of the Marriage Bed.* The last work abounds in Richardsonian situations, often presented in brief narratives and dialogues, and among many other matters argues against "clandestine or forced marriages." But when it comes to protracted fictitious narrative, adventures and projects have the right of way in Defoe, and limit the use he is disposed to make of auxiliary forms and devices like the dialogue, the letter, and the informal essay.

II

Following the second part of *The Family Instructor* came the great series of works of fiction on which the attention of the general reader will always be concentrated—*Robinson Crusoe* (1719-20), *Memoirs of a Cavalier* (1720), *Captain Singleton* (1720), *Moll Flanders* (1722), *A Journal of the Plague Year* (1722), *Colonel Jacque* (1722), *The Fortunate Mistress,* usually known as *Roxana* (1724). To Defoe and his contemporaries this most memorable chapter in his career seems to have appeared as a mere variant of his extensive labors in journalism and pamphleteering; there is no adequate recognition of a remarkable mutation, no critical excitement about the appearance of a "new way" or "new species" of writing such as attended the first major novels of Richardson and Fielding.

Each one of these works is in autobiographical form; Defoe creates a character and assumes the role. It may be well to begin with "H. F.," the London saddler who records his experiences during the Plague, since he offers a very simple case of impersonation and is very close in status and point of view to Defoe himself. His professed purpose is to tell his fellow citizens what an outbreak of the plague is like, and what to do if the plague should come again, and to this end he subordinates his own personality:

> I have set this particular down so fully, because I know not but it may be of moment to those who come after me, if they come to be brought to the same distress, and to the same manner of making their choice; and therefore I desire this account may pass with them rather for a direction to themselves to act by than a history of my actings, seeing it may not be of one farthing value to them to note what became of me. (IX, 9)
> I come back to my three men. Their story has a moral in every part of it, and their whole conduct, and that of some whom they joined with, is a pattern for all poor men to follow, or women either, if ever such a time comes again; and if there was no other end in recording it, I think this a very just one, whether my account be exactly according to fact or no. (IX, 140)

The *Journal* could profess to be practical and timely; the appearance of the plague at Marseilles was calling forth much literature on the subject. The citizen's concern with ways and means is brought to a dramatic height, and the commonplace streets and houses of London become a tragic scene. Though Defoe uses numerous authentic sources, the work is a hasty and inaccurate compilation if considered as history.[30]

But apart from literal veracity, the *Journal* draws power from the deep-rooted memories of the populace. Defoe might remember something of the Plague, and he had always heard his elders talk about it. H. F., though a moderate Churchman, no doubt takes the attitude toward the Plague that prevailed among the Dissenters in Defoe's early years. As he tries to decide what to do, he considers "particular providences" and seeks to interpret them as signs of God's will. Thus the story is closely connected with the *exempla,* the cautionary tales to show the workings of Providence; the godly citizen might well believe that the wicked London of the Restoration deserved to be smitten in this way. "The immediate finger of God" may work by natural means: "Among these causes and effects, this of the secret conveyance of infection, imperceptible and unavoidable, is more than sufficient to execute the fierceness of Divine vengeance, without putting it upon supernaturals and miracle"

(IX, 223) . And yet "nothing but the immediate finger of God, nothing but omnipotent power," could have stopped the Plague. Defoe's other work on the subject, *Due Preparations for the Plague,* published a little earlier in 1722, shows characters discussing their religious attitudes in time of plague at great length, in the set dialogue of the literature of edification. H. F. tells us that he also retired at times and wrote religious meditations, which he does not intend to publish, but the *Journal,* he says, is based on the "memorandum" of his "observations without doors." Details are not presented according to a chronological or logical plan; the apparently random sequence heightens the immediacy and vividness of the record—another example of how Defoe's apparently deliberate reduction or simplification of method produces what seems to be a cunningly devised effect. The subject itself prescribes unity of place and tone.

The *Journal* is full of Defoe's interest in economics and statistics, but is likewise suffused with an intense feeling for physical actuality; there are the bills of mortality and there are also the ghastly burial carts and the great pit in the churchyard at Aldgate. The narrative is steeped in atmosphere to a degree unusual in Defoe, or rather we may say the subject provides its own atmosphere. Blazing stars or comets appear, and strange prophecies circulate; the people are filled with superstitious dread, and ghosts are visible in open day. There is the palpable present horror and also the vague terror: the Pie Tavern episode, with a ribald group of fellows jeering at the mourners (IX, 73-79) , invites comparison with the plague scene at the opening of Chaucer's Pardoner's Tale. The *Journal* is a book of London, a book of the community, but carries man at a stroke from the temporal to the eternal; the same conception comes through to our time in the pages of Camus' *La Peste.* Within the framework of the great metropolis and its crowded life there is the solitude created by the coming of death: "Passing through Tokenhouse Yard, in Lothbury, of a sudden a casement violently opened just over my head, and a woman gave three frightful screeches, and then cried, 'Oh! death, death, death!' in a most inimitable tone, and which struck me with horror and a chillness in my very blood. There was nobody to be seen in the whole street, neither did any other window open, for people had no curiosity now in any case, nor could anybody help one another, so I went on to pass into Bell Alley" (IX, 92). The horrors of plague time had been vividly presented before, as in Dekker's pamphlets, but H. F. is of essential value in giving tone and perspective, and his very limitations lend strength to his report.

A Journal of the Plague Year has been considered first in the hope that, in spite of its exceptional qualities, its method will help to make clear the status and character of the protagonist in Defoe's other long narratives. The essential step is the assumption of a role that fits Defoe's utilitarian and objective approach. This does not mean that the reader is expected to approve all the actions of the adventurer, the pirate, the pickpocket, or the prostitute; but that, beyond the intrinsic interest of the report as such, he always finds common ground with the principal character in an underlying inclination to accept a current social, moral, and religious code. Arranged in a kind of scale are the various objectives,—merely surviving or getting by, energetic action for its own sake, the winning of social approval, saving one's soul by doing the will of God. At the bottom of the scale, human nature being what it is, Defoe sometimes feels that necessity knows no law: "I am of the opinion that I could state a circumstance in which there is not one man in the world would be honest. Necessity is above the power of human nature, and for Providence to suffer a man to fall into that necessity is to suffer him to sin, because nature is not furnished with power to defend itself, nor is grace itself able to fortify the mind against it."[31] This is an extreme statement; it gives the right of way to the irresistible pressures of modern naturalism. What could a street boy like Colonel Jacque do except become a thief? What chance did society give Moll Flanders? Both still have the rudiments of a conscience, as well as some desire to conform to an approved social ideal, but their needs override their scruples. And once they get into the game, they play it with all their might. The Defoe character is driven to an incessant quest for advantage which, as we have noticed, may be described in the idiom of trade. And the means to an end, when steadily pursued, itself becomes an end: *"Gain* is the Tradesman's Life, 'tis the Essence of his Being, as a qualified Tradesman. Convenience, and the Supply of necessary Things for Life, were the first Causes indeed of Trade; but the Reason and End of the Tradesman is to get Money: 'Tis the Pole-Star and Guide, the Aim and Design of all his Motions; 'tis the Center and Point to which all his Actions tend; 'tis the Soul of Business, the Spur of Industry, the Wheel that turns within all the Wheels of his whole Business, and gives Motion to all the rest."[32] The quest for gain gives Defoe's central characters a dogged and consistent purpose kept within the limits of a practical program which is typical rather than idiosyncratic; they are not allowed to develop into "nonpareils" like Chaucer's, eminent and extreme examples of their kind with markedly individual peculiarities. At the same time, this profit motive is not identified with original sin, or on the other hand with the Puritan tradition of zeal in one's calling in the world, of which recent popular theories of the relation of Protestantism to capitalism have made so much. On the contrary, a Defoe character on the make illustrates the mixed nature of man; the profit motive is natural, and yet when pushed far enough it comes into conflict with accepted standards of morality and religion.

But the history of man in action cannot be fully written either in terms of deliberate self-interest or in terms of conformity to an established religious or ethical ideal. A man will choose a course and stick to it, he knows not why—out of sheer infatuation or perversity. Robinson Crusoe can say:

But my ill fate pushed me on now with an obstinacy that nothing could resist; and though I had several times loud calls from my reason and my more composed judgment to go home, yet I had no power to do it. I know not what to call this, nor will I urge that it is a secret overruling decree that hurries us on to be the instruments of our own destruction, even though it be before us, and that we rush upon it with our eyes open. Certainly nothing but some such decreed unavoidable misery attending,

THE EARLY MASTERS OF ENGLISH FICTION

and which it was impossible for me to escape, could have pushed me forward against the calm reasonings and persuasions of my most retired thoughts, and against two such visible instructions as I had met with in my first attempt. (I, 14)

This theological idiom describes man as the victim of irresistible passions and impulses that keep him headed in the wrong direction. If Defoe had concentrated on this theme he would have developed his own version of bourgeois tragedy; from such an "overruling decree" can be derived the opposition of Richardson's Lovelace and the Harlowes, or the career of Hardy's Michael Henchard. Defoe keeps the theme steadily in mind in *Robinson Crusoe;* his hero becomes a prosperous planter in Brazil, but gratuitously undertakes a wicked and ill-advised slaving expedition: "All these miscarriages were procured by my apparent obstinate adhering to my foolish inclination of wandering abroad, and pursuing that inclination in contradiction to the clearest views of doing myself good in a fair and plain pursuit of those prospects, and those measures of life, which Nature and Providence concurred to present me with, and to make my duty" (I, 41). Much of the time, of course, we see Crusoe merely following his "rambling designs." He does not always live in the presence of Fate or Providence, but some-times remarks in a matter-of-fact way that he cannot give good reasons for what he did:

I had no more business to go to the East Indies than a man at full liberty, and having committed no crime, has to go to the turnkey at Newgate and desire him to lock him up among the prisoners there and starve him (II, 183).
I will not say but that I might, by my loose and unhinged circum stances, be the fitter to embrace a proposal for trade, or indeed for any-thing else; whereas otherwise, trade was none of my element. However, I might, perhaps, say with some truth, that if trade was not my element, rambling was; and no proposal for seeing any part of the world which I never had seen before, could possibly come amiss to me (II, 211-12).

Among all these perverse or casual actions a premonition or warning often comes. The theme carries over from the life to the fiction, and Defoe tells us of himself: "I know a man who made it his rule always to obey these silent hints, and he has often declared to me that when he obeyed them he never miscarried; and if he neglected them, or went on contrary to them, he never succeeded."[33] The relative prominence of this theme in *Robinson Crusoe* again points to the underlying connection between Defoe's fiction and the literature of remarkable providences. These intimations help to give Defoe's world what depth it has. "Let no man despise the secret hints and notices of danger which sometimes are given him when he may think there is no possibility of its being real. That such hints and notices are given us, I believe few that have made any observations of things can deny; that they are certain discoveries of an invisible world, and a converse of spirits, we cannot doubt; and if the tendency of them seems to be to warn us of danger, why should we not suppose they are from some friendly agent, whether supreme, or inferior and subordinate, is not the question, and that they are given for our good?" (I, 279-80) Sometimes the question arises whether these obsessions and impulses are for good or for evil. When Crusoe was dogged by the desire to return to his island, his wife told him "she believed there was some secret powerful impulse of Providence upon me, which had determined me to go thither again" (II, 4). At first he does not accept this view, and tries to overcome his desire, but it masters him at last. He is almost "fey," as Scott might have said.

The influence of *Robinson Crusoe* has been so enormous as to be incalculable; it has spread everywhere like a folktale, or, if we prefer, a "myth." We can consider the book here only in some of its obvious connections with the history of prose fiction. Defoe's interest in episodes centering about material things, his utilitarianism, moralism, and religiosity, are now united with the travel and adventure pattern. There had been other stories of shipwrecked solitaries; Defoe's art makes the difference. Meager though Crusoe is, he gives the story its coherence and significance. The way of life on the island establishes a dominant pattern seldom to be found in Defoe. The situation makes Defoe substitute a tighter analysis of a situation for the loose travel and adventure formula, enables him to attain the range and variety of adventure within the compass

DANIEL DEFOE. Frontispiece of *A True Collection of the Writings of the True Born Englishman*. 1703.

SAMUEL RICHARDSON. Portrait by Joseph Highmore in the National Portrait Gallery, London.

of the strictly relevant. We may illustrate Defoe's plotting here by Ker's distinction between heroic epic and romance; the epic concentrates on "the defence of a narrow place against odds," whereas romance turns the hero loose to encounter what adventure may come.[34]

Even though Defoe does not use elaborate psychological notation, Crusoe's anxiety and anguish are vividly presented, and interest us more than his heavy piety.[35] His strongest feelings are translated into physical reactions; the James-Lange theory of emotion would be congenial to Defoe. "I ran about the shore, wringing my hands, and beating my head and face, exclaiming at my misery, and crying out, I was undone, undone" (I, 75). "I walked about on the shore, lifting up my hands, and my whole being, as I may say, wrapt up in the contemplation of my deliverance, making a thousand gestures and motions" (I, 50). A striking example is the description of his intense desire for companionship when he sees the wrecked vessel with no survivor: "Such were these earnest wishings, that but one man had been saved! 'O that it had been but one!' I believe I repeated the words, 'O that it had been but one!' a thousand times; and the desires were so moved by it, that when I spoke the words my hands would clinch together, and my fingers press the palms of my hands, that if I had any soft thing in my hand, it would have crushed it involuntarily; and my teeth in my head would strike together and set against one another so strong, that for some time I could not part them again."[36] The emphasis by simple repetition and concrete circumstance is characteristic. Eighteenth century writers inherited a tradition of rhetorical speech and gesture appropriate to strong emotions, and this formal grammar of the passions is regularly used by the novelists and their illustrators; but in such passages as this in Defoe, and more extensively in Richardson and Sterne, we can realize the importance of a tendency to use in place of these stock attitudes and expressions a more minutely particularized account of spontaneous mannerisms and gestures.

But the story deals with Crusoe's triumphs as well as his disasters.   On the island he has a unique opportunity to control the situation, to realize within natural limits and with comparative innocence man's desire for domination. "In the first place, I was removed from all the wickedness of the world here: I had neither the lust of the flesh, the lust of the eye, or the pride of life: I had nothing to covet, for I had all I was now capable of enjoying; I was lord of the whole manor, or, if I pleased, I might call myself king or emperor over the whole country which I had possession of; there were no rivals; I had no competitor, none to dispute sovereignty or command with me" (I, 142). This passage inspired the opening lines of Cowper's "Verses Supposed to Be Written by Alexander Selkirk," but Defoe does not like Cowper dwell chiefly on the tragedy of solitude. Nor is Defoe's emphasis the same as in Steele's account of Selkirk's story: "This plain man's story is a memorable example, that he is happiest who confines his wants to natural necessities."[37] Defoe is interested in giving priority to Crusoe's most pressing needs, and though he provides him with abundant supplies from the wreck, has him play the game largely without using these supplies. But the impulse is toward simplification, not toward primitivism. Crusoe and Defoe want as much civilized life as can be had under the conditions. This triumph on a modest scale in a simpler-than-real-life program is a principal reason for the story's universal appeal. There is some rudimentary treatment of social and political problems in Part II, when Crusoe tries to order things among the Spaniards, the savages, and the English, but this theme is not carried far, and Defoe does not make Crusoe a great colonizer or *entrepreneur*.

On or off the island, other characters count only as they help or hinder Crusoe. In Part I we have the good boy Xury, the famous Friday himself, and the Portuguese captain who manages Crusoe's Brazilian estates faithfully. But his obligations to the helpers do not go deep. Such timely aid is like finding money, but Defoe does not build upon it a world of comradeship and love. Robinson's experiences of himself and others do not transform his later career. The most notable example

THE EARLY MASTERS OF ENGLISH FICTION

of the helper is of course Friday, and Dickens could never forgive Defoe for burying him without a fitting tribute. Sheer utilitarianism can be in its way as offensive as the later excesses of sentimentalism. Yet Defoe's apparent insensibility is regularly moderated by decent human feeling, and at his best he can set up an unenthusiastic bond of sympathy that connects author, character, and reader. He understands plain practical people, and is endowed with a remarkable insight into primitive minds—the child, the savage, the poor and ignorant servant. Such intuitions sometimes remind us of another Anglo-Saxon exponent of the active life, Rudyard Kipling.

Robinson Crusoe was a "surprise" success, like Richardson's *Pamela* twenty years later. *The Life and Strange Surprizing Adventures of Robinson Crusoe* was published in April, 1719, and there were three more editions and at least two piracies in London before the end of the year, and another in Dublin. There was also a piratical abridgment by Thomas Cox, centering of course on the island story. Serial publication in the *Original London Post,* beginning in October, 1719, was another evidence of popularity, and the story was translated into French the next year. *The Farther Adventures of Robinson Crusoe; Being the Second and Last Part of his Life* appeared in August, 1719, with another edition before the end of the year. *Serious Reflections during the Life and Surprising Adventures of Robinson Crusoe: with His Vision of the Angelic World* (August, 1720), though of interest to students of Defoe's religious views, must have been a disappointment to booksellers and public.

Defoe proceeded by trial and error. Even within the wonderful years 1719-1724 it is impossible to arrange his major works of fiction in a sequence that will clearly show development by artistic self-discovery. To illustrate his characteristic point of view, I have discussed the *Plague Year* before *Crusoe.* But his output was so rapid and voluminous that he seems to be moving in several directions at once, to be reverting to old ways as well as to be advancing and experimenting. I leave out of account the *History of the Life and Adventures of Mr. Duncan*

Campbell (1720), since the style shows this work to be not wholly Defoe's. *The Life, Adventure, and Pyracies of the Famous Captain Singleton* (June, 1720) is somewhat akin to the extra-island part of *Robinson Crusoe;* Singleton seeks his fortune on the high seas and in undeveloped continents. Defoe presents the career of this hero in terms of his own interest in travel, overseas trade, and navigation, and also under the stimulus of his interest in piracy, which had been shown in his recent *King of Pirates; Being an Account of the Famous Enterprises of Captain Avery* (December, 1719). Like Colonel Jacque and Moll Flanders, Singleton is an outcast who has never had a fair chance. He is well disposed, eager to learn, and shows ability as a leader—an able youth accidentally gone wrong. His need of a helper is illustrated by a striking anecdote at the beginning of the story, much admired by Charles Lamb:

> The pilot of the ship, an old seaman, seeing me look very dull, came to me, and speaking broken English to me, told me I must be gone. "Whither must I go?" said I. "Where you will," said he, "home to your own country, if you will." "How must I go thither?" said I. "Why, have you no friend?" said he. "No," said I, "not in the world, but that dog," pointing to the ship's dog, (who, having stolen a piece of meat just before, had brought it close by me, and I had taken it from him, and ate it), "for he has been a good friend, and brought me my dinner."
> Well, well," says he, "you must have your dinner. Will you go with me?" "Yes," says I, "with all my heart." In short, the old pilot took me home with him, and used me tolerably well, though I fared hard enough (VI, 4-5).

Others cross his path,—a stray Englishman in the interior of Africa, and most important of all, the shrewd Quaker William Walters, who stands by him throughout his profitable career as a pirate. Defoe likes the canny William, "the dry gibing creature," and lets him talk at length; the dialogue expands in a way not usual for Defoe outside his conduct-books. William enforces the point that the only thing to do is to keep one's ill-gotten gains and use them for good purposes. Singleton has less inner life and is a less commanding figure than Crusoe; he is not overruled by fate or visited with premonitions, and we do not share his hopes and fears; the problem of ways and means on earth and in heaven is largely taken over by Quaker William.

Attention shifts from the adventurers to the adventures—especially the operations around Madagascar, the famous journey across Africa, and the career of piracy. Defoe was deeply interested in these subjects, but skilful compilation cannot do all, and the insertion of a long extract from one of his sources, Robert Knox's *Historical Relation of the Island Ceylon,* shows that the novelist is flagging.

Memoirs of a Cavalier is a notable addition to the 1720 group, and Trent finds here "some evolution in the art of writing fiction," since Defoe now deals with the past, though it would be easy to argue that the *Plague Year* is really better history. The *Memoirs* is dominated by Defoe's idea of history as standard informative and profitable fare for readers and writers. As in Scott's formula, the fictitious character whose point of view is maintained encounters historical situations and persons. But the Cavalier has no romantic ardor, though he shares Defoe's own admiration for Gustavus Adolphus, under whom he served on the Continent, and for the Parliamentary leader Fairfax, "this noble enemy." At the outset he was little better than a mercenary. "I confess, when I went into arms at the beginning of this war, I never troubled myself to examine sides: I was glad to hear the drums beat for soldiers, as if I had been a mere Swiss, that had not cared which side went up or down, so I had my pay. I went as eagerly and blindly about my business as the meanest wretch that 'listed in the army; nor had I the least compassionate thought for the miseries of my native country, till after the fight at Edgehill" (V, 134). His larger view is a concern for military methods and leadership, and an abiding conviction that a war is bound to be a complicated and irrational affair, full of mistakes. "But what signifies reason to the drum and the trumpet!" (V, 212) Defoe's moderation as he looks back on the wars of the last century reminds us somewhat of Scott, who will not allow his young heroes like Waverley and Morton to be fired too intensely by partisan zeal, and who enjoys a mercenary like Dugald Dalgetty. But the evocation of the past is far less vivid than in *The Plague Year,* and the mass of military detail here is not so interesting as the social and geographical detail that forms the basis of compilation in Defoe's most effective works. He may have had material on hand from the years before the heightened consciousness of fiction that began about 1719; much of the *Memoirs* is comparable to his *History of the Wars of his Present Majesty Charles XII* (1715), attributed to "a Scots Gentleman in the Swedish Service." The record of reprints indicates but little interest in the Cavalier during the rest of the century.

In *Moll Flanders* (January, 1722, dated 1721), above all the other works, Defoe combines his conception of character as brought out by immediate practical problems, his sense of social and economic reality, his selective and vivid presentation of detail significant for action, his application of a bourgeois success philosophy in a dangerous hinterland beyond the limits of respectability. Moll is a victim of society, showing the workings of economic and social compulsion; an unfortunate adventuress, showing the workings of chance and random circumstance; a cool exponent of self-interest, systematically trying to figure profit and loss in business, love, and crime. Though an outcast from the middle class, she carries many of its standards with her. A foundling at Colchester, she is educated above her station as a servant girl, and is lured into an illicit affair with the elder son of the family, and then honestly sought in marriage by the younger son. We begin somewhat on the level of the domestic conduct-books, with a Pamela-like situation which turns in the direction of scandalous incident. "He would have me, and I was not obliged to tell him that I was his brother's whore" (VII, 55). "Mrs. Betty," as she is called, cannot keep for long her aspirations to be a "little gentlewoman," and though after the death of this first husband she marries a gentleman-tradesman (the very term condemns him), with his bankruptcy she breaks away from respectability. Interest in money takes the place of the more intangible manifestations of pride and vanity. The later discovery that the Virginian planter she has married is her half-brother mars the narrative with the coarse incest motive that sometimes intrudes in early popular fiction. After six years more in England as another man's mistress she still longs for a "settled life." Her next lover is an Irish adventurer, and he and Moll get married under false expectations as to each other's fortune; but both meet the situation in a good-natured way, and even with something approaching disinterested attachment, or at least spontaneous sexual attraction. While he is off seeking his fortune—he really turns highwayman—she marries a staid citizen and until his death seems to be in a safe harbor. A new period begins when under the tutelage of an old midwife or "governess" she becomes a skilful pickpocket and shoplifter. The nickname "Moll Flanders," which she had apparently acquired before this, now becomes especially appropriate if we can take "Moll" as almost a generic name for a female criminal. The governess, who appears and reappears at various points, is one of the most remarkable instances in Defoe of the helper type of character. Moll has great success in her new calling, and becomes the greatest artist of her time, but she falls a prey to the infatuation that overtakes Defoe's protagonists, and will not leave off. Defoe here dwells on the methods of London thieves, and shows himself versed in the tricks of the town, pretending that he is putting honest citizens on guard against such wiles. Though London is not described at length, the physical presence of the city is intensely realized. Moll is finally caught, and faces destiny in some remarkable scenes in Newgate, but her repentance is not so convincing as her anguish at the thought of being caught, or her pervasive fear of being stranded without money. She would confirm Samuel Butler's dictum that money losses are the hardest of all to bear. With her highwayman-husband she is transported to Virginia, where she reëstablishes herself, and finally returns to lead a settled life in England. Fate, or the convention of a happy ending, has restored to her the most congenial of her numerous husbands.

The action has been summarized to show that much bizarre and sensational incident enters into the record, only to be leveled out by a monotonous evenness of emphasis. Moll reports everything from incest to the contents of a stolen bundle with a dead-pan attitude that may remind us of the strict neutrality of naturalism. She compiles data on her husbands as Defoe compiled statistics. This simplification of her attitude is more drastic and less natural than the enforced simplification of Crusoe's attitude on the island. Moll is craftier than Crusoe, and has less mysticism; she indulges in no religious meditations, and feels few secret promptings from guardian spirits, though at least once she seems to be in telepathic communication with her favorite husband. Common decency requires that she should swoon and weep on being reprieved, but her feelings are not elaborated. Yet natural humanity is not completely leveled out. Moll has promptings toward honesty and loyalty, and she can even fall in love in her way, but she feels that she cannot afford to indulge such impulses, though other things being equal she would rather have intelligence and virtue. " 'Tis something of relief even to be undone by a man of honour rather than by a scoundrel" (VII, 155). "I would gladly have turned my hand to any honest employment if I could have got it" (VIII, 5).

I was now a loose, unguided creature, and had no help, no assistance, no guide for my conduct; I knew what I aimed at, and what I wanted, but knew nothing how to pursue the end by direct means. I wanted to be placed in a settled state of living, and had I happened to meet with a sober, good husband, I should have been as true a wife to him as virtue itself could have formed. If I had been otherwise, the vice came in always at the door of necessity, not at the door of inclination; and I understood too well, by the want of it, what the value of a settled life was, to do anything to forfeit the felicity of it; nay, I should have made the better wife for all the difficulties I had passed through, by a great deal; nor did I in any of the times that I had been a wife give my husbands the least uneasiness on account of my behaviour. (VII, 131)

Crusoe is the victim of infatuation and wanderlust; he deliberately leaves the state of security that Moll is struggling to attain. Moll is more completely the prisoner of the immediate situation than Crusoe is even on the island. As a practical woman she has to consider the immediate future, but she does not take long views; she reports her own attitudes and calculations, but she does not look steadily within and struggle with a divided mind. Like the Wife of Bath, she has had five husbands, "withouten

THE EARLY MASTERS OF ENGLISH FICTION

oother compaignye in youthe," but she could never sum up her career with such reflections as these:

> But, Lord Crist! whan that it remembreth me
> Upon my yowthe, and on my jolitee,
> It tikleth me aboute myn herte roote.
> Unto this day it dooth myn herte boote
> That I have had my world as in my tyme.

Throughout her story she uses a stereotyped practical and moralistic style; Defoe's triumph is that he convinces us that it is her personal style. She is so completely occupied with explicit detail bearing on ways and means that she is not disposed to take the aesthetic attitude required to render fully the immediately experienced present, or the imaginative coloring of recollection and anticipation. It has recently been suggested that the moral inconsistencies in *Moll Flanders* and *Roxana* are due to the gap between the state of mind at the time of action and the state of mind at the time of record: that is, Moll and Roxana have repented at long last, and incongruously put their repentant attitude into their report of their original misdeeds.[38] The difficulty with this theory is that Defoe is not much interested in the time-span and the changes wrought by time; he is never keenly conscious of the double point of view involved when a character is talking about his own past. But it should be added that when Defoe is at his best the character at the time of the wicked action is not so oversimplified as to be unconvincing. The marvellous episode of the child's necklace may be quoted to show how Moll's colloquial style, weak compunctions, and ruthless purposes are fused into imaginative unity:

I went out now by daylight, and wandered about I knew not whither, and in search of I knew not what, when the devil put a snare in my way of a dreadful nature indeed, and such a one as I have never had before or since. Going through Aldersgate Street, there was a pretty little child had been at a dancing-school, and was agoing home all alone; and my prompter, like a true devil, set me upon this innocent creature. I talked to it, and it prattled to me again, and I took it by the hand, and led it along till I came to a paved alley that goes into Bartholemew Close, and I led it in there. The child said, that was not its way home. I said, "Yes, my dear, it is; I'll show you the way home." The child had a little necklace on of gold beads, and I had my eye upon that, and in the dark of the alley I stooped, pretending to mend the child's clog that was loose, and took off her necklace, and the child never felt it, and so led the child on again. Here, I say, the devil put me upon killing the child in the dark alley, that it might not cry, but the very thought frighted me so that I was ready to drop down; but I turned the child about and bade it go back again, for that was not its way home; the child said, so she would; and I went through into Bartholemew Close, and then turned round to another passage that goes into Long Lane, so away into Charterhouse Yard, and out into St. John's Street; then crossing into Smithfield, went down Chick Lane, and into Field Lane, to Holborn Bridge, when, mixing with the crowd of people usually passing there, it was not possible to have been found out; and thus I made my second sally into the world.

The thoughts of this booty put out all the thoughts of the first, and the reflections I had made wore quickly off; poverty hardened my heart, and my own necessities made me regardless of anything. The last affair left no great concern upon me, for as I did the poor child no harm, I only thought I had given the parents a just reproof for their negligence, in leaving the poor lamb to come home by itself, and it would teach them to take more care another time.

This string of beads was worth about £12 or £14. I suppose it might have been formerly the mother's, for it was too big for the child's wear, but that, perhaps, the vanity of the mother to have her child look fine at the dancing-school, had made her let the child wear it; and no doubt the child had a maid sent to take care of it, but she, like a careless jade, was taken up perhaps with some fellow that had met her, and so the poor baby wandered till it fell into my hands.

However, I did the child no harm; I did not so much as fright it, for I had a great many tender thoughts about me yet, and did nothing but what, as I may say, mere necessity drove me to.   (VII, 203-4)

The hypothetical matter about the parents and the maid is a striking example of the way Moll's mind works, and Defoe's.[39]

Moll's sexual escapades have always given the book a bad name; its immediate success (three editions in 1722, another edition and an abridgment in 1723) was no doubt due in large part to its supposed scandalous character. Defoe's full title shows how the book made its market: "The fortunes and misfortunes of the famous Moll Flanders &c. who was born in Newgate, and during a life of continu'd variety for three-score years, besides her childhood, was twelve years a whore, five times a wife (whereof once to her own brother) twelve years a thief, eight years a transported felon in Virginia, at last grew rich, liv'd honest, and died a penitent, written from her own memorandums." Chapbooks put the story within the reach of all, and it was supposed to corrupt the morals of the young. Hogarth's idle apprentice chooses to read *Moll Flanders* (perhaps a broad-side ballad version) rather than *The Apprentice's Guide*. As late as 1916 Professor Trent said that the full title was unprintable, and gave no extracts from *Moll Flanders* in his excellent book on Defoe. But here there is nothing to compare to the insistent emphasis on sex in Richardson and Sterne, to say nothing of the twentieth century. Moll may be *tout entière à sa proie attachée*, but not in the same sense as Venus. Like a good many other people, she is after all concerned with the social and economic pre-conditions for sexual union. She is too business-like to be either demure or lascivious, and she is so consistently on the make that she imposes strict limits on the range of Defoe's compilation. Here is Defoe's closest approach to deliberate realism according to a program, and it is this anticipation of the hard-boiled novelist of later times that gives the story its present high position. The reduction of the entire record to acquisition and calculation and the spiritual impoverishment implied in the practical and moral warnings that echo through the story operate on us with the effect of a marvellously constructed piece of art—no one could be so monolithic by accident. In the use of casual and apparently unstudied detail which always bears on the main point, even though given in a repetitious and colloquial style, Defoe has some advantage over the novelist of later times who professes to document fully and richly, and also over the fastidious artist who handles discriminated detail with a manifest intention to be poignant and precious and symbolic. Defoe's position is the stronger because he can never go on a walk with J. Alfred Prufrock. This is not to belittle later fiction with its collateral influences from poetry and science, but simply to assert that Defoe's apparent unstudied simplifications yield a result which justifies our crediting him with genuine artistic intent.

Closely associated with *Moll Flanders* is *Colonel Jacque* (published December, 1722, dated 1723). The full title of the story, inaccurate as regards the ending, suggests that the booksellers hoped to match the success of *Moll Flanders* by appealing to the interest in miscellaneous and somewhat scandalous adventures: "The History and Remarkable Life of the truly Honourable Colonel Jacque, commonly call'd Col. Jack; who was Born a Gentleman, put 'Prentice to a Pick Pocket, was Six and Twenty Years a Thief, and then Kidnapp'd to Virginia. Came back a Merchant; was Five times married to Four Whores; went into the Wars, behav'd bravely, got Preferment, was made Colonel of a Regiment, came over, and fled with the Chevalier, is still abroad compleating a Life of Wonders, and resolves to dye a General." The first part of the narrative is the best. Jack, as he was called, begins as a waif in the London streets, and his early experiences are unsurpassed in their kind in English fiction. Defoe does not let philanthropic intention and sentimental piety mar his realism; Jack, with a boy's natural eagerness, innocence, and curiosity, thinks of picking pockets as an apprenticeship to a trade, and wishes to return to his victims the valuable bills he can't use. Nothing could be more graphic or plausible than his embarrassment at having a large sum of money—shall he put it in his shoe, hide it in a tree, or what? The boy's point of view is presented unaffectedly: thus when he and his companions enjoy a good meal with stolen money the best part for them is that the servants keep saying, "Gentlemen, do you call?" In general, the treatment of childhood in eighteenth century fiction is perfunctory, or sentimental, or both. And if we go farther and compare the early part of *Colonel Jacque* with the account of Oliver Twist's life in the underworld, and the sentimental treatment of Oliver's natural goodness, we can realize more fully the fine quality of Defoe's work, even though he does not invest the slums with Dickens' strange enchantments. His action is imaginatively fused with his setting, and at this point he tops his success in the London low-life part of *Moll Flanders*. The rest of the story, including Jack's life as bondservant, overseer, and planter in Virginia, his military service, and his checkered matrimonial career, does not surpass work that Defoe had already done. The hero's moral improvement in America, his success on the plantation, and his long discussion of humane principles in the treatment of slaves, offer a variation of the self-help with reformation theme. He often represents the lighter side of Defoe's eagerness for experience: "I could not prevail with myself to live a private life: I had got a wandering kind of taste, and knowledge of things begat a desire of increasing it, and an exceeding delight I had in it, though I had nothing to do in the armies or in war, and did not design ever to meddle with it again; yet I could not live in the world and not inquire what was doing in it" (XI, 71). His restlessness and curiosity make him a wanderer, an observer, and a commentator, but we miss "the defence of a narrow place against odds," the impact of the obsession and infatuation of Crusoe and Moll.

With *Moll Flanders* it is also natural to compare *The Fortunate Mistress: or, a History of the Life and Vast Variety of Fortunes of Mademoiselle de Beleau, afterwards call'd the Countess de Wintselsheim, in Germany. Being the Person known by the name of the Lady Roxana, in the Time of King Charles II*. Like Moll, the heroine begins life in the middle class and marries a stupid tradesman, but, as the title shows, the story transposes vicious and mercenary intrigue to high life. There is an approximation to the *chronique scandaleuse*, the report of illicit amours among the fashionable and the aristocratic, the kind of thing that was being done by Mrs. Aubin and Mrs. Haywood. When Roxana deliberately chooses to be a mistress rather than a wife, or puts her own lover to bed with her maid Amy, we meet a degree of corruption which outruns Defoe's usual doctrine of unscrupulous self-help. In the veiled manner of the "secret history" it is hinted that the heroine became the mistress of Charles II—an anachronism, of course, since she came to England as a small child in 1683. The name Roxana and the story of her Turkish costume are drawn from Abel Boyer's translation of Anthony Hamilton's *Memoirs of Grammont* (1714). But Defoe is no heir of the Restoration. Roxana herself, in spite of her supposed French vivacity, is not a gay heroine, and is subject to the usual compunctions and compulsions. ["I confess I had strong natural aversions to the crime at first, partly owing to a virtuous education, and partly to a sense of religion; but the Devil, and that greater devil of poverty, prevailed" (XIII, 15-16).]She is eventually deprived of the economic argument for selling her virtue, for she becomes rich; but she still argues with some cogency that matrimony is a bad bargain for a woman of means, and takes what may be called an advanced feminist position. As she asks her Dutch merchant after he has helped her to escape from France to Holland, why should she sell her independence and buy a mere lodging for thirty thousand pounds? *Moll Flanders* and *Roxana* deal with matrimony and "whoredom" in terms of economic distress and advantage, but admit the possibility of a cordial and practical comradeship between man and woman, along with the struggle for money and sexual gratification.[40]

"Helper" characters are extensively used—Amy the maid, the honest Dutch merchant, and later a friendly Quakeress. In Amy this type of character rises to a level of almost primary interest. Vice and calculations of profit and loss can get dull, but Defoe never tires of Amy: "I might have interspersed this part of my story with a great many pleasant parts and discourses which happened between my maid Amy and I; but I omit them on account of my own story, which has been so extraordinary" (XII, 92). Amy's loyalty amounts to the kind of obsession found in Defoe's best pieces of characterization. Moreover, in looking after the interests of her mistress she makes up stories and devises intrigues, and thus widens the range of the narrative, producing in a small way an effect like that of the fabricated stories in the *Odyssey* or the elaborate deceptions of Richardson's Lovelace.

After her career in high life, Roxana returns with the help and protection of her Quakeress to the middle class, and we have a suggestion of the contrasting social settings which were to figure so largely in eighteenth century fiction. [She is now disposed to change her views and mend her morals, though she is not converted like Crusoe. "There was not the least hint in all this from what may be called religion or conscience, and far from anything of repentance" (XIII, 15). Something like remorse appears in the later part of the story, and Defoe describes it in emphatic stereotyped phrases—"a dart struck into the liver" or "a secret hell within" (XIII, 85), but it is really connected with fear of discovery. Roxana has married her Dutch merchant, but instead of enjoying her wealth in security and in duly repentant mood, she is driven to despair by the prolonged threat of discovery and exposure by her daughter, one of the children formerly disposed of by Amy. Later editions underwent extensive revision by other hands, and acquired more than one spurious conclusion, the most important a vigorous treatment of the drama of the reappearing daughter, which is broken off abruptly in Defoe's own version.[41] Apparently Defoe here builds up to and then shies away from a situation that would naturally force him to follow a tightly constructed story through to the end. What happens gives some support to the theory that he was at times an artist in spite of himself, or at least did not always have the leisure and inclination to work out problems imposed on him by the development of his story. But the persistence of the daughter gives a fine effect of merciless iteration, and Defoe goes some distance toward developing the method of incremental repetition later used by Richardson. For example, Roxana had already made much of the Turkish dress in which she had won the favor of the court, and which had given her her romantic nickname; the daughter tells the story over again, and Roxana's past assumes new significance. Defoe is probably getting into a tighter story than he had bargained for, but he can rise to the occasion and is capable of fine strokes like this: "I cannot help confessing what a reserve of pride still was left in me; and though I dreaded the sequel of the story, yet when she talked how handsome and how fine a lady this Roxana was, I could not help being pleased and tickled with it; and put in questions two or three times of how handsome she was; and was she really so fine a woman as they talked of; and the like, on purpose to hear her repeat what the people's opinion of me was, and how I had behaved" (XIII, 116-17). This is a real reversal of fortune for Amy and Roxana, but instead of going on to the full development of the catastrophe Defoe vaguely intimates that Amy made away with the daughter, and gives an abrupt and perfunctory biographical conclusion.

This last important situation is only the most striking instance in this story of a tendency to lay emphasis on the reappearance of characters and to work out the consequences of previous acts. Another unusual point is that scenes at which the principal character is not present are on a few occasions given at length.[42] The story moves closer to the later norm of the novel of manners. Yet the scandals and the technical novelties did not win for *Roxana* the popular success of *Moll Flanders,* and this work has in the long run been the most neglected of Defoe's major fictions, though the dramatic situation at the end attracted the special attention of William Godwin and Charles Lamb.

III

Defoe did not consolidate or extend his gains in prose fiction after 1724. His later fiction includes the tracts on criminals like Jack Sheppard and Jonathan Wild, the *General History of the Robberies and Murders of the Most Notorious Pirates* (1724), *The Four Years Voyages of Capt. George Roberts* (1726), *The Memoirs of an English Officer* or *Memoirs of Captain George Carleton* (1728), *Madagascar: or, Robert Drury's Journal* (1729), and other titles. The last three works named, if substantially Defoe's, represent his rewriting of a given body of material rather than creative recombination. Up to a certain point his work in fiction is stimulated by the tremendously wide range of his nonliterary interests, and then checked by the dispersal of his attention. Moreover, a limit is imposed on his experiments and attainments in prose fiction by his lack of interest in literary *genres* and his complete acceptance of the current situation in the literary market and the reading public. Demand at the pamphlet shops no doubt encouraged fictionalized

TOBIAS SMOLLETT. Portrait by an unknown artist (probably Italian) in the National Portrait Gallery, London.

LAURENCE STERNE. Portrait by an unknown artist in the
National Portrait Gallery, London.

biography and autobiography embodying success and failure, profit and loss, travel and amours, scandal in high life, crime in low life; current journalism perhaps encouraged him to include the plague, realistic social studies, and maritime and military affairs. But we cannot say that there is free transfer of topics of current interest; we do not get the life of coffeehouse and theater, of middle-class and upper-class families, of the English parish, nor does he give us a tale of bubbles, projects, and stock-jobbing, a theme that attracted his attention during the early twenties. No one could fairly demand that he should have innovated more than he did; the point to remember is that the strong conventional limitations on the content of fiction made all innovations in this field remarkable.

Throughout Defoe's fiction the position that the story is true is substantially maintained. He is always ready to trade on the supposed superiority of fact to fiction, as in the opening address of *The History of Jack Sheppard* (1724): "His history will astonish; and is not composed of fiction, fable, or stories placed at York, Rome, or Jamaica, but facts done at your door, facts unheard of, altogether new, incredible, and yet uncontestable" (XVI, 172). But for the implied theory of fiction it is important to note, first, that the story is sometimes said to be profitable and pleasant in itself, that is, without regard to authentication, and even modified, if not made up, to that end; and second, that the shadowy form of an editor, writer, or narrator, other than the principal character, almost always appears.

The admission of even the slightest fictitious element is regularly accompanied by strong claims that the story is substantially true, and unquestionably profitable and diverting. This seems to be the purport of the Preface of *Crusoe* Part I, and is stated more clearly in the Preface to Part II:

The Editor believes the thing to be a just history of fact; neither is there any appearance of fiction in it: and, however, thinks, because all such things are despatched, that the improvement of it, as well to the diversion as to the instruction of the reader, will be the same. And as such, he thinks, without farther compliment to the world, he does them a great service in the publication.[43]

The just application of every incident, the religious and useful inferences drawn from every part, are so many testimonies to the good design of making it public, and must legitimate all the part that may be called invention, or parable in the story.

The second part, if the Editor's opinion may pass, is (contrary to the usage of second parts) every way as entertaining as the first, contains as strange and surprising incidents, and as great a variety of them; nor is the application less serious and suitable, and doubtless will, to the sober as well as ingenious reader, be every way as profitable and diverting. (II, vii)

Such a position was natural in the current apologies for fiction. Thus the author of *The Compleat Mendicant: or, Unhappy Beggar* (1699) begins by saying that his story, consistent, natural, and familiar as it obviously is, can be considered as matter of fact, but even supposing that it is a well-contrived fable, "I can see no Reason, why the fabulous Life of a Vertuous Mendicant should not be as acceptable to the World as an *English* Rogue, a *Gusman Lazerillo,* or any other *Romantick* History of Villanous Tricks." Defoe restates much the same position in the Preface to *Colonel Jacque:* "If discouraging everything that is evil, and encouraging everything that is virtuous and good— I say, if these appear to be the whole scope and design of the publishing this story, no objection can lie against it; neither is it of the least moment to inquire, whether the Colonel hath told his own story true or not; if he has made it a History or a Parable, it will be equally useful, and capable of doing good" (X, xvi). The fiction, if fiction there be, is the Colonel's, and the story is either history or parable. It may be noted that the rewritten version of this Preface as in the fourth edition (1738) speaks of "moral Romance" instead of parable. It may be doubted whether Defoe would use the phrase "moral Romance." He never says that his principal characters are fictitious, but at most that they may deviate from truth in a substantially true narrative. The account of Rob Roy called *The Highland Rogue* (1723) is no longer admitted to the Defoe canon, so that the opening sentence of the Preface may be taken to be the words of some contemporary turning against Defoe his claim of authenticity: "It is not a romantic Tale that the Reader is here presented with, but a real History: Not the Adventures of a

Robinson Crusoe, a *Colonel Jack,* or a *Moll Flanders;* but the Actions of the *Highland Rogue;* a Man that has been too notorious to pass for a meer imaginary Person."

A basic assumption is that the principal character needed some help in getting recorded and published. In *Crusoe* an editor is supposed to provide the Prefaces, though no editorial work is described. The "I" of the Preface to *Moll Flanders* is an editor who has cleaned up Moll's language and in general put the story into new words. In *Roxana* there is an intermediate "writer" or "relater" who can vouch for the substantial truth of the story, though he wishes to avoid real names. "If we should be always obliged to name the persons, or not to relate the story, the consequence might be only this—that many a pleasant and delightful history would be buried in the dark, and the world deprived both of the pleasure and the profit of it" (XII, xiv). Defoe may here be taking advantage of the double game played by the *chronique scandaleuse,* which found an advantage in suggesting and then withholding complete identification of characters and circumstances. The relater is not expurgating the story, as in *Moll Flanders;* on the contrary, the story as Roxana herself told it was both diverting and instructive, and if there are any defects in the published narrative, "The relater says it must be from the defect of his performance, dressing up the story in worse clothes than the lady whose words he speaks, prepared for the world." The exact methods imputed to the assumed editor in *Moll Flanders* and the "relater" in *Roxana* remain in doubt. How far did they use documents? Did they interview the ladies? We are here within measurable distance of the "editor" who was soon to prepare Pamela's letters for publication. In Richardson the role is explicitly assumed; in Defoe it is rather vaguely suggested. Thus we find ourselves on the threshold of important developments in which the novelist may be at the same time the impersonator of feigned characters, the impersonator of the reporter of the actions of feigned characters, the impersonator of the editor of documents recording the action of feigned characters.

The development of these methods in practice ran far ahead of the novelist's discussion of his methods. Even Richardson, a mature artist, was reluctant to use the Preface which Bishop Warburton provided for *Clarissa* because it discussed the work as an outright work of fiction: "Will you, good Sir, allow me to mention, that I could wish that the *Air* of Genuiness [*sic*] had been kept up, tho' I want not the Letters to be *thought* genuine; only so far kept up, I mean, as that they should not prefatically be owned *not* to be genuine: and this for fear of weakening their Influence where any of them are aimed to be exemplary; as well as to avoid hurting that kind of Historical Faith which Fiction itself is generally read with, tho' we know it to be Fiction."[44] In the Preface to *Sir Charles Grandison* Richardson at first wrote of his three novels: "How such remarkable Collections of private Letters fell into [the Editor's] hands, he hopes the Reader will not think it very necessary to enquire." This conventional claim to documentation was dropped after the first edition. On the title-page of *Clarissa,* the words "Published by the Editor of Pamela" were dropped after the second edition (1749); and on the title-page of *Grandison* the words "Published from the Originals, By the Editor of Pamela and Clarissa" were dropped after the third edition (1754). In different ways and to different degrees Defoe and Richardson accept the booksellers' working idea that stories supposed to be true will be more readily approved and will sell better, so that a novelist will do well to screen himself behind what Richardson calls "the umbrage of an editor's character." With Fielding the situation is different. His narrator is still formally considered to be an historian or reporter rather than a deviser of feigned narrative. But the emphasis is now shifted from a claim to actuality to a claim to probability, particularly as regards the possibilities of human nature. "To say the truth, if the historian will confine himself to what really happened, and utterly reject any circumstance, which, though never so well attested, he must be well assured is false, he will sometimes fall into the marvellous, but never into the incredible. He will often raise the wonder and surprise of his reader, but never that incredulous hatred mentioned by Horace. It is by falling into fiction, therefore, that we generally offend against this rule, of deserting probability, which the historian seldom, if ever, quits, till he forsakes his character and commences a writer of romance." Historians of public events can produce the most extreme examples of virtue and vice, a Nero and a Caligula. "But we who deal in private character, who search into the most retired recesses, and draw forth examples of virtue and vice from holes and corners of the world, are in a more dangerous situation. As we have no public notoriety, no concurrent testimony, no records to support and corroborate what we deliver, it becomes us to keep within the limits not only of possibility, but of probability too."[45]

Yet Defoe does not move exactly in the direction of the later novel of manners. It is clear that Defoe's domestic conduct-books and Richardson's early work are close together, but the work of Richardson and Fielding is much more clearly influenced by contributory literary forms like the essay, the drama, and the model letter, and by contemporary ethical theory, and Richardson and Fielding deal much more systematically with the interrelations of social classes. Thus Defoe was in a sense without successors, and because of his dubious reputation as a journalist and political agent, and because he wrote much of low life, and professed to pay little attention to literary canons, his great popularity was in large part sub-literary. His success was discounted in such words as these: "If popular Applause were always a Proof of Merit, such ribald and impure Writers as Sir *Roger L'Estrange, Settle, Daniel De Foe,* and many of the same Class, are fixed on that Standard."[46] The following passage gives us the tone of much talk about Defoe's fiction in the 1720's:

The Age of Gallantry I observe seems to roll round again, for certainly Plays, Novels, and Romances were never more in Vogue than at this Juncture . . . . It must be confess'd, that it is very rueful to behold the Quill-Drivers of the present Age, so egregiously Triumphant over those of the Last, for now *Shakespear* and *Ben Johnson,* must give way to *Robinson Crusoe,* and Colonel *Jack,* as well as *Dryden* and *Otway* to *Moll Flanders* and *Sally Salisbury.* And I myself am terribly afraid that the Voyages and Adventures of Captain *Richard Falconer,* must in a short Period of Time strike to Sir *John Mandeville's* lying Travels, and Mademoiselle *Beleau's* unheard of Intrigues [*Roxana*].[47]

A passage in the *Dublin Journal* equates the new fiction with criminal biography: "Such are the fabulous Adventures and Memoirs of *Pirates, Whores,* and *Pickpockets,* wherewith for some time past the Press has so prodigiously swarmed. Your *Robinson Crusoe's, Moll Flanders's, Sally Salisbury's,* and *John Shephard's,* have afforded notable Instances how easy it is to gratify our Curiosity, and how indulgent we are to the *Biographers* of *Newgate,* who have been as greedily read by People of the better sort, as the Compilers of *Last Speeches* and *Dying Words* by the Rabble."[48] One would like to have more evidence about the currency of Defoe's fiction among "People of the better sort," but it does not appear to have amounted to critical acceptance. And unless there was critical support, great popular success in itself aroused suspicion and contempt: "However, it is certain, that the Sale of a Book chiefly depends on the Universality of the Subject, and that the most excellent do not meet with the greatest Success; and accordingly we find, that *Robinson Crusoe* sells quicker than *Locke* on Human Understanding, and the Beggar's Opera than the best Comedy: nay, is it not sufficiently known, that some have acquired Estates, by printing Tom Thumb, Riddles, Songs, Fables, the Pilgrim's Progress, and such like common Trumpery?"[49]

It is hard to analyze a bygone reading public: we can only speculate about various levels and attitudes and their interaction, about the relation between the persistence of popular traditions of a semi-literary or sub-literary kind, and the emergence and acceptance of great innovators who change the course of things. Bunyan and Defoe, writers of high quality and superb ability, tended for generations to be reabsorbed into the popular current. If a writer of no greater inherent ability than they, like Richardson, does actually appear to change the course of things immediately, it must be because he elicits sharper direct responses from the elite or self-conscious reading public. Meanwhile the great substratum of popular fiction remained com-

THE EARLY MASTERS OF ENGLISH FICTION

paratively inert and unprogressive. In illustration of these uncharted areas or depths we may quote an advertisement of 1736, offering "A Choice, Instructive, and very Entertaining Collection of memorable and genuine Histories." This long announcement at least shows the ingredients of popular appeal as one bookseller saw them only four years before *Pamela:*

This Collection, which is calculated for the Entertainment of all Sorts of Readers, will contain a far greater Variety of surprizing and remarkable Events than any Work yet extant; and the Tracts are generally vouched for true by the respective Authors. Besides many notable Instances of the ruinous Effects of Hatred, Lust, Envy, Avarice, Revenge, &c. with shining Examples of Chastity, Love, Fidelity, Constancy, Honour, Generosity, Fortitude, and their Contraries, it includes the detestable Lives, and deserved Punishments of a great Number of most notorious Murderers, Robbers, Thieves, Sharpers, &c. As also unexpected Sea-Deliverances, and strange Escapes from Slavery. As to the Rest; tho' the Bulk of this Work is to consist of Stories really Tragical, yet, for Variety Sake, such as are not so are not to be wholly excluded, but shall be here and there interspersed. Neither shall I so far confine myself to Foreign Histories, as absolutely to neglect inserting occasionally some of the Growth of our own Country; but always such as are far from being common. As very few, if any, of the Foreign Relations were written within a Century of Years, possibly some Phrases and Expressions may, by modern Critics, be thought to savour of the Times wherein they were penn'd. However, all convenient Care shall be taken to render the Narrative smooth, easy, and intelligible to every Capacity, without any affected Nicety of Stile. I must also animadvert, that the Foreign Authors I extract from commonly screen the unhappy Parties they treat of under fictitious or borrow'd Names, to avoid the Displeasure of their surviving Friends and Relatives: And consequently I am oblig'd to do the like in my Translations, tho' sometimes even the Places, nay, Countries, are so disguis'd, that the whole Story carries with it the Air of a Romance: However, this is not very frequent. It was likewise the Humour, or rather the Vice of those Times, to affect a prolix, sermonizing Way of telling a Tale; but I shall studiously omit all those tedious and tiresome Superfluities, sticking close to Facts only, and leaving my Readers at Liberty to make thereon what Reflections they think proper. Few Books can be more useful and necessary in Families than this Collection, it abounding with Morality, and directing Youth to the Love of Virtue, as also deterring them from vicious Courses, by very notable Examples.[50]

Here we are still at the level of the collections of *exempla* which Defoe could read in his early days.

If we consider the general situation from 1700 to 1740, we may be surprised that the middle-class novel of manners did not develop until a generation after the *Tatler* and the *Spectator*, or directly and immediately from the *Tatler* and the *Spectator*. We have discussed the limitations of the direct development from Defoe. The actual contributions of once favored forms of French romance must have been very limited indeed, although Professor Boyce has recently shown that such a contribution was possible.[51] In the interval between Defoe and Richardson a complete account would reckon with a new wave of influence from France in the works of Le Sage, Marivaux, and Prévost. These writers, by their sense of form and style, and by their systematic attention to dominant tone and calculated range of effect, undoubtedly helped to prepare the English reading public for the work of Richardson, Fielding, and Smollett. It is hard to determine exactly how far these French writers were approved and read in Great Britain; their influence on English novelists is also hard to assess, and appears much more clearly after than before the pioneering of Richardson and Fielding, but there can be little doubt that they wrought a rather rapid change in the climate of English fiction in the 1730's.

II

Samuel Richardson

I

On June 2, 1753, Samuel Richardson sent a long autobiographical letter to one of his admirers and translators on the Continent, the Reverend Johannes Stinstra of Harlingen. This letter is the only source of our knowledge of Richardson's early life, and is here reprinted in full.[1]

My Father was a very honest Man, descended of a Family of middling Note in ye County of Surry; but which having for several Generations a large Number of Children, the *not* large Possessions were split & divided; so that he & his Brothers were put to Trades; & the Sisters were married to Tradesmen. My Mother was also a good Woman, of a Family not ungenteel; but whose Father & Mother died in her Infancy within half an Hour of each other in the London Pestilence of 1665.

My Father's Business was that of a Joiner, then more distinct from that of a Carpenter, than now it is with us. He was a good Draughtsman, & understood Architecture. His Skill & Ingenuity, & an Understanding superior to his Business, with his remarkable Integrity of Heart & Manners, made him personally beloved by several Persons of Rank, among whom were the Duke of Monmouth & the first Earl of Shaftesbury; both so noted in our English History. Their known Favour for him, having, on the Duke's Attempt on the Crown, subjected him to be looked upon with a jealous Eye, notwithstanding he was noted for a quiet & inoffensive Man, he thought proper, on the Decollation of the first-named unhappy Nobleman, to quit his London Business & to retire to Derbyshire; tho' to his great Detriment; & there I, & three other Children out of Nine, were born.

He designed me for the Cloth. I was fond of this Choice: But while I was very young, some heavy Losses having disabled him from supporting me as genteelly as he wished in an Education proper for the Function, he left me to choose at the Age of 15 or 16, a Business; having been able to give me only common School-Learning: I chose that of a Printer, tho' a Stranger to it, as what I thought would gratify my Thirst after Reading. I served a diligent Seven Years to it, to a Master who grudged every Hour to me, that tended not to his Profit, even of those Times of Leisure & Diversion, which the Refractoriness of my Fellow-Servants *obliged* him to allow them, & were usually allowed by other Masters to their Apprentices. I stole from the Hours of Rest & Relaxation, my Reading Times for Improvement of my Mind; & being engaged in a Correspondence with a Gentleman greatly my superior in Degree, & of ample Fortunes, who, had he lived, intended high things for me; those were all the Opportunities I had in my Apprenticeship to carry it on. But this little Incident I may mention; I took Care, that even my Candle was of my own purchasing, that I might not in the most trifling Instance make my Master a Sufferer (& who used to call me the Pillar of his House) & not to disable myself by Watching or Sitting-up, to perform my Duty to him in the Day-time.

These, Sir, are little things to trouble you with: But my Circumstances were little, & your Enquiries are minute.

Multitudes of Letters passed between this Gentleman & me. He wrote well, was a Master of ye Epistolary Style: Our Subjects were various: But his Letters were mostly narrative, giving me an Account of his Proceedings, and what befell him in ye different Nations thro' which he travelled. I could from them, had I been at Liberty, & had I at that time thought of writing as I have since done, have drawn great Helps: But many Years ago, all ye Letters that passed between us, by a particular Desire of his (lest they should ever be published) were committed to the Flames.

I continued 5 or 6 years after ye Expiration of my Apprenticeship (Part of ye Time, as an Overseer of a Printing-House) working as a Compositor, & correcting ye Press: As I hinted, in a better Expectation. But *that* failing, I began for myself, married, & pursued Business with an Assiduity that, perhaps, has few Examples; & with ye more Alacrity, as I improved a Branch of it, that interfered not with any other Person; & made me more independent of Booksellers (tho' I did much Business for them) than any other Printer. Some of them even thought fit to seek me, rather than I them, because of the Readiness I shewed to oblige them, with writing Indexes, Prefaces, & sometimes, for their minor Authors, *honest* Dedications; abstracting, abridging, compiling, and giving my Opinion of Pieces offered them. I have been twice married; to good Women both times. My Business, Sir, has ever been my chief Concern. My Writing-time has been at such times of Leisure as have not interfered with that. From what I have written you will gather an Answer to your Question, "In what kind of Life I have been conversant from Youth?"

You complement me, Sir, in your next Question, with a Knowlege of the Manners of Mankind, & ask, Whence I attained this kindly-imputed Knowlege? I had greater Opportunities than I made use of, from the Correspondence I mentioned above. From my earliest Youth, I had a Love of Letter-writing. I was not Eleven Years old, when I wrote, spontaneously, a Letter to a Widow of near Fifty, who, pretending to a Zeal for Religion, & who was a constant Frequenter of Church Ordinances, was continually fomenting Quarrels & Disturbances, by Backbiting & Scandal, among all her Acquaintance. I collected from ye Scripture Texts that made against her. Assuming the Stile and Address of a Person in Years, I exhorted her; I expostulated with her. But my Handwriting was known: I was challenged with it, & owned ye Boldness; for she complained of it to my Mother with Tears. My Mother chid me for the Freedom taken by such a Boy with a Woman of her Years: But knowing that her Son was not of a pert or forward Nature, but, on y^e

contrary, shy & bashful, she commended my Principles, tho' she censured the Liberty taken.

As a bashful & not forward Boy, I was an early Favourite with all the young Women of Taste & Reading in the Neighbourhood. Half a Dozen of them when met to Work with their Needles, used, when they got a Book they liked, & thought I should, to borrow me to read to them; their Mothers sometimes with them; & both Mothers & Daughters used to be pleased with the Observations they put me upon making.

I was not more than Thirteen when three of these young Women, unknown to each other, having an high Opinion of my Taciturnity, revealed to me their Love Secrets, in order to induce me to give them Copies to write after, or correct, for Answers to their Lovers Letters: Nor did any one of them ever know, that I was the Secretary to the others. I have been directed to chide, & even repulse, when an Offence was either taken or given, at the very time that the Heart of the Chider or Repulser was open before me, overflowing with Esteem & Affection; & the fair Repulser dreading to be taken at her Word; directing *this* Word, or *that* Expression, to be softened or changed. One, highly gratified with her Lover's Fervor, & Vows of everlasting Love, has said, when I have asked her Direction; "I cannot tell you what to write; But (her Heart on her Lips) you cannot write too kindly:" All her Fear only, that she sh^d incurr Slight for her Kindness.

I recollect, that I was early noted for having Invention. I was not fond of Play, as other Boys: My Schoolfellows used to call me *Serious* and *Gravity:* And five of them particularly delighted to single me out, either for a Walk, or at their Fathers' Houses or at mine, to tell them Stories, as they phrased it. Some I told them from my Reading as true; others from my Head, as mere Invention; of which they would be most fond: & often were affected by them. One of them, particularly, I remember, was for putting me to write a History, as he called it, on the Model of Tommy Potts; I now forget what it was; only, that it was of a Servant-Man preferred by a fine young Lady (for his Goodness) to a Lord, who was a Libertine. All my Stories carried with them, I am bold to say, an useful Moral.

I am ashamed of these Puerilities: But thus, Sir, when I have been asked a like Question by others, to that you put, have I accounted for a kind of Talent; which I little thought of resuming; or thinking it worth while to resume. As a Proof of this, let me say, that when I had written the two first Vol^s. of Pamela, & was urged by a particular Friend to put it to the Press, I accepted of 20 Guineas for two Thirds of the Copy-Right; reserving to myself only one Third.

You ask, "If I had a Model before my Eyes, in some of my Pieces?" The Story of Pamela had some slight Foundation in Truth. Several Persons of Rank were guessed at, as having in my Mind sat for the two principal Characters in that Piece: But no one Conjecture came near the Truth; nor was it likely that it should; for I myself knew no more of the Story, than what I recollected a Gentleman told me of it Fifteen Years before I sat down to write it; & as it was related to him by an Innkeeper in the Neighbourhood of the happy Pair: & which Gentleman had been, at the Time, several Years dead.

The writing it then, was owing to ye following Occasion:—Two Book-

SAMUEL RICHARDSON

49

sellers, my particular Friends, entreated me to write for them a little Volume of Letters, in a common Style, on such Subjects as might be of Use to those Country Readers who were unable to indite for themselves. Will it be any Harm said I, in a Piece you want to be written so low, if we should instruct them how they should think & act in common Cases, as well as indite? They were the more urgent with me to begin the little Volume, for this Hint. I set about it, & in the Progress of it, writing two or three Letters to instruct handsome Girls, who were obliged to go out to Service, as we phrase it, how to avoid the Snares that might be laid against their Virtue; the above story recurred to my Thought: And hence sprung Pamela. This Volume of Letters is not worthy of your Perusal. I laid aside several Letters after I had written them as too high for the View of my two Friends. But I will send it to you.

I have been raillied on a warm Scene or two in Pamela, as well as for the Fire Scene in Clarissa, by a few of my Friends, Lovers of Virtue; & who, knowing that my Life from Youth upwards, had not been very censurable, wondered how I came by them. To such it has been answered for me, that there were Scenes of a quite contrary Nature, to those guilty ones, & Characters too, that might be no less the Subject of Wonder, my Situation in Life considered, & especially Female ones: But it may not misbecome me to assure my Reverend Friend Mr. Stinstra, that he may not from the Jewkes's, the Sinclair's, the Mr. B's, the Lovelaces, & others of both Sexes, of like Characters, be ashamed for his Correspondent, that I never, to my Knowlege, was in a vile House, or in Company with a lewd Woman, in my Life. So I have in Pamela described, with Approbation, a Masquerade Scene; yet never was present at one.

Clarissa is a Piece from first to last, that owes its Being to Invention. The History of my Good Man is also wholly so.

I have some little Pleasure, for the Sake of my Acquaintance & Friends, in being able to say, that no one of them can challenge either for Praise, or for Dispraise, his or her Picture in any of the three Pieces; for I am equally an Enemy to Flattery and personal Abuse. I have no Spleen to gratify, by the one, nor Interest to court by the other. Hence, Sir, you will not see a Dedicatory Epistle to one of the Histories; tho' I have the Honour of being esteemed by several Persons, who by their Rank & Fortunes, as well as Merits, would be a Reputation to any Work. I will be bold to say, that never Man of a small Fortune, & obscure Birth & Station, was more independent. God & my own Diligence were ever my chief Reliance. Pardon, Sir, the Boaster.

You ask, Whether any other Pieces than Pamela & Clarissa have been written by me? None, I think, worthy of your Notice. I have told you, Sir, that the little Volume of Letters, to which Pamela owes her Being, is not worthy of it. I was requested to revise the numerous editions of Aesop's Fables in English, & to give the Public one I would commend for Children. I will send you one of those: But as I have given some Account of it in the Preface, shall say nothing of it here; only that I choose not to set my Name to either of the little Volumes; nor indeed to any thing I have written. A few other little Things of the Pamphlet-kind I have written; all with a good Intention; But neither are they worthy of your Notice.

I have been engaged in Epistolary Correspondencies, chiefly with

Ladies. I am envied, Sir, for the Favour I stand in with near a Score of very admirable Women, some of them of Condition; all of them such as w^d. do Credit to their Sex, & to the Commonwealth of Letters, did not their Modesty with-hold them from appearing in it. Yet with several of them, I have charming Contentions, on different Parts of what I have written. Should I ever have the Pleasure to see you in England, I would shew you Volumes of Epistolary Correspondencies; And to these, as a very agreeable Amusement, when I have attended my good Man thro' the Press, I propose to confine my Pen, should Life be spared me any time. For, Sir, I am in an advanced Age; & have by too intense Application, fallen into Nervous Maladies: In short, am almost worn out, as to my Health; tho' I bless God, my Mind, at times when not too much oppressed by bodily Disorders, is not very sensible of Decay.

Only, I should say, that I intend to give to my good Pamela, my last Hand. I find I shall correct it much; but shall have a particular Regard to preserve the Simplicity of the Character.

I will not bespeak your Favour for my new Piece. I am sure you will approve of my *Intention* when you come to peruse it. There are some of my Friends, who speak very highly of what they have seen of it. But the Partiality of Friends must be allowed for. This only I will say, It is entirely new & unborrowed, even of myself; tho' I had written so voluminously before. It is said to abound with delicate Situations. I hope it does; for what indelicate ones can a good Man be involved in?—Yet he must have his Trials, his Perplexities—And to have them from good Women, will require some Management. In Clarissa, my Favourite Clarissa, there is a twofold Correspondence necessary, one between her and Miss Howe; the other between Lovelace and Belford. The Subject of one Letter arose often out of another. It was necessary it should. In the new Work (except one or two Letters of each of the Respondents, as I may call them) the Answers to the Letters of the *Narratist* are only supposed, & really sunk; yet Seven Volumes are, to my Regret, made of it, when I have scratched out the quantity of two, & should have been glad to have comprized the whole in Four—Whence you will judge that the unpublished Work, whether it will be thought equal or not, must have cost me most Pains: As indeed it has. But I designed it as my last Work; & as the completion of my whole Plan—If a Man may be allowed to say *Plan*, who never was regular enough to write by one; & who when he ended one Letter, hardly knew what his next would be.

Richardson was fifty years old when he changed the course of English fiction by writing and publishing *Pamela*. His career as apprentice, journeyman, and master printer helps to explain, though of course it does not explain completely, his career as an author, and has recently been closely studied.[2] The early Richardson seems so conventional, so industrious, and so docile that we are sometimes disposed to liken him to Francis Goodchild, Hogarth's industrious apprentice, or even to the subservient shopkeeper in Defoe's *Complete English Tradesman*. After his apprenticeship to John Wilde, he served, as he tells us, as "Overseer and Corrector" in an unidentified printing office until he set up for himself, and from about 1720 we find him established in Salisbury Court, Fleet Street, where he lived and worked for the rest of his long life. Within twenty years he had built up one of the largest and most prosperous printing businesses in London, doing work for many booksellers, and also printing some periodicals and numerous books brought out by subscription. An important part of his profits came from the official printing he did for the House of Commons. Later he was joint patentee in the office of Law Printer to His Majesty. Much of his printing was nonliterary, of course, but his work also brought him into contact with literary circles, and with writers such as Aaron Hill, James Thomson, and Edward Young. Evidently Richardson was not a projector like Defoe; he lacked Defoe's versatility and curiosity, and was much more of an introvert and a creature of habit.

From his routine work as a printer his earliest writing developed. The "Indexes, Prefaces," and *"honest* Dedications" to which he confesses can never be identified. The earliest known work from his pen is *The Apprentice's Vade Mecum: or, Young Man's Pocket Companion,* evidently published in 1733, though the only known copies are dated 1734.[3] Richardson, having written a letter of advice to his nephew on taking him apprentice in 1732, added to this piece enough material to make a little manual on the subject. The *Vade Mecum* is related to the sections of conduct-books which treat of the duties of servants; apprentices had come in for a good deal of attention in this literature. We are here very close to Defoe, whose domestic conduct-books, as has already been noticed, Richardson printed in part and no doubt endorsed. Along with the usual exhortations, the *Vade Mecum* goes on record about drama by censuring Restoration comedy, the popular pantomimes of the day, and the new theater in Goodman's Fields, and bestows memorable praise on Lillo's *London Merchant:* "I know but of one Instance, and that a very late one, where the Stage has condescended to make itself useful to the City-Youth, by a dreadful Example of the Artifices of a lewd Woman, and the Seduction of an unwary young Man; and it would savour too much of Partiality, not to mention it. I mean, the Play of *George Barnwell*, which has met with the Success that I think it well deserves; and I could be content to compound with the young City Gentry, that they should go to this Play once a Year, if they would condition, not to desire to go oftner, till another Play of an equally good Moral and Design were acted on the Stage" (p. 16). A kind of sequel to this little treatise is *A Seasonable Examination of the Pleas and Pretensions of the Proprietors of, and Subscribers to, Play-Houses, Erected in Defiance of the Royal Licence* (1735), in support of Sir John Barnard's bill for the regulation of the theaters, a pamphlet printed by and almost certainly written by Richardson.[4] It is also possible that a reference to the *Vade Mecum* and other details in the 1738 edition of Defoe's *Complete English Tradesman* point to Richardson's hand in the revision of this work, just as he certainly had a main hand at about this time in the revision of Defoe's *Tour thro' England and Wales*.

Richardson's early work as a didactic writer is extended in the volume of model letters whose origin he describes in the report to Stinstra. Miss Hornbeak has demonstrated the relation between this manual and the domestic conduct-books with great precision, and has shown how middle-class standards and prudential moralizing had long before appeared in the collections of model letters, so that Richardson's program of showing how to think and act was by no means a novelty.[5] It is clear that he was following the tendencies already shown in Henry Care's *Female Secretary* (1671), John Hill's *Secretary's Guide* (1687, and later editions), *The Experienc'd Secretary* (1699), and G.F.'s *Secretary's Guide* (1710, and later editions). All these share the intention to offer practical advice to plain or humble people, and are in conscious opposition to the rhetorical style of other manuals in what we may call the *Academy of Compliments* tradition. Meager as the artistic pretensions of these little bourgeois manuals are, they offered models for specific literary exercises in an approved anti-romantic and didactic vein. Richardson, working in this direction, added new topics "suggested to him . . . by various periodical essays, courtesy books, domestic conduct-books, apprentices' guides, and his own editorial activities."[6] He sustains the plain style more evenly. He evidently enjoyed the variety of characters and situations opened up to him by the letter formulary, and wrote longer and more numerous letters than his predecessors. He pays more attention to women and to love and courtship, as well as to the affairs of tradesmen and apprentices. He also goes beyond previous manuals in developing groups of letters which tell a continuous story, and he introduces various situations that could easily be developed further—the apprenticeship of William (I-VI), the courtship of Polly (XV-XXI), the marriage of Nancy (XXVIII-XXX), the poor tenant (CV-CVIII), the rivalry between a fop and a formal suitor (CLXI-CLXV), and several others. As we look at the possibilities here, and note the effective plain style and the view of homely actuality in the manner of Defoe and Franklin, we may wonder why the bourgeois letter writer had not already led to the development of a bourgeois novel. A partial explanation is that this type of manual was too rigid and conventional. When Richardson did go on to the epistolary novel, he postponed further work on his letter book and wrote the two volumes of *Pamela* rapidly, expanding a theme which in the letter writer itself or in a periodical essay would have been disposed of in a few pages. "Little did I think," he wrote to Aaron Hill, "of making one, much less two volumes of it."[7] But he thought such a simple story might turn the young from "the pomp and parade of romance-writing" and "might tend to promote the cause of religion and virtue . . . I therefore gave way to enlargement: and so Pamela became as you see her." He carries over from the bourgeois manuals the letter form, the presentation of the servant's point of view, the plain style and practical moralizing, and the professed opposition to romance. His success in business now afforded him leisure to follow his bent in expanding "epistolary correspondencies." Not only did he have the time

THE EARLY MASTERS OF ENGLISH FICTION

to write the story at any length the subject might seem to require, but he had the option, unusual for an author, of printing it when and if he chose to do so.

In speculating about the prehistory of *Pamela*, it seems best to pass over lightly or disregard previous works of fiction in letter form, although attempts have been made to establish connections.[8] To the bourgeois manuals and the didactic purpose, and the assiduity of the experienced printer used to paper-work, we may add a somewhat vaguer consideration, the conception of letter-writing as a profitable exercise for one's leisure. Richardson tells us that he exchanged many letters with his unnamed patron, and there is some evidence to show that ambitious young men in trade might be anxious to educate themselves by engaging in systematic correspondence. For example, about 1716 a young man named William Cotesworth wrote from Cambridge to his brother Robert, who was in a "commercial school" in London:

The writing of Letters would be a very proper exercise for your leisure hours and if you have nobody to write to, invent someone; . . . then you must labour that subject very diligently for a man that would compose nicely must reject many more thoughts than he inserts. Never be weary nor think you compose too slowly but if you write one letter in the week, if you do it nicely, think you have done enough. To read all the letters you can lay your hands upon is the best way to stock you with subjects and to read letters wch you meet with by chance wou'd please me better than any Collection that is printed for in print there is always something aim'd at wch often runs the author into a necessity of being bombast, whereas between Friends a letter is commonly free and unconfined wch is certainly the most acceptable way of writing.[9]

Pamela was published in two volumes in November, 1740; an inferior continuation, into which Richardson was forced by the appearance of a spurious sequel, appeared in December, 1741. *Pamela I* enjoyed a popular success comparable to that of *The Beggar's Opera* or Hogarth's prints, though many people thought of the book as on the outer fringe of literature. As far as we can tell, there had been nothing quite like this *réclame* before; *Pamela* at its inception was "low" in subject matter and style, and the "low" in literature, it was thought, needed clear justification. If a plain or "low" work was written as a record of miscellaneous adventure, as a deliberate literary burlesque, or as a piece of humble piety for low or middling people, one could understand that, but *Pamela* did not fit neatly into any of these categories. Even in our own day, people who would never think of evaluating contemporary fiction in terms of subject matter are content to smile pityingly at the report of a servant girl, graceful, demure, and conventionally virtuous and pious, who is the victim of some extraordinarily clumsy attempts at seduction on the part of her young master Mr. B—, but who sincerely or shrewdly holds out for marriage, and thus wins her man. It is a simple and popular plot, with many analogues, and not without precedent in the society of Richardson's day. A letter of 1733 may be quoted in illustration of the theme as it appears in the contemporary English scene:

> If it is no way uneasy to you, as I believe it is not, to write a letter to my Lady Bab. Herbert to recommend her as a servant, I should be very glad. And if you will send the letter by this bearer to me, I will give it to the woman to carry. This woman did live with Mrs. Hanbury, when I was at Scarborough, and is certainly a very good creature. She has sense, which I have seen by letters to Grace, she is very handy, and upon any occasion can make things for a dessert, which is often very convenient, though Lady Bab. Herbert has a housekeeper. Sometimes one may be in a place, and not have all one's servants with one. The reason of her coming from Mrs. Hanbury's was, that her third son, who is very amorous, was fallen so passionately in love with this woman, who was extremely modest and honest, that Mrs. Hanbury apprehended he would marry her. And therefore she put her away. This Mrs. Hanbury wrote herself to me, and that she would recommend her to anybody. I don't wonder that Mrs. Hanbury was frighted, for nobody would be pleased to marry their son to their woman. However, if you write to my Lady Bab. Herbert, I think it is best to say nothing of that, because it is not easy to make everybody understand it.[10]

The Earl of Egmont wrote in his diary for February 4, 1745, that various maidservants and others of low degree had recently married dukes and earls.[11] In a letter to Hill, Richardson said that he had heard such a story from a friend some years before,[12] and we have seen that he repeated this statement to Stinstra. But *Pamela* is not a mere story of a *mésalliance,* or merely a scandalous account of the wiles of a would-be seducer, though it combines the two familiar themes in its own way. Neither is it merely a Puritan conduct-book, or a manifesto of middle-class piety.

Richardson wrote it *con amore,* the subject kindling his interest.

> While I was writing the two volumes, my worthy-hearted wife, and the young lady who is with us, when I had read them some part of the story, which I had begun without their knowing it, used to come in to my little closet every night, with—'Have you any more of Pamela, Mr. R.? We are come to hear a little more of Pamela,' &c. This encouraged me to prosecute it, which I did so diligently, through all my other business, that by a memorandum on my copy, I began it Nov. 10, 1739, and finished it Jan. 10, 1739-40. And I have often, censurable as I might be thought for my vanity for it, and lessening to the taste of my two female friends, had the story of Moliere's Old Woman in my thoughts upon the occasion.[13]

Richardson's term "enlargement" gives us the key, along with another favorite phrase of his, "writing to the moment." The presentation of a situation in letter form suggested the idea of changing the scale of the narrative by giving a minutely particular account of thoughts, actions, and accompanying circumstances at such frequent intervals as to make up a current record rather than a retrospective summary. There is a connection or parallel here with English empirical philosophy, with its emphasis on the primary value of immediate experience from one conscious moment to another, and this connection is later elaborated and made explicit by Sterne.[14] But it would be pretentious to tie up Richardson closely with epistemology; an alert literary intelligence might "write to the moment" without going to school to the philosophers. Chaucer centuries before had noted the unrealized possibility of fiction on such a scale. "Now, perhaps, some one may expect me to recount every word, message, glance, or expression that Troilus used in communicating with his dear mistress. That would be a long story, to describe all the words and looks of a man in such a difficult situation. To tell the truth, neither I nor anyone else ever heard of such a thing being done, and even though I wanted to do it, I couldn't; a single one of their letters might be half as large as this book. The writer I am following didn't choose to put such a document on record—how then should I be expected to write a line of it?" (*Troilus,* III, 491-504)

And Cervantes evidently felt that a vast circumstantial narrative needed the defense his playful commentary could supply:

"In very truth, all who enjoy stories like this should show their gratitude to Cide Hamete, its first author, for his meticulousness in recording its minutest details, leaving nothing, however trivial, which he does not bring clearly to light. He depicts thoughts, reveals intentions, answers unspoken questions, clears up doubts, in fact elucidates the slightest points the most captious critic could raise. O most renowned author!"[15] Dostoevsky puts the novelist's double program of inclusion and exclusion with characteristic directness and simplicity: "But I see I can't go on like this, partly because some things I did not hear, others I did not notice, and others I have forgotten, but most of all because, as I have said before, I have literally no time or space to mention everything that was said and done."[16] And Stendhal asks with similar directness, "How am I to find space for all the arguments, all the ways of looking at what was happening to him which, for three mortal hours on end, kept this impassioned man in torment?"[17]

The details in both Defoe and Richardson always bear more or less directly on the question of what the central character is to do in a given situation, but this situation is presented in more complex terms in Richardson, and there is more careful subordination of external detail and incident. Thus when Goodman Andrews sets out to discover the truth about his daughter: "He put on a clean Shirt and Neckcloth, (which he brought in his Pocket) at an Alehouse there, and got shav'd; and so, after he had eat some Bread and Cheese, and drank a Can of Ale, he set out for my Master's House, with a heavy Heart, dreading for me, and in much fear of being brow-beaten. He had, it seems, asked at the Alehouse, what Family the 'Squire had down here, in hopes to hear something of me; and they said, A House-keeper, two Maids, and, at present, two Coachmen, and two Grooms, a Footman, and a Helper. Was that all? he said. They told him, there was a young Creature there, belike, who *was*, or *was to be,* his Mistress, or somewhat of that nature; but had been his Mother's Waiting-maid. This, he said, grieved his Heart, and confirmed his Fears."[18] We note the lists of items, as in

Defoe, but Defoe would have given the inquiries at greater length; and Fielding might have given a longer alehouse scene. Richardson gets on to what is for him the main point—the confrontation of Mr. B— and Goodman Andrews, and the old man's attempt to grasp and interpret what Mr. B—says to him. Dialogue and "air and manner" are important as clues to the attitudes and reactions of other people. As Richardson's heroine Clarissa says at the beginning of her story: "And then you will always have me give you minute descriptions, nor suffer me to pass by the air and manner in which things are spoken that are to be taken notice of; rightly observing, that air and manner often express more than the accompanying words" (I, 8). His "minute descriptions" are selective. His way of "writing to the moment" is not indiscriminate expansion of descriptive detail, but a running record of significant circumstance and fluctuating feeling from the point of view of the letter-writer.

Such a record gives the reader a continuous and cumulative impression of living through the experience, and thus creates a new kind of sympathy with the character whose experiences are being shared. It is not merely that the character's feelings and observations are systematically presented; this in itself might, and sometimes does, lead to a tedious and trivial record. The point is that here we have the close linking of memory and current impression with anticipation of what is to come—a future not merely conceived as ultimate outcome—will Pamela's chastity be violated? will the story end with wedding bells?—but a future emerging directly from the specious present—what is to be done next, whether Pamela is to be sent to Mr. B—'s sister Lady Davers, or home to her parents, whether Mr. B— is to marry someone else, whether Pamela might be married off to the chaplain Mr. Williams, whether Mr. B—, as Pamela is warned, plans to entrap her by a mock-marriage. One question about the immediate future leads to another, and we get a very close *liaison des scènes*. For example, if Pamela is about to go home to her parents, what clothes shall she wear? This leads to the "rustic garb" scene, a very skilful performance, in which minor details point back to significant major tensions. Richardson is not afraid to reiterate the minor questions; when he is at his best he is not concerned with asking himself how they would sound in a pulpit or a drawing room.

It is just this resolution not to exclude the apparently undignified or trivial that marks Richardson's art. Defoe is concerned with such questions of policy too, but he does not steadily elaborate them within what we may call the domestic milieu. Naturally Richardson's procedure was not described in this way in the 1740's; those who were fascinated by the book could perhaps give less adequate explanations than those who were vexed by it. There was sometimes a combination of irritation and fascination which appears with particular clearness in the French comments, but contemporary criticism was on the whole inarticulate and inadequate. Contemporary readers did not oblige posterity by saying the right things. *Pamela* could be called low, hypocritical, tedious, at times indecent. Much of the discussion is carried on in terms of formal piety, material goods, and literal physical chastity. Richardson of course deliberately adopts a plain colloquial style for Pamela's reports, and he forgoes many things that might seem to be of advantage to the novelist. Pamela is isolated, first at the Bedfordshire estate of her master and then at his Lincolnshire estate, where she is kept prisoner at Mr. B—'s orders. The rest of the cast is made up of Mr. B— and a few servants and dependents, the good Mrs. Jervis, the bad Mrs. Jewkes, the inept but well-meaning Parson Williams. Pamela's mistress, Mr. B—'s mother, is dead; if she had lived she would have complicated the plot considerably, but affairs are worked out between Mr. B— and Pamela before his family, in the person of his redoubtable sister Lady Davers, asserts itself. Richardson gives us glimpses of the English household of his time, but it is not one of his primary purposes to do so, and in *Pamela* he deliberately avoids the presentation of a full family circle. He does not devise a wide range of episodes, but works out his effects from a few simple premises. Such devices as sending the characters on a circumstantially reported journey, or putting the central character in London or Bath, to watch the people go by, are not for him. Nor does he allow Pamela's parents, to whom her letters and journals are directed, to take effective action; in fact, he artificially limits outside intervention.

On the positive side, Richardson cultivates intensively the area he covers, and the letter form is a means to this end. In *Pamela* he follows a simple plan: the "narratist" sends letters or keeps a journal, but does not regularly receive and answer letters. Why, we may ask, should not this account have been presented as simple narrative in the first person? The letter convention emphasizes the medium and the method, and may be open to the objection that it is clumsy and ostentatious, that it obtrudes itself on the attention somewhat to the same effect as an elaborate story in a news-weekly about its wonderful method of getting news, or a television show about the marvels of producing a television show. Documents must be provided at any cost, and readers have smiled at Pamela's indomitable determination to write, even when there seems to be little prospect that anyone will read what she has written, even when correspondence has been cut off and she has to hide supplies of writing materials. And in the same way Richardson's heroine Clarissa says, "I must write on, altho' I were not to send it to anybody" (III, 221). As developed in *Clarissa* the system requires not only indefatigable correspondents but servants who devote much of their time to carrying letters. When letters cannot be written or sent immediately, the character may be occupied in keeping a journal or in making minutes, rough notes, and memoranda. And as I have said elsewhere, "The writing of the letters is only the beginning; they are copied, sent, received, shown about, discussed, answered, even perhaps hidden, intercepted, stolen, altered, or forged." Endless variations are possible here: thus when Clarissa expects her room to be searched by her family, she leaves in view a letter "which affording arguments suitable to my case, may chance (thus accidentally to be fallen upon) to incline them to favour me" (II, 330).

In *Pamela* the variations on the letter form are comparatively simple. Without going into full detail, we may note that when Mr. B— at last gets a chance to read Pamela's journal entire, he recalls her after he has given her full permission, her trials now over, to return to her parents; thus not only the earlier action but the record of the earlier action and the analysis and reception of that record condition the story. The writing of the novel is part of the action of the novel.[19]

If *Pamela* had been merely a Puritan conduct-book it would now be forgotten, like Defoe's *Family Instructor*. In writing his continuation of the story Richardson discovered that his analysis of a situation after it had become static ended in listless verbosity, and that the defect could not be remedied by drawing on conduct-books and collections of commonplaces concerning education, family life, and other social relationships. An added complication was that he now wanted to retreat from the radical democracy implicit in *Pamela I;* the original case of the virtuous serving maid does not fit easily into the accepted view of society set forth in *Pamela II*. And yet *Pamela II* gave Richardson valuable experience and taught him the danger of relying on miscellaneous letters. In the desire to elevate Pamela's style and in the plan to keep her writing long letters at any cost, Richardson may have been influenced from an early stage by the educational theory of polite correspondence which I have already mentioned; such a theory was probably necessary to get him beyond the brief and meager models of the epistolary manuals. No matter how spontaneous and independent an artist is, he cannot dispense entirely with preconceived doctrine about genre and style. The peril was that such preconceptions might have checked Richardson's development. He and his daughters came to be somewhat ashamed of the "low" style of *Pamela I*.

Yet it was *Pamela I* that was the great success, and the success was popular rather than literary. There were dramatizations, Pamela poems, spurious continuations and imitations, waxworks, pictures, fans, as well as derisive comments on Pamela's virtue by Fielding and others, but these matters need not detain us here, save as affording full illustration of the phenomenon of the best seller. *Pamela* never became a universal book like *Robinson Crusoe*, but aroused more immediate excitement with an appeal to sex and sentimental democracy; Upton Sinclair has recently recaptured in part the spirit in which the book was first received by imitating it sympathetically in *Another Pamela: or Virtue Still Rewarded* (1950). An unusual contemporary example of what we may call mature and yet spontaneous literary criticism of *Pamela* appears in an early letter of Richard Hurd's:

I thank you, good Sir, a thousand times for recommending Pamela to me. I had some how conceiv'd such an unaccountable prejudice agst: it, that nothing less than your good Opinion could have induc'd me to read it. But what a treasure of Beauties had I then lost! to say the least of a work, of wch. the most one can say is too little, I never saw Nature in such perfection before. I make no scruple to say there never were any characters more justly drawn, with greater propriety & exactness, or of a more glowing likeness to the life. The whole is literally a speaking Picture, & by reason of the several distressful Incidents, that are work'd up in it, as moving a one as ever did credit to any pencil. As a draught of Nature then I must read, love, & admire it, & stand amaz'd that any Reader of Taste should hazard his reputation so much as to own a dislike of it. But in it's moral capacity I am not so positive. On the other hand I incline to suspect more danger from it to the generality of young readers, than advantage. M^r. B's character is a little too engaging to make a Debauchee sufficiently distasteful to the youth of his quality & fortune; & the very nature, that strikes so much in Pamela's narrative of her own distresses is, I fear, still more dangerous to most female Fancies. 'Tis hazardous, nay I'll go further 'tis hurtful to paint Nature in such cases too faithfully. The too lively representation warms & inflames—the passions kindle at the view, & want more than the fair complainants ejaculations, & reflections to cool them again. This, Sir, I cannot but fear will be the probable consequence of some part of Pamela's charming Journal to the unconfirm'd virtuous of both Sexes. I mention it not as an Objection to the work, (for I am satisfy'd 'tis the very perfection of it) but as a hindrance to it's moral Design. 'Twill be a pleasure to find myself mistaken, & too apprehensive in this point, for 'tis with reluctance I observe anything in the lovely piece, that may keep it from being generally read.[20]

But the immediate effect of the book might appear to be a mere vogue or craze; there was little formal literary endorsement or support. The more important direct results of *Pamela*, indeed, appeared in *Joseph Andrews* and *Clarissa*.

SAMUEL RICHARDSON

II

Clarissa (1747-48) shows a much higher degree of self-realization, a term which may be taken to include a rise in social position, a heightening of literary dignity, and a more complex and profound art. These things go together to a certain extent, but the social conditioning, though important, should not be given precedence over the art. Both *Pamela* and *Clarissa* have heroines who assert themselves within and partly in opposition to a social framework. In *Pamela* the immediate framework is the household rather than the family, and centers about the master-servant relationship; in *Clarissa* the framework is the upper middle-class family. In both stories the heroine is sought, or we may say assailed, by a man of higher rank; in both there is an interplay of attraction and repulsion; as the heroine tries to protect herself, to assert her personality and ideals in a sexual crisis, we pass from a social document to a novel of personality. Richardson's convention of letter-writing gives a one-way report of this struggle in *Pamela;* his use of several major correspondents in *Clarissa* means that he presents with shifting point of view a triangular situation in which Clarissa, her family, and the lover-abductor-seducer Lovelace are each engaged in an intense, bitter, and protracted struggle with the other two. Clarissa has set herself up, she says, "presumptuously, as a middle person between flaming spirits" (III, 126).

We must then try to get our social bearings in order to interpret plot and characters. Professor Sale has recently remarked in a brilliant essay that when the Harlowes are transplanted from the city to the country, their ignoble materialism stands out larger than life against their aspirations to gentility.[21] We are not told how they got their money, but Clarissa's paternal grandfather had a large estate of his own making; of his three sons, John and Antony made money in mines and in the East India trade, and Clarissa's father married the only daughter of a viscount, with a large dowry. He has built a large and pretentious mansion, Harlowe Place, apparently in Hertfordshire. Clarissa's brother James, the only male heir in his generation, wants to consolidate the family fortunes in his own and to rise to a peerage, and at the same time envies and distrusts the aristocracy he would emulate. But at this stage in the family history the opposition between the Harlowes and Lovelace must be defined in terms of personal quality and attitude rather than in terms of social status. The Harlowes were by now so high in the social scale that better things might reasonably be expected of them. Lord M., Lovelace's kinsman, who ought to know, does not speak of them as mere upstarts: "Their family is of standing. All gentlemen of it, and rich, and reputable. Let me tell you, that many of our coronets would be glad they could derive their descents from no worse a stem than theirs" (VI, 240). Clarissa herself attempts to distinguish between legitimate and illegitimate family pride. When it is reported that Lovelace speaks contemptuously of the Harlowes, she records her comment: "I replied, That he was a very unworthy man, if it were true, to speak slightingly of a family, which was as good as his own,'bating that it was not allied to the Peerage: That the dignity itself, I thought, conveyed more shame than honour to descendents, who had not merit to adorn, as well as to be adorned by it: That my Brother's absurd pride, indeed, which made him everywhere declare, he would never marry but to *Quality,* gave a disgraceful preference against ours: But that were I to be assured, that Mr. Lovelace was capable of so mean a pride as to insult us or value himself on such an accidental advantage, I should think as despicably of his sense, as every-body else did of his morals" (II, 240). At the same time, she continues, it should be considered "whether the value some of my friends put upon the riches they possess (throwing perhaps contempt upon every other advantage, and even discrediting their own pretensions to family, in order to depreciate his) might not provoke him to like contempts."

The honors of birth and the honors of wealth should alike be borne with moderation, but the fact remains that the man of unquestioned rank and inheritance is likely to stand the test better. Miss Howe endorses Lovelace's conception of the choice manners which he himself illustrates: " 'That upon *true* quality, and *hereditary* distinction, if good sense were not wanting, *honour sat as easy as his glove;* That, with *as* familiar an air, was his familiar expression; 'while none but the prosperous upstart, MUSHROOM'D into rank (another of his peculiars) was arrogantly proud of it' " (I, 291). In backing the pretensions of the "prosperous upstart" Solmes to Clarissa's hand, the Harlowes are untrue to the standards which they should have accepted or should be acquiring, and thus they wantonly aggravate the differences between themselves and Lovelace. The social barrier was by no means impassable. Yet Richardson would never assert categorically, like Defoe, that the merchant at his best and as such could vie with the nobility. Though a prosperous City man himself, Richardson never deals sympathetically with the newly rich; he dislikes their "crass aspirations," belittles the "nominal honours" they can buy, and deprecates matches between trade and titled families. This attitude toward low wealth was the approved view of the period, and was shared by Richardson and Fielding, as can be shown by a brief passage in Mrs. Miller's narrative in *Tom Jones:* "The mother of this lady had been a servant to my grandmother; and, having inherited a vast fortune from her father, which he had got by pawnbroking, was married to a gentleman of great estate and fashion. She used my sister so barbarously . . . that I believe she at length broke the heart of the poor girl" (XIV, v). This is what one might expect of Solmes. The point appears also in the contrast of the Nightingale brothers in Fielding's story: both were bred to trade, but one continued to deal in money and thought of nothing else; the other used a modest fortune to purchase a small estate in the country, whither he retired, marrying the daughter of an unbeneficed clergyman (XIV, viii). The second brother thus adopted the ideal of a virtuous and modest retreat within an approved social system. The ideal life for the Harlowes would be a more splendid version of the same plan. From the vantage point of a secure retreat in a commodious or even magnificent country house one could oppose both the plutocrat and the arrogant aristocrat. This position was to be greatly elaborated in Richardson's third and last novel, *Grandison.*

In *Clarissa,* then, we cannot speak without qualification of a conflict between the aristocracy and the middle class. Social distinctions are a necessary but not a sufficient condition for the development of the action; the principal characters are not primarily representative of a class, and we find that they are on their own at last. If the social background is elaborated as compared with *Pamela,* the central figures are elaborated in even greater proportion. The result is a certain distortion, if the novel is considered in respect to normal life, and this has no doubt helped to promote the mistaken idea that Richardson conceives his principal characters primarily in terms of exaggerated vice or virtue. There is exaggeration and romantic heightening in *Clarissa,* yet Richardson shows skill in merging these heightened themes with a world which the eighteenth century could accept as real. Except in *Roxana,* Defoe had never tried to combine the scandalous love story of an aristocratic "novel" with his own kind of realism. *Clarissa* in bald outline would be a scandalous story of abduction and rape, but Richardson goes much farther than any of his predecessors in referring the action to its ultimate origins in society and in individual character. Richardson's actual world is conceived of as a field for self-assertion, as posing problems in the resolution of relations among such contending forces as individual pride, personal loyalties and attachments, and social and religious authority. Far from sentimentalizing and glorifying the family as an institution, Richardson describes the whole area of domestic relations as a battlefield. Clarissa is willing to accept family authority to almost any degree short of the last extremity, but she refuses finally to submit to her father's usurpation of authority. There is a double warfare, a struggle within the family and a combat between the sexes, and the plot consists in the connection of the two. Lovelace, Clarissa, and the other Harlowes all have pride, and are alike in wanting to control the situation and at the same time to justify themselves in terms of accepted standards. Yet Clarissa and Lovelace are both in a sense quixotic in their pride, and stand in contrast to many of the surrounding characters who are bogged down in convention and give automatic responses, facile and superficial answers to the questions that beset the principals. The two major characters inevitably assert themselves, and this points to a tragic outcome. In a really tight situation Richardson does not believe that bad people are naturally good; he deplores "the specious, yet foolish hope of subduing riveted habits, and . . . of altering natures" (VII, 365-66).

What has just been said of Richardson's presentation of character can be restated in terms of his use of letters. The correspondents report conflict and offer commentary. The conflict is not typically a head-on collision between one correspondent and another, assertion and reply; rather it is presented largely within the letters of a dominant correspondent, who makes his report in great detail. Each principal correspondent undertakes to report and comment on various aspects of a complex situation, may be hard put to it to formulate immediate or long-range aims, and thus presents the spectacle of the "divided mind." Conflict and doubt inhere in the present, and are projected into the past and the future. This is preëminently true for Clarissa and Lovelace. For Clarissa's confidante Miss Howe and for Lovelace's confidant Belford, the provision of comment outweighs the report of conflict, but when Richardson is at his best there is an organic connection; that is, significant commentary on the action is a complication and advancement of the action. Secondary characters may be given over to one aspect or the other: the Harlowes represent a brutal and sullen form of conflict, and are not intelligent or articulate enough to provide their own commentary. About all that James and Arabella Harlowe can do is to be, as Richardson says, "affrontive." In his own correspondence, and in the original Preface to *Clarissa,* Richardson showed misgivings about the great length to which his method carried him, and was inclined to justify his bulky collection of letters as conveying "instruction," yet his final position was that his method was artistically justified, that the *"instantaneous* Descriptions and Reflections" of the principal characters and "the Lives, Characters, and Catastrophes" of the secondary are always relevant. For *Clarissa* he asserted that "long as the Work is, there is not one Digression, not one Episode, not one Reflection, but what arises naturally from the Subject, and makes for it, and to carry it on."[22] Essentially the same assertion appears in the Preface to *Grandison:* "There is not one Episode in the Whole; nor, after SIR CHARLES GRANDISON is introduced, one Letter inserted but what tends to illustrate the principal Design."

Clarissa is a paragon of beauty, intelligence, and virtue. She is originally conceived as an ideal heroine of the post-*Spectator* generation, plying a ready pen in the cause of virtuous sagacity. Like Clara, the niece of "Henry Stonecastle" in the *Universal Spectator,* October 21, 1732, she has profited by "Lessons of Virtue and Piety," has been taught the "finest Arts of *Visit* and *Conversation,*" excels in her judgment of "Cases, relating to the *Unmarry'd World,*" and "writes *Letters* and *Essays* to those of her own Sex." At the beginning Clarissa is loved and admired by all except her jealous and arrogant brother James and her sister Arabella. The libertine Lovelace appears as a suitor first for Arabella and then for Clarissa herself; James and Arabella are able to use against her the guarded relationship with Lovelace into which she is forced, and succeed in inducing the heads of the family to try to compel her to marry the inept and ugly Solmes. Although the conduct-books denied the daughter the right to marry against the parents' will, the accepted creed also denied the parents, at least in theory, the right to force a daughter to marry a man to whom she had insuperable objections. In real life, however, the exercise of this veto power by the daughter might be very difficult. One of Trollope's heroines, Lady Glencora, remarks more than a century later: "We talk with such horror of the French people giving their daughters in marriage, just as they might sell a house or a field, but we do exactly the same thing ourselves. When they all come upon you in earnest, how are you to stand against them? How can any girl do it?"[23] But Clarissa is perfectly clear on the central issue. As soon as the proposal about Solmes is made, she sees the position she must take, though without realizing all the tragic complications that lie ahead: "But surely *they* will yield—Indeed *I* cannot. I believe the gentlest spirits when provoked (causelessly and cruelly provoked) are the most determined. The reason may be, That not taking up resolutions lightly—their very deliberation makes them the more immoveable.—And then when a point is clear and self-evident, how can one with patience think of entering into an argument or contention upon it?" (I, 93)

Clarissa's predicament forces her into continuing secretly a correspondence with Lovelace that had been begun openly. Family authority is exerted with almost irresistible force: Clarissa again and again tries to negotiate with her obdurate kinsfolk, and is at last, half by accident and half by Lovelace's plot, forced to take flight with him. He now finds that he is in command of the situation, and hesitates between marriage, which he now thinks of as a concession or surrender, and further elaborate plans leading to seduction. A summary of the action gives no idea of the quality of the book. Richardson now realizes to the full his new scale and tempo of narration, and the possibility of manipulating the point of view afforded by the letter form. As Clarissa is beset and entrapped, he achieves an effect of slowly mounting tension within a prolonged deadlock. At first Lovelace remains in the background, and makes a delayed entrance. Clarissa herself tells most of this part of the story, sent journal-wise to her friend Anna Howe. Though the two-way correspondences of this novel represent an important technical achievement, it is still true that for a given part of the story there is usually a dominant correspondent, even as between Anna and Clarissa, or Belford and Lovelace. Anna's part is to present a non-tragical antitype to Clarissa; she helps to anchor the story in social reality by giving us a view of an ordinary world in which girls can innocently quarrel with suitors and parents. At the same time she shows that even wit, spirit, and sense fall short of solving Clarissa's tragic problem; her advice is good, but it is never adequate for Clarissa's needs. Yet she often gets to the point: "You can no more change your nature than your persecutors can change theirs." Another remark of hers formulates what Richardson no doubt thought to be the fundamental contrast between these two characters: "Were *your* character, and *my* character, to be truly drawn, mine would be allowed to be the most natural. Shades and Lights are equally necessary in a fine picture. Yours would be surrounded with such a flood of brightness, with such a glory, that it would indeed dazzle; but leave one heartless to imitate it" (III, 226).

More clearly in *Clarissa* than in *Pamela*, Richardson made his own use of the character-types established in the kind of drama with which he was familiar. Both Clarissa and Lovelace quote sententious bits from tragedy, culled largely, it appears, from Bysshe's *Art of Poetry*.[24] Richardson himself discusses, only to reject, the analogy with Rowe's *Fair Penitent,* Lovelace being much more like the gay Lothario than Clarissa is like Calista (VII, 133-34), and in general the novelist was inclined to find fault with the attitudes and motives of important characters in current tragedy, even while he profited by their example.[25] Lovelace's attitudes lead him to use a style which blends a half-playful use of the rhetoric of tragedy and heroic play with the colloquialisms of the fine gentleman of comedy. His conscious inclination to adopt one role and then another is an essential part of his characterization. And on the level of comedy, as Professor John Harrington Smith has recently pointed out, the contrasts within and between the couples in *Clarissa* and *Grandison* develop from dramatic models.[26] Though Richardson does not make direct use of the "gay" and the "serious" couple, he pairs a serious suitor with a lively or "difficult" lady, Hickman with Anna Howe and later of course Lord G. with Charlotte Grandison. Clarissa and Lovelace conform less exactly to the pattern of serious lady and lively suitor, though the analogy is helpful for their lighter scenes. The gay correspondents, Anna and Lovelace, provide color and spirit. Aside from the pairing of couples, these characters are closely related to the coquette and the rake of didactic literature. But both characters—Lovelace to a much greater degree—are pushed beyond the "reformation of manners" level. Meanwhile, Richardson gets remarkable effects from the lighter utterances of Anna Howe and Lovelace. The passages in which Miss Howe gives brief imaginary sketches of Hickman, Solmes, and Lovelace as boys, and the "Rosebud" idyll of Lovelace, describing an innocent country girl whom he spares and befriends, show an extremely skilful use of the light style.

The end of Clarissa's ordeal in Harlowe Place leads into the other and greater ordeal of London, where she is held a virtual prisoner by Lovelace and his infamous agents. We may feel that the machinations of Lovelace are much too elaborate; from the beginning it seems improbable that even he could reduce the Harlowes to "so many puppets danced by his wires"; and the improbability increases as Clarissa is more and more hopelessly deceived. She continues to think that marriage with Lovelace is still easily possible, that she has only to accept his formal offer made under proper terms, and she cherishes the hope, cruelly and falsely promoted by Lovelace, that a reconciliation with her family is still possible. The story consists largely of an elaborate system of stipulations and conditions proposed but never carried out, a phantasmagoria of orderly negotiation counterbalanced by Lovelace's phantasmagoria of conspiracy. All plans are misdirected: the Harlowe family, Anna Howe and her friends, the creatures who surround Clarissa in London, Lovelace and his fellow rakes, the futile group of well-meaning women in Hampstead when Clarissa takes refuge there—all are misled. We cannot, however, condemn Lovelace's insane persistence, his passion for disguise and his other elaborate contrivances on the mere ground of improbability; the age of the atomic bomb is in no position to deny that a life of obsessive drives and intricate techniques may assume this febrile quality, or that a protracted nightmare of this kind could begin in dull and stodgy Harlowe Place and develop within the prosaic London setting. This is the history of victory that is no victory: Lovelace comes to see that he has become the victim of his own contrivances, and that the victory he has plotted for will undo him. On the other hand, Clarissa's early hopes of a solution that will satisfy her pride and her personal standards are necessarily futile; Professor Sale has well pointed out that her pious utterances should not blind us to the tragic situation in the here and now.[27] Her conception of her own personality fixes her proud resolve to avoid the appearance of being "giddy, unsteady, and precipitate," but from an early point in the action she could exclaim, "How wise have I endeavoured to be! . . . yet all my wisdom now, by a strange fatality, likely to become foolishness" (II, 76). Her legitimate resistance to her family and to Solmes makes her *ipso facto* unable to cope with the brutal actuality of Lovelace's designs. She cannot at first afford to accept the simple and literal truth when she hears it from the lips of the despised Solmes: "Mr. Lovelace is a declared *Marriage-hater,* and has a design upon your honour" (II, 244). Once she has left Harlowe Place and before the conspiracy completely closes in on her in London, she shows an excessive regard to propriety even as the proprieties go by the board. Meanwhile Lovelace exults in the delicacies of intrigue as he takes over epistolary dominance in his long series of letters to his friend and correspondent Belford. "I have ever had more pleasure in my contrivances, than in the End of them. I am no sensual man, but a man of spirit" (III, 249). The social standards of Clarissa's world call for matrimony, but she wishes to marry Lovelace without admitting coercion. Tragic irony carries even the early London phase of the story beyond the limits of the novel of manners. It is perhaps Clarissa's misjudgment of successive situations in these early parts that led Dr. Johnson to say that "there is always something which she prefers to truth."[28] This remark may be interpreted not as a criticism of Clarissa's character but as an informal description of the role of self-deception in tragedy.

Against this hope for an unattainable solution, actual circumstances move in the direction of an ugly *chronique scandaleuse*. Angered by a stratagem (worthy of Pamela's Mr. B—) by which Lovelace raises a false alarm of fire in order to get access to her bed, Clarissa escapes and takes refuge in Hampstead. Lovelace follows her thither, intercepting warning letters from Miss Howe. Abandoned women masquerading as Lovelace's relatives finally lure Clarissa back from Hampstead to London, where she is drugged and violated. Lovelace tells this part of the story; later Clarissa tells it again to Anna Howe, and Richardson here shows his skill in getting reiterated effects from the letter form. Hereafter the mirage of a happy ending on earth persists only as a desperate and fantastic hope. Anna Howe moves farther from the center, and advises marriage long after it is out of the question. Lovelace is kept by his egotism and his unbridled will from realizing or at least from admitting the true situation. In the period from the violation of Clarissa to her second escape from Lovelace we have less effective conspiracy by Lovelace, and less elaborate negotiation. The so-called "penknife scene" marks at long last the end of Lovelace's plotting and establishes Clarissa's spiritual and dramatic dominance. Lovelace is reduced to impotence and bravado: "Have her I will, tho' I marry her in the agonies of death" (VII, 89).

Our impatience with Richardson's circumstantial concern with sex and his pietistic idiom should not obscure our understanding of Clarissa's tragic quest for integrity and her inevitable martyrdom. The story hangs together whether or not we share the concern of Richardson and Fielding for the reward of virtue in another world.[29] There is an underlying logic in Clarissa's final separation from Lovelace, from Miss Howe, from her own family. A lax sentimentalist would have staged final confrontations. These separations may be called the severing of earthly ties, but what we really have here is isolation as an essential part of the tragedy of personality. From isolation imposed by mere physical restraint, as in *Pamela* and some parts of *Clarissa*, Richardson works his way to something more profound. Richardson and Sterne come to such a close reckoning with inner experience as makes them the forerunners respectively of tragic and comic intransigeance as the basic themes of the later novel.

It is not, then, an adequate view to consider Clarissa primarily as an example of deflowered virginity, of the death-wish with which sexual desire is associated, as a signal instance of Christian martyrdom and the workings of divine grace, or as the embodiment of an ideal produced by a certain society ("Puritan" and "bourgeois," of course).[30] Such considerations bear on components of the work, particularly on the imagery, but the tragedy of personality does not yield its ultimate secret to such catalytic treatment. The use of the term "myth" for such a story solves no problems: "myth," we may say, presents plot and characters in the light of ultimate moral and religious sanctions, but an explicit emphasis on such sanctions leads us back to the old didactic point of view; or if we choose not to tie up myth with formal systems and say that it inheres in some mysterious internal force operating through personality, what more are we saying than that the integral force of personality under stress is significant, mysterious, and ultimate? Similarly, much is lost if we consider Lovelace exclusively in terms of male sexual aggression or aristocratic libertinism; labels will not take us all the way, whether we call him sadist, rake, or Prince of Devils. This is not to deny that the novelist and the reader are confronted with the problem of evil. The reconciliation of sexual self-realization with transcendental or absolute values may well be the ultimate challenge to humanity, and calls for an imaginative reading of life which was beyond Richardson's power. There had long been a conflict between "troubadour love of women" and "Christian love of God," and recantation of sexual love had become part of the tradition. This explains the conclusion of the *Troilus,* when the frustrated lover is translated to the spheres and looks down with scorn on earthly passion; the resolution of the conflict is the principal theme in Dante, whose spiritual drama transcends the imperfect rendering of love, however beautiful and ardent, in Guido Guinizelli and Arnaut Daniel.[31] There is a similar hiatus between Don Quixote's devotion to chivalry and his recovery of his senses as he makes a good Christian end.

It is Richardson's lack of the idiom of poetry, that is, his failure to reach the ultimate degree of imaginative concentration, that keeps *Clarissa* from being great tragedy. Stevenson put it in his own way when he said that *Clarissa* did not create the pictures or images that come home to the imagination.[32] This is to judge by the highest standards; nevertheless Richardson attains a height seldom surpassed in the novel of manners. Clarissa's second escape from Lovelace and her refuge in Covent Garden, with the final false arrest by Lovelace's agent Mrs. Sinclair, confirm her isolation and martyrdom. The account of her arrest is pathetic rather than dramatic, but it is powerfully told. She is thereafter regularly visited by Lovelace's friend Belford, who for a time becomes the central letter-writer, and she is also in communication with Lovelace's relatives, with her friendly kinsman Colonel Morden, and with other correspondents such as the good clergyman Dr. Lewen who serves as intermediary between her and her family. Lovelace has to reckon with his own family, and there are other secondary interchanges of letters, but all are centered about Clarissa. Arrangements are even made within the story for the final gathering and editing of the letters by Belford and Miss Howe, though Belford at last seems to be the active editor. The machinery of the outward action continues to operate, and stands in a kind of ironic contrast to the static situation; the pedantic clergyman Brand, who is as stupid as any pompous bureaucrat in Ibsen, portentously investigates the case of Clarissa, with a view to reporting back to her family, and solemnly comments on the impropriety of Belford's visits; Lovelace, just as he had invaded Clarissa's hiding place at Hampstead, now tries to make a last swaggering visit to Covent Garden, though he is destined never to see her again; he engages in fierce and tense parleys with Morden; the Harlowe family moves in a clumsy and futile way toward reconciliation; both

THE EARLY MASTERS OF ENGLISH FICTION

the Harlowes and Lovelace discuss at length and oppose for different reasons Clarissa's appointment of Belford as her executor. Tragic irony, which in the earlier part of the story had centered in Clarissa's own attitude, is now diffused through a system of social relationships; Clarissa's own situation is pathetic rather than ironic. This may be taken as a restatement of Dr. Johnson's remark that the first two volumes of *Clarissa* were the best, "for give me a sick bed, and a dying lady, and I'll be pathetic myself."[33]

Richardson's style and method are not fully adapted to sustained irony, and in the last volumes he may seem to be surrounding his central characters with a mass of circumstantial talk, but another feature of his narrative method should be noted here, the occasional and memorable direct stroke. We have had it before—"Your Clarissa has gone off with a man"—"All is over—Clarissa lives" (Lovelace to Belford after the rape). There are some powerful strokes of this kind toward the end. Thus Belford announces the death of Clarissa to Lovelace: "I have only to say at present—Thou wilt do well to take a Tour to Paris; or wherever else thy destiny shall lead thee!!!" (VII, 464) This is the entire letter, and though the exclamation points are irritating, how could Richardson have done more in two lines? Or how could he have bettered the consolations of Lovelace's crass companions? "We told him as how she was but a woman, and an obstinate perverse woman too; and how could he help it?" (VII, 466) Less successful are the cautionary scenes described by the reformed Belford, the tale of the sad end of their fellow-rake Belton, and the ghastly deathbed of the wicked woman Sinclair. No doubt there were readers who thought of the last volumes of *Clarissa* and of the *Night Thoughts* of Richardson's friend Young as treatises on Christian deathbeds, and on the consequences of transgression of the formal law. These are impediments, but Richardson uses the swift stroke again when Lovelace goes to the Continent and falls in a duel with Morden at Trent, exclaiming at last, "Let this expiate!" The novelist tells this final episode with the utmost brevity; far from being anticlimactic, it gives the inevitable close, with social code and personal tragedy finally fused. Richardson, illustrating social and moral excellence, could avert duel after duel in *Grandison,* but this was one that had to be fought.

It often seems to us that the eighteenth century gives the wrong reasons for admiring *Clarissa.* Here we have to reckon not only with a difference in taste but with a difference in critical technique and vocabulary. Of the first volumes of *Clarissa,* Fielding wrote in the *Jacobite's Journal,* January 2, 1748:

> My chief Delight hath always been in reading; and as Works of Imagination afford me the greatest Pleasure, you may easily imagine that I have many Years ago run through all the Books (for they are not numberless) which ancient or modern Authors have produced of that kind. Indeed I have read them all so often, that their Beauties, from too much Familiarity, begin to pall upon my Mind.
>
> How charmed am I therefore when I meet with a new Production in the Region of Fancy, capable of giving me the same Delight which I have received from my most favourite Authors at my first Acquaintance with them. The most learned Botanist, who discovers a new Plant; or the surfeited Epicure, who invents a new Dish, may perhaps have some faint Idea of my Pleasure, at perusing such Works from any of my Cotemporaries.
>
> When I tell you I have lately received this Pleasure, you will not want me to inform you that I owe it to the Author of *CLARISSA.* Such Simplicity, such Manners, such deep Penetration into Nature; such Power to raise and alarm the Passions, few Writers, either ancient or modern, have been possessed of. My Affections are so strongly engaged, and my Fears are so raised, by what I have already read, that I cannot express my Eagerness to see the rest. Sure this Mr. *Richardson* is Master of all that Art which *Horace* compares to Witchcraft,
>
> —Pectus inaniter angit,
>
> Irritat, mulcet, falsis terroribus implet,
>
> Ut Magus.—
>
> With what Indignation do I therefore hear the Criticisms made on this Performance. *Clarissa* is undutiful; she is too dutiful. She is too cold; she is too fond. She uses her Father, Mother, Uncles, Brother, Sister, Lover, Friend, too ill, too well. In short, there is scarce a Contradiction in Character, which I have not heard assigned from Reasons to this poor Girl; who is as much the Object of Compassion as she can be, and as good as she should be described.

It would be a mistake to dismiss this utterance as a mere piece of amiability and sensibility. And we can now get a closer view of Fielding as a reader of *Clarissa* from his letter to Richardson, October 15, 1748, written on receiving the fifth volume of the novel, referring to the Hampstead scenes, the return to London, and the outrage, and thus commenting directly on the crucial issues of the plot and the characterization:

In all the Accounts which Loveless Gives of the Transactions at Hampstead, you preserve the same vein of Humour which hath run through the preceding Volumes. The new Characters you Introduce are natural and entertaining, and there is much of the true Comic Force in the Widow Bevis. I have seen her often, and I Promise you, you have drawn her with great exactness. The Character of Loveless is heightened with great Judgment. His former Admirers must lose all Regard for him on his Perseverance, and as this Regard Ceases, Compassion for Clarissa rises in the same Proportion. Hence we are admirably prepared for what is to follow.—Shall I tell you? Can I tell you what I think of the latter part of your Volume? Let the Overflowings of a Heart which you have filled brimfull speak for me.

When Clarissa returns to her Lodgings at St. Clairs the Alarm begins, and here my Heart begins its Narrative. I am Shocked; my Terrors ar[e ra]ised, and I have the utmost Apprehensions for the poor betrayed Creature.— But when I see her enter with the Letter in her Hand, and after some natural Effects of Despair, clasping her Arms about the Knees of the Villain, call him her Dear Lovelace, desirous and yet unable to implore his Protection or rather his mercy; I then melt into Compassion, and find what is called an Effeminate Relief for my Terror, to continue to the End of the Scene. When I read the next Letter I am Thunderstruck; nor can many Lines explain what I feel from Two.

What I shall say of holding up the License? I will say a finer Picture was never imagined. He must be a Glorious Painter who can do it Justice on Canvas, and a most wretched one indeed who could not do much on such a Subject. The Circumstance of the Fragments is Great and Terrible; but her [Clarissa's] Letter to Lovelace is beyond anything I have ever read. God forbid that the Man who reads this with dry Eyes should be alone with my Daughter when she hath no Assistance within Call. Here my Terror ends and my Grief begins which the Cause of all my Tumultuous Passions soon changes into Raptures of Admiration and Astonishment by a Behaviour the most Elevated I can possibly conceive, and what is at the same time most Gentle and most natural. This Scene I have heard hath been often objected to. It is well for the Critick that My Heart is now writing and not my Head. During the Continuance of this Vol. my Compassion is often moved; but I think my Admiration more. If I had rec'd no Hint or Information of what is to succeed I should perceive you paving the way to load our admiration of your Heroine to the Highest Pitch, as you have before with wonderfull Art prepared us for both Terror and Compassion on her Account. This last seems to come from the Head. Here then I will end: for I assure you nothing but my Heart can force me to say Half of what I think of *the* Book.[34]

Noteworthy here are the references to compassion and terror as appropriate to the story and as a test of virtue, and the use of

"Admiration" as a critical standard, an important element in the current theory of tragedy. We should mark also that Fielding the humorist recognizes a "vein of Humour" not always conceded to Richardson by later readers. The modern student would wish that Fielding and other contemporary critics had written "from the Head" rather than from the heart. If one of Richardson's admiring young ladies had put her overflowing feelings on record in this style, the letter would now be dismissed as negligible sentimentalism. But if Fielding is not to be discredited as a critic—and he was certainly more interested in criticism than any other novelist of the age—we must try to get at the serious purpose underlying his references to terror, grief, and compassion. He is undertaking to evaluate *Clarissa* as a tragedy within the framework of the novel of manners. The élite to whom *Clarissa* appealed, in contrast to *Pamela* with its broad popular appeal, may after all have used their heads as well as their hearts in judging the book, though their terminology is not ours. At their best they appreciated and understood both *Clarissa* and *Tom Jones;* with the notable exception of Dr. Johnson, perhaps they kept the balance between the two masterpieces as well as the twentieth century can.

Richard Payne Knight at the end of the eighteenth century attempted to account for a decline in the reputation of *Clarissa* by pointing out that "tragedy is an exhibition of general nature, and comedy of the exceptions from it: for all personal peculiarities are more or less ridiculous; and local and temporary habits are merely personal peculiarities."[35] It follows that Richardson is handicapped by incongruity between general conception of character and minute detail: "The author of the novel of Clarissa Harlowe attempted to make his fictions interesting by the same sort of minute precision and exactitude in the detailed relations of all common circumstances [as in *Gulliver*]; and, in some scenes, he has succeeded admirably: but, in general, he has failed through want of talent to fill up properly and consistently those bold outlines of character, which first introduce his fictitious personages to the knowledge of the reader" (*ibid.,* pp. 285-86). This may for our purpose be roughly paralleled with Yeats's comments on the course of poetic drama: "Suddenly it strikes us that character is continuously present in comedy alone, and that there is much tragedy, that of Corneille, that of Racine, that of Greece and Rome, where its place is taken by passions and motives, one person being jealous, another full of love or remorse or pride or anger. In writers of tragicomedy (and Shakespeare is always a writer of tragicomedy) there is indeed character, but we notice that it is in the moments of comedy that character is defined."[36] Perhaps we can keep historical perspective if we consider the "manners" in *Clarissa* to be in the tradition of tragicomedy, and the protracted moral, religious, and psychological commentary as in some sense a substitute for earlier dramatic lyricism. It is in the extended commentary that Richardson falls short, or at least shows a serious deficiency of style. But his transcription of manners in relation to the tragic theme is a unique contribution. If we consider the later elaboration of manners as locating the characters more specifically in place and time, as well as throwing emphasis on particular circumstances rather than general theme, we can see that this later elaboration divided up the broad field of manners in various ways, as witness Smollett, Mrs. Radcliffe, Jane Austen, and Walter Scott, without allowing an easily assignable place to the tragicomedy of Richardson.

III

One of Richardson's purposes in portraying an ideal gentleman in *Sir Charles Grandison* (1753-54) was to present an antitype to Lovelace and Tom Jones. The complacent assumption that polite society can stand, when properly purged of vice and error, was easily made by Richardson and his public; the novelist could be shaken loose from such an assumption only by an exceptionally intense situation such as develops in *Clarissa*. The ideal of the "gentleman," though fortified by the prestige of the ruling classes and the whole Western tradition, hampered the novelist in so far as it substituted a carefully defined type or standard for an ultimately unclassifiable human being. The name suggests the aristocracy, and Richardson may have remembered a work which he had helped to print, the English translation of Giannone's *History of Naples* (1729-31), which was dedicated to the Earl of Grandison and his son Viscount Falkland: "I have at hand the noble Historian, who, in his Catalogue of Heroes (great as any *Greece* or *Rome* ever produc'd) has not two more beautiful Characters, than those of *Falkland* and *Grandison*." Richardson's Grandison is a baronet, not a peer; the ideals of reason and nature must be realized within the fixed system imposed by his status. He is invariably courteous, rational, and benevolent, but his attitudes toward much of the world are formal and somewhat remote—toward the lower classes and the trading classes, toward politics and public life. He executes a virtuous and rational retreat or semi-retreat to private life, which, as noted above in the discussion of *Clarissa,* could be opposed alike to the evils of new wealth, the arrogance and licence of the old aristocracy, and the follies of fashion. His accomplishments are social rather than cultural; he is not a poet like his libertine and extravagant father. He is the center of a large group of kinsmen, friends, and dependents, and above all he dominates a circle of refined and admiring women.[37] These relationships are conceived of as an extension of the family.[38] It is within such a circle that the virtuous man will naturally find a wife; this is preëminently true of Sir Charles Grandison and Harriet Byron, and the important principle of the domestic and socially approved setting for the love affair, the exact opposite of *mésalliance,* passes into later fiction.

Sir Charles's ideals are within reach for his time and place, so that he can never go to war with his world or be involved in the quixotic clash of ideal and real. On the other hand, he is too composed and complacent to succumb to the ennui that security and success might bring, like M. Pococurante. Though he is more disposed than Fielding's Mr. Allworthy to give authoritative moral judgments, both good men avoid mortal struggle with society and with themselves, and illustrate Fielding's

THE EARLY MASTERS OF ENGLISH FICTION

dictum that "the wisest man is the likeliest to possess all worldly blessings in an eminent degree."[39] As a conduct-book *Grandison* builds on the program of Steele, thus briefly described in an ideal play to be written by one of his disciples: "There are, I find, to be in [his drama] all the reverend Offices of Life, such as Regard to Parents, Husbands, and honourable Lovers, preserved with the utmost Care; and at the same Time that Agreeableness of Behaviour, with the Intermixture of pleasing Passions as arise from Innocence and Virtue, interspersed in such a Manner, as that to be charming and agreeable, shall appear the natural Consequence of being virtuous."[40] Behind Sir Charles stands the figure of Bevil in Steele's *Conscious Lovers,* pointing the way to a program of benevolism in which the ideal of the gentleman is identified with an extension of "the reverend Offices of Life" to include an entire society. In practice, as has been remarked, benevolism as dramatized must be limited by personal experience and interest, but in theory it is all-embracing. The good man's benevolence is "diffusive," to use a favorite term of the moralists, and seeks out occasions. "The communicating advice and comfort, assistance and support, according to the various exigencies of those with whom he converses, is his constant endeavour, and most pleasing entertainment. . . . [He] seeks for opportunities to be useful; 'tis part of the stated employment and business of his life. . . . You can't lay a greater obligation upon him than by proposing ways in which he may be useful, or enlarge his sphere of usefulness: For this is the point in which all his views, all his desires, all his satisfaction, center."[41]

Grandison was written with more regard to the presence of Richardson's friends and advisers than its two predecessors. It reflects their views to some extent, but it also shows the novelist at work as a self-conscious artist. Of the many references to *Grandison* among Richardson's correspondents, a brief report by Dr. Thomas Birch will suffice to show us the situation: "Mr. Richardson, the Printer, is employing himself in a Work, for which the Men will be as much oblig'd to him, as the Ladies have hitherto been, having, as he own'd to me some days ago, resum'd the Subject, which you heard him mention at your own House, of the virtuous & generous Gentleman. He complains to me of the Difficulty of enlivening it with proper Incidents: But we may safely trust to his Invention, which is inexhaustible upon all Occasions. He has desir'd me to give him an Hour or two's Attention on the reading of his Plan."[42]

Historically *Grandison* opened the way for the later Richardsonian novel of manners; here characters are brought from the isolated and sinister house in town or country into a cheerful society that frequents drawing rooms rather than the public haunts of fashion. Richardson had now served a long apprenticeship in fiction, and could skilfully vary setting and characterization, though he does not now seem to be markedly eager for experiments in technique. The interest is spread over a wider area than in the earlier books. The prefixed "Names of the Principal Persons" number fifty, "Men, Women, and Italians." and the elaborate Index includes about three times that number. We begin with the heroine Harriet Byron and her circle of friends in Northamptonshire at a time when she is about to go up to London—a kind of beginning which becomes almost standardized for this type of novel. She is twenty years old—it is time for her to be married. Lucy Selby's opening sentence, "Your resolution to accompany Mrs. Reeves to London has greatly alarmed your three lovers," suggests a direct narrative which does not develop. The letters begin by giving us an elaborate and lightly touched social record. Harriet herself feels that she is virtually on the point of creating an epistolary novel: "Shall I tell you what I imagine each person of the company I am writing about (writing in character) would say of me to *their* correspondents?—It would be digressing too much, or I would" (I, 66). "What a length have I run! How does this narrative Letter-writing, if one is to enter into minute and characteristic descriptions and conversations, draw one on!" (I, 86) "What a great deal of writing does the reciting of half an hour or an hour's conversation make, when there are three or four speakers in company; and one attempts to write what each says in the *first* person! I am amazed at the quantity, on looking back. But it *will* be so in narrative Letter-writing" (II, 414). The scale and method of some of these performances suggest the structure of the Boswellian record. Continued attention is paid to details of gesture: "Once, indeed, he tried to speak: His mouth actually opened, to give passage to his words; as sometimes seems to be his way before the words are quite ready: But he sat down satisfied with the effort" (I, 60). This we may call the late Richardsonian treatment of mannerism, approaching Sterne.

As to the plot, Harriet is beset with lovers. The libertine Sir Hargrave Pollexfen plans a forced marriage and abducts Harriet, who is rescued by Sir Charles. Thus the hero makes an impressive delayed entrance, and we are introduced to the Grandison circle, dominated by Sir Charles and his sister Charlotte. The history of the Grandison family is given by Harriet, who is provided with documents and information for the purpose. But Richardson's letter-writing narratists are also interested participants, and Harriet is of course destined to fall in love with Sir Charles. The hero himself is not an important letter-writer. As far as the reader is concerned, he comes ready-made; we do not really see him developing or changing. There is of course elaborate illustration of his virtues—his numerous benefactions, his lofty intervention in the tangled affairs of kinsmen, friends, or even strangers, and his notoriously effective way of placating and disarming men who want to fight duels with him. All this has counted heavily against him with readers of later times. As Mark Twain says somewhere, "Few things are harder to put up with than the annoyance of a good example."

The plot is complicated by Sir Charles's Italian involvements, his conditional betrothal to Clementina della Porretta. Despite the plan or outline which Richardson had, he hesitated as to how much emphasis to give to the Italian story. On October 22, 1751, he wrote to William Duncombe:

Clementina's Fate is not yet come to my Knowledge. I have been hinder'd from enquiring after her; in other words, from pursuing her story. But I think she rises upon me. And as I know not what to offer next, being too irregular a scribbler to be able to write by a plan, I seem to be at a loss, to know what to do with her, or to fetch up Harriet again, and make her the principle Female character. . . .

I want more time than my Business will allow me, now her story is become arduous, to adjust, reconcile, retrospect, connect, etc. I have half a Mind to lay by the Work for ever. A very little inducement will make me resolve to do so. Do you think it right at my time of life, and shook by maladies, that affect me mentally as well as corporally, to write Love Stories, and fill my head with Nugatories of Boys and Girls.[43]

Richardson ends by duplicating effects rather extensively. Clarissa, Harriet, and Clementina all meet social and moral obstacles as they are drawn into unavowed or imperfectly avowed attachments; all undergo various degrees of compulsion; all are confronted with the argument, "If you aren't really in love with A, why should you refuse to marry B?" The Porrettas persecute Clementina as the Harlowes persecute Clarissa, though of course Clementina never becomes a Richardsonian heroine in the full sense because she never becomes a major correspondent. Richardson here tries to repeat the gigantesque effect of *Clarissa* in a relatively facile and theatrical way, to execute a romantic variation of the novel of manners. It is significant that when John Scott of Amwell discusses the possibility of striking illustrations for Richardson's novels he notes that *Grandison* "abounds with fine situations" and refers particularly to the Italian heroines, Clementina herself and the jealous and passionate Olivia, who actually draws a dagger on Sir Charles:

> Now from the page of Richardson bestow
> On Clementina's face the lines of woe;
> Or let sweet Harriet's livelier beauty wear
> The soul-fraught eye and apprehensive air;
> Or draw the proud Olivia's rage-flush'd charms,
> When the calm hero seiz'd her deadly arms;
> And paint that hero, firm in trial prov'd,
> Unaw'd by danger, and by vice unmov'd.[44]

Though admired by contemporaries, the Italian story seems to us to be at the same time colorless and theatrical, and Sir Charles's toplofty embarrassment, with the ideally eligible

Harriet in England and the tragic Clementina in Italy, does not command our full interest and sympathy. After protracted negotiations which do not "engage the heart" like the deadlock in *Clarissa* or even the predicament of Pamela, Sir Charles is made free to marry Harriet by Clementina's scruples about marrying a heretic. It is interesting to mark Richardson's preference between the two heroines: " 'Will I give you Leave to think. that Harriet is superior to Clementina?' Indeed I will. I have owned the Superiority to our dear Lady B. And have reflected upon the Judgment of those who are struck with the Glare of a great Action, which was owing principally to a raised Imagination. Your beloved Sister is of Opinion with you, Madam, in preferring Harriet: And I will not choose for my Judges of the Work, any of those, who are of a contrary one."[45] This verdict, like others pronounced in that period on the characters in the novels, appears to be based on the moral qualities of the character rather than on the success of the characterization; yet Richardson probably had enough power of self-criticism to realize that his Italian story, when compared with his best work, represented a failure of the imagination.

Next to Anna Howe, Charlotte Grandison is the most important of Richardson's lively ladies, and does much to sustain the level of the comedy of manners. She was a more important character for contemporary readers than she has been for later generations; her good and bad qualities were much discussed, and many agreed with the more sedate Harriet in blaming her for her perverse treatment of her husband, her "froppishness," to use one of Richardson's words. The Lord G.-Charlotte and Harriet-Charlotte contrasts, as has been said, come from the cross-pattern of grave and lively characters in current comedy. The plan of *Grandison* permits the expansion of such roles. The duplication of themes from *Clarissa* is not confined to the Italian story, though most of the situations are toned down. Even the unscrupulous Sir Hargrave aims at enforced marriage, not seduction, and is far from being a complex egotist like Lovelace; other rakes and men of pleasure, like Sir Everard Grandison, are silly and futile rather than dangerous. Sir Thomas Grandison, the libertine father of Sir Charles, domineers over his daughters, but shows himself to be more sprightly and less sullen than Clarissa's father. The approved social circles in *Grandison* contrast on the one hand with the domestic tyranny of the Harlowes and on the other hand with the folly and frivolity of fashionable life. Didacticism persists, but finer distinctions are being made, and the promptings of the comic spirit are beginning to make it easier to distinguish folly from wickedness. Within the groups presented the discriminated characteristics of the various ages of man count for much; the old, the middle-aged, and the young are all depicted, and we are expected to remember that Sir Charles's father is a middle-aged cynic, Harriet herself a girl of twenty (a year or two older than one would expect an unmarried beauty to be), the naïve Emily Jervois fourteen, and so on.

Impulse may be evil in the arrogant or wicked, but delightful, admirable, even playful in the virtuous, though untrustworthy in a whimsical person like Charlotte; on the other hand, mere impulse is so completely controlled in a moral paragon like Sir Charles that his actions often seem pompous and formal, whatever we are told about his feelings. This may be called sentimentalism if we mean by that term a harmonizing of the true, the good, and the beautiful, which is at the same time a harmonizing of self-love or self-approval with benevolence; but it is not sentimentalism in the sense that it exalts a mere release of feeling which carries with it the guarantee of its own virtue. Richardson's ethical position is well stated in one of Henry Grove's papers in the *Spectator:* "The Desire of doing Good . . . though antecedent to Reason, may yet be improved and regulated by it, and, I will add, is no otherwise a Virtue than as it is so."[46] Or, as Grove later put it, "the *virtue* of benevolence" is not to be identified "with the *instinct* called by that name"— an identification erroneously made, he says, by Hutcheson in his *Inquiry into the Original of Our Ideas of Beauty and Virtue.* For Richardson and Sir Charles the natural goodness of human nature is not a fixed dogma, but a working assumption convenient for the didactic novelist and the philanthropist.

Surely, Dr. Bartlett, human nature is not so bad a thing, as some disgracers of their own species have imagined. I have, on many occasions, found, that it is but applying properly to the passions of persons, who, tho' they have not been very remarkable for benevolence, may yet be induced to do right things in *some* manner, if not always in the *most* *graceful*. . . . We should not too soon, and without making *proper* applications, give up persons of ability or power, upon conceptions of their general characters; and then, with the herd, set our faces against them, as if we knew them to be invincible. How many ways are there to overcome persons, who may not, however, be naturally beneficent! Policy, a regard for outward appearances, ostentation, love of praise, will sometimes have great influences. (IV, 156-57)

Richardson is at great pains to show that the good man's feelings and opinions must issue in deeds, and to avoid the common objection that sentimentalism substitutes feeling for action. The novelist's Concluding Note points out that such deeds are within the power of any man so situated, and that the purpose of the story is "to shew, by a series of facts in common life, what a degree of excellence may be attained and preserved amidst all the infection of fashionable vice and folly" (VI, 329). "The Chevalier Grandison, said the kind Jeronymo, speaks by *action:* It is his way. His head, his heart, his lips, his hands, are governed by one motion, and directed by one spring" (IV, 227-28). This is a restatement of the ideal of harmony that underlies sentimental ethics.

Love between the sexes of course poses the supreme problem in the harmonizing of passion with rational esteem and moral approval. The theme is always present in Richardson's novels from the first clumsy advances of Mr. B— to the concluding tableaux at Grandison Hall, though it reaches tragic heights only in *Clarissa*. Through much of *Grandison* this engrossing issue is discussed as in a long-drawn-out session of a bourgeois or genteel court of love. When Charlotte writes in anti-romantic vein, "Love-matches, my dear, are foolish things," Harriet replies: "I remember, you once said, It was well that Love is not a passion absolutely invincible: But, however, I do not, my dear, agree with you in your notions of all Love-matches.

Love merely *personal*, that sort of Love which commences between the years of fifteen and twenty; and when the extraordinary *merit* of the object is not the foundation of it; may, I believe, and perhaps generally *ought* to, be subdued. But Love that is founded on a merit that every-body acknowledges—I don't know what to say to the vincibility of *such* a Love" (V, 70, 72).

This moral seriousness in a settled system, expressed in socially acceptable forms and in detailed illustrations and nice distinctions, imparts a sense of security and encourages lightness of touch. The feminine point of view prevails. As Clarissa herself had remarked, "Who sees not that those women who take delight in writing, excel the men in all the graces of the familiar style? The gentleness of their minds, the delicacy of their sentiments (improved by the manner of their education) and the liveliness of their imaginations, qualify them to a high degree of preference for this employment" (VIII, 224). The tone of the later Richardsonian letter, abundantly illustrated in *Grandison* and in the novelist's own correspondence, is thus suggested in a letter to Miss Westcomb:

And shall the modest Lady have nothing but her Silence to commend her? Silence indeed to me is a Commendation, when worthy Subjects offer not, and nothing but Goose-like Gabble-Gabble-Gabble (Begging their Flippancies' Pardon) is going forward; For Air, and Attention, and Non-Attention, as Occasions require, will show *Meaning* beyond what Words can; to the Observing: But the Pen will show *Soul*, and *Meaning* too!—Retired, the modest Lady, happy in her self; happy in the Choice she makes of the dear Correspondent of her own Sex (for ours are too generally Designers) Uninterrupted; her Closet her Paradise: Her Company, her self, and ideally the Beloved absent; there she can distinguish her self! By this Means she can assert and vindicate her Claim to Sense and Meaning—And shall a modest Lady then refuse to write? Shall she, in other Words, refuse to set down her Thoughts, as if they were unworthy of her self, of her Friend, of her Paper?—A Virtuous and innocent Heart to be afraid of having its Impulses *embodied* as I may say!—Tell it not in Gath—Lest the Daughters of the Philistines (the Illiteratae, if you please) rejoice!—Shall she refuse to give herself, by Use, a Facility, in so commendable an Employment; which on so many Occasions may be no less *useful* than commendable?—Shall she deny her self a Style, and, as I may say, an Ability to judge of the Style or Sense of others; or even of what she reads?—Hard, very hard, would she think it, if our Sex were to make a Law to deny hers, the Opportunities she denies her self.[47]

THE EARLY MASTERS OF ENGLISH FICTION

We enjoy the new style better when it gives us not the sentimental and didactic meditations of the "closet" but the notation and analysis of social detail. Amid the festivities and self-congratulations of the wedding day, Charlotte can write: "The coach-way was lined with spectators. Mr. Selby, it seems, bowed all the way, in return to the salutes of his acquaintance. Have you never, Lady L., called for the attention of your company in your coach, to something that has passed in the streets, or on the road, and at the same time thrust your head thro' the window, so that nobody could see but yourself? So it was with Mr. Selby, I doubt not. He wanted every one to look in at the Happy Pair; but took care that hardly any-body but himself should be seen" (V, 374). One interesting result is the *ingénue* type of letter, written, but not at great length, by Emily Jervois, and afterwards further developed by Fanny Burney. There are even hints that the lighter letters could be made a delicate instrument for high comedy, that is, for criticism of the basic assumptions made by the characters in the book. Harriet is not always excessively solemn about her troop of suitors: "Bless me, my dear, how am I to be distressed on all sides! by *good* men too; as Sir Charles could say he was, by good women" (IV, 41). And when it appears that Harriet is magnanimously giving up all hope of Sir Charles, and preferring the happiness of Clementina to her own, the facetious Uncle Selby contributes one of the subtlest comments in the whole work: "My Uncle, in particular, says, the very pretension is flight and nonsense: But, however, if the girl, added he, can *parade* away her passion for an object so worthy; with all my heart: It will be but just, that the romancing elevations, which so often drive headstrong girls into difficulties, should now-and-then help a more discreet one out of them" (IV, 56). Charlotte's picture of the eternal friendship struck up between Harriet and Clementina, heroines both, "each admiring herself *in* the other," raises large issues and opens an important page in Meredith's Book of Egoism.[48] Charlotte and Harriet can speak of Sir Charles with salutary irreverence; the inevitable critic of the Egoist is an intelligent woman, as Fitzwilliam Darcy,

Sir Austin Feverel, and Sir Willoughby Patterne were to discover. "After all, he ill brooks to be laughed at," says Charlotte (V, 5). There is a minor strain of uneasiness after the hero's return from Italy, a hint of impatience or dissatisfaction with his very virtues. Should he come unannounced to Selby House to claim, as all expect, the hand of Harriet? Should he send word in advance? "Or does he think," asks Harriet, "we should not be able to outlive our joyous surprize, if he gave us not notice of his arrival in these parts before he saw us?" (V, 88) Harriet had already hit the target with a remarkable bit of analysis: "Do you think, my dear, that had he been the first man, he would have been so complaisant to his Eve, as *Milton makes Adam* [So contrary to that part of his character, which made him accuse the woman to the Almighty]—To taste the forbidden fruit, because he would not be separated from her, in her punishment, tho' all *posterity* were to suffer by it?—No; it is my opinion, that your brother would have had gallantry enough to his fallen spouse, to have made him extremely regret her lapse; but that he would have done *his own duty,* were it but for the sake of posterity, and left it to the Almighty, if such had been his pleasure, to have annihilated his first Eve, and given him a second" (IV, 362). At times Richardson taxes the letter form beyond the limits of his own scrupulousness and propriety. Once he goes so far as to record at length a troubled dream of Harriet's, recapitulating with broken imagery the principal events of the story (V, 257-59). "Incoherencies of incoherence!" she cries, and her "resveries" are not greatly extended, as they might be in modern stream-of-consciousness fiction, but even here Richardson is experimenting with his forms and testing their possibilities to the last.

Grandison furnishes the most striking illustration of the tendency of Richardson's novels to impart to the reader a feeling of close acquaintanceship or intimacy with a group of characters set in the framework of a familiar society. There is always a disposition to project the characters of fiction into the plane of actuality: quixotism in this sense has a long history, from the time when women might weep because "Amadis is dead," down to the days when the country folk, according to the story, rang the bells of the parish church to celebrate Pamela's marriage, to the famous leader in the *Times* beginning, "Soames Forsyte is dead," and to the state of mind of innumerable listeners who cannot be kept from sending in wedding presents if a character in a radio serial is getting married. Readers of *Grandison* thought of the characters as actual members of contemporary society; some of Richardson's circle took nicknames from the novel, and Continental readers enjoined their friends who were traveling to England to visit their favorite characters. "Je vous prie," says a Frenchman in Diderot's *Éloge de Richardson*, "de voir de ma part Miss Emilie, M. Belford, et surtout Miss Howe, si elle vit encore." It was this new intimacy, as well as the mere multiplication of novels, that set the moralistic critics of fiction to evaluating the works in terms of their overt teaching as supported by their social and psychological plausibility. More subtly, this extrapolation from books into life had a marked effect on literary criticism in general, notably in the new criticism of Shakespeare's characters which treated them as "real people" existing in a moral, social, and psychological system independent of the plays. This subject deserves further exploration.

Richardson's influence on the later eighteenth century novel has often been considered in contrast to that of Fielding, but such an opposition is oversimple or exaggerated. His position has likewise been defined in terms of sentimentalism. But Richardson's influence on later sentimentalism is hard to isolate; when it can be identified it works for artistic rigor and for minute and consistent analysis of detail. A full-scale Richardsonian imitation must be serious (with tragic possibilities), and at the same time finely analytical of manners and morals. The danger was that the serious would go into violence and sensationalism, that the analytical would run into triviality. The innumerable stories which give us a sprightly-serious correspondence between a heroine and her friend, a daring libertine, an abduction, and a seduction, are only superficially Richardsonian. It is unhistorical to see Richardson in every bourgeois seduction story—in the story of Faust and Gretchen, for example, as has been done by an able scholar.[49] Moreover, the story of Clarissa did not lend itself completely to the uses of the conduct-book. When the heroine of a novel of 1764 leaves her home to avoid a loveless marriage, her friend carefully explains to her angry father: "Your child, sir, only desires a bare negative in a point whereon all her peace and felicity is dependent; she sets up no will of her own against you, nor has she presumed to make a clandestine, indiscreet choice. She has, indeed, flown from your house, but her flight was single, no giddy lover to assist, no unworthy confident [sic] to impel her to the commission of an action, that would have blasted your every hope and expectation."[50] When Maria Susannah Cooper revised one of her novels, she explained that she had originally erred in making her heroine too independent of "the earliest duty of life": "Emilia's heart was devoted to an object worthy of its attachment, but she engaged herself by a promise which abridged the right of parental authority. This defect in example lessened the influence of her precepts. The writer has now endeavoured to draw a perfect pattern of filial obedience, and female delicacy."[51] Lovelace was endlessly imitated, not without moral misgivings and serious doubts about the probability of his elaborate plots, as in the utterances of one would-be seducer who happens to be named Lord Lovell: "With your noble way of thinking you will probably wonder that I have not recourse to some stratagem, or even violence, to get her person into my possession, and so take the shortest way with my fair dissenter. But those schemes of rapes, or running away with women, are, in the first place, what I have always detested and despised: besides, they rarely or ever answer the end, and, in this country especially, are next to impracticable. But as to Clara, for many reasons that I could give you, the probability of succeeding in such an attempt would hardly be less than that of a Sallee rover's cruizing above bridge, and making prize of a Thames-wherry carrying a company to Vauxhall."[52]

The ineffectual imitations and modifications of the *Clarissa* plot force us to the conclusion that *Grandison* was imitated to more purpose than *Clarissa*. Yet, if it was only too easy to substitute commonplace melodrama and didacticism for the tragic issues of personality in *Clarissa*, it was also easy to reduce *Grandison* to conventional standards:

Then asking, what book she had in her hand, Miss Spendlove told her, It was Sir Charles Grandison. And are you not charmed, my dear, resumed my sister, with Richardson's manner of writing? In my opinion, his works are better calculated for public utility, than any of his contemporaries—What justness, and delicacy of sentiment! What fine rules of morality! What a thorough knowledge of nature!—But are you not particularly pleased with the artless simplicity of Emily? How noble an effort was hers, to conquer a passion, that stole into her breast beneath the veil of gratitude, and which she indulged, as a generous sentiment. Miss Spendlove's embarrassment betrayed her. After a pause, she answered, with frequent hesitation, "Certainly, Madam. she was a noble girl—Yes—'twas a proper resolution—And to be sure—But don't you think Lady Grandison had a tincture of jealousy in her composition?—Lady Grandison's concern, my dear, reply'd my sister, with a sigh she could not suppress, seems rather to proceed from affection, and apprehension, for a fair friend, than a jealous suspicion. Indeed, whilst she suffered the pain of uncertainty, we cannot wonder at her fears; but after having received Sir Charles's addresses, she had such perfect confidence in his love and honour, that friendship only could give rise to her solicitude. Emily's resolution was highly praise-worthy, and she pursued the only method which could restore her heart, unwarily entangled in an illaudable passion.[53]

This is not contemptible, though perhaps it is drawn too fine for us. A discerning reader can still easily understand why *Grandison* was one of Jane Austen's favorite novels. Richardson handed on to Jane Austen the tradition of a judgment of society by the intelligent feminine mind, secured by an accepted social and moral system. The individual within the system is under close surveillance by the critic, and the questions raised are those of the interplay of personality and convention, the correction of one's judgments of people and situations, the adjustment of "candor" to the facts of life, the reconciliation of spontaneity and good manners, the art of being not too pliable and not too stubborn, the art of saving oneself from one's friends, the art of living with bores, stuffed shirts, and egoists, including members of one's own family. Jane Austen's titles denote these topics without any attempt to be ornamental or oblique—*First Impressions, Sense and Sensibility, Pride and Prejudice, Persuasion;* her themes represent the exquisite distillation of the social comedy of the *Grandison* tradition combined with a serious though not tragic treatment of family relationships which derives from *Clarissa.* On the "vincibility" of love and liking, and the place of "merit" in matchmaking, Jane Austen occupied common ground with Harriet and Charlotte. From *Grandison* also stems the treatment of the libertine as fool rather than villain; his position is often reduced to absurdity, and we get Willoughby in *Sense and Sensibility,* Wickham in *Pride and Prejudice,* and Sir Edward Denham in *Sanditon.* In this tradition the social comedy can never be separated from a basic system of moral judgments; the release of free and humorous criticism or irony, as it is now fashionable to call it, is never irresponsible though it may well be lighthearted; as an aspect of the art of the novelist it stands in vital relationship to a plot structure which embodies a social structure.

For convenience the modern tendency to revise our estimate of Richardson may be illustrated by Professor E. A. Baker's significant statement:

He gave our literature the first example of that novel of personality, that history of the struggle for self-realization, which was to wait a century, for the recognition of a more enlightened scale of values, before other novelists could take it up and develop it. But of this, which was the real greatness of his achievement, Richardson was unaware, or aware very obscurely; nor did his contemporaries see what he was doing. To them and to himself he was simply the novelist of sensibility, and it was the value and interest of human feeling, as exhibited in his three novels, that riveted attention. No one observed that this was necessarily bound up with a new sense of the value and inexhaustible interest of the individual man or woman.[54]

Professor Baker later adds, "The study of feeling leads directly to the study of motive; the whole system of volitions and actions is opened up" (p. 71). In accepting in essentials this estimate of Richardson's position one may possibly give the novelist more credit for his own achievement, doubting whether long complex works can be created in utter ignorance of their real significance; there is some ground for considering *Pamela* an accident, but we can hardly dispose of *Clarissa* and *Grandison* in the same way. The critical formulas of Richardson and his age are not ours, and it is also true that many readers in the eighteenth century admired him for what we should consider the wrong reasons, and that many writers of the next generation, if they imitated him, imitated him in the wrong way. Despite his immense prestige in Western Europe, the exact extent of his influence in fiction of high value and significance, notably *La Nouvelle Héloïse* and *Werther*, remains questionable. Actual imitation is often insignificant, on a minor or secondary level. The history of Richardson's reputation, which cannot be reviewed here, shows that his special qualities were not completely submerged in the tide of sentiment, and in particular that the generation of Jane Austen and Lady Louisa Stuart, Coleridge and Hazlitt and Lamb, read him with greater intelligence and discrimination than it has been his fortune to meet with since, unless indeed the balance is being redressed at the present time. He remains the novelist of introversion and introspection, of scrutinized motives and attitudes, of the interplay of impulse and interest with code and convention that constantly ripples the surface of society and sometimes subjects the individual to an ordeal of crucial importance.

III
Henry Fielding

I

If the work of Defoe and Richardson can be related to facile generalizations about the middle class, Fielding tempts us to use the stereotype of an aristocratic background in manners and culture. But it must be kept in mind that all these class formulas can be misleading, and should not be applied mechanically. From the life of the ruling class in town and country Fielding moves into literary and professional circles. He is never the amateur in letters; he must have felt an urgent need to write for a living, and his genius and his education qualified him for discriminating compliance with the current demand for moral and professional responsibility, a demand which crossed class lines. On the whole, the spirit of the age promoted a sense of responsibility among authors with respect both to moral and artistic standards; the true author can be distinguished from the lordly amateur, the venal hack, or the servile suppliant for patronage. At his best Defoe works his way free to some extent from hurried pamphleteering and opportunist journalism; Richardson, well established in trade, proceeded to write in comparative security and leisure. With the following three major novelists such a development was heightened by humanistic education, or professional training, or both: Fielding was a student of the humanities at Eton and Leyden, and later read law in the Temple; Smollett studied medicine; and Sterne's highly individual performance presupposes bookishness and a scaffolding of scholastic and miscellaneous learning.

Thus Fielding had a thorough classical and some legal education, wide reading in modern literature, and a popular dramatist's extensive experience of the town, before he began to write novels. The drama as he practised it was in the long run an inadequate vehicle for his genius, and its significance for his literary apprenticeship should be neither ignored nor exaggerated. For the historian of fiction, the dramas should be taken as important evidence for Fielding's literary theory and practice, but should not be set apart from other models and influences. The theories suggested by the terms satire, humor, burlesque, and farce extended to nondramatic literature. In fact they could be better realized when Fielding was not immediately concerned with pleasing a given audience at a given juncture. His dramatic pieces show him to be the victim of topicality; they echo current town talk and town ways, and in the course of the 1730's fell in with the literary campaign against Walpole. Fielding is particularly fond of burlesquing current modes in the theater by means of farcical "rehearsal" pieces (*The Author's Farce, Tom Thumb, Pasquin*). His attempts at high or polite comedy in the Restoration tradition are not very successful; he does not show himself a master of witty dialogue on that level. Molière's combination of farce and satiric penetration of the fundamental issues of character must have appealed to him profoundly. But nothing is pushed very far; we do not get analytical continuity, but scattered strokes and hits. Fielding repeats himself hurriedly without following things up, despite his brilliant competence. The plays did not give him the opportunity to provide a unifying commentary from his own point of view. The novel at least gives a writer like Richardson or Fielding or Scott or Thackeray room to expatiate—a chance to use or abuse the privilege of dilation. As with Scott's poems and Thackeray's early sketches, Fielding's plays show talents not fully realized within the medium in which the young writer is exercising himself. A detailed analysis of the plays is not possible here, though the modes of satire in the plays are an important step toward the novels. But we must not take a single-line approach.[1] Outside of the drama, the examples of Cervantes, Scarron, and Marivaux were important. What we may call the official theory of the corrective function of comedy and satire is not complex enough to explain Fielding's practice. The biographical evidence shows that his controversial career as a dramatist had made him a good many enemies, and this accumulated hostility was to affect the reception of his novels. Thus an anonymous piece called *The Satirist* (about 1738) advises against writing plays and speaks of Fielding's turning to the law:

> Tell *F——* that—But *F——* is no more—
> Betaken now Reports and *Coke* to pore—
> The scurril Jest, all the licentious Rage,
> Behold! absorpt in the dry cumbrous Page. (p. 8)

The obvious thing to say about Fielding's shift to the novel is that there was a great change of scale. The burlesque on *Pamela* called *Shamela* (April, 1741) is certainly his, and represents the scale on which he worked in his plays.[2] It also uses the method of the plays, a burlesque inversion of scene after scene in *Pamela*, with hits at Colley Cibber, Conyers Middleton, Whitefield and the Methodists, and possibly other targets. By the time he wrote *Shamela*, Fielding must have known that Richardson was the author of *Pamela*, but his attack is directed at what he considers the unwholesome and hypocritical contents of the story, not at the author.

Joseph Andrews, published in 1742, is aimed at the same targets as *Shamela*, but it is possible that this work was planned as a full-scale novel from the beginning, as something beyond a mere anti-*Pamela*, though it begins with the heroine's chaste brother Joseph and with the lascivious Lady Booby's playing the role of her nephew Mr. B—. The genesis of the book cannot be exactly retraced, and it is impossible to say just when the plan as formulated in the full title presented itself to Fielding—*The History of the Adventures of Joseph Andrews and of his Friend Mr. Abraham Adams, Written in Imitation of the Manner of Cervantes, Author of 'Don Quixote.'* Since Fielding in an early chapter calls Lady Booby "the heroine of our tale" (I, viii), we may perhaps conjecture that he had at least a half-formed plan to make the novel a sustained satirical treatment of high

THE EARLY MASTERS OF ENGLISH FICTION

life, just as *Jonathan Wild* was a sustained ironical treatment of a criminal career. To satire of high life Fielding was to return in *Tom Jones* and *Amelia;* that it once occurred to him as a basic possibility for *Joseph Andrews* is at least a harmless surmise. Such an intention might be concurrent with the influence of Marivaux' *Paysan Parvenu* in the early chapters.

We may ask whether the classic Preface, the most important critical document in the history of English prose fiction up to this time, was written before or after the work itself. It is perhaps inevitable that the practice of a great humorist should outrun his theory. What Fielding says he is doing is based on a formal doctrine of the "ridiculous" (not the "comic" in the broadest sense) which forces him to describe his "comic epic in prose" as primarily aimed at exhibiting and censuring vice and folly—a didactic and corrective program. The human scene may be broadly presented, but this presentation is justified primarily in terms of the instruction. A good statement of the approach to this theory is to be found in Fielding's praise of Hogarth: "I esteem the ingenious Mr. *Hogarth* as one of the most useful Satyrists any Age hath produced. In his excellent Works you see the delusive Scene exposed with all the Force of Humour, and on casting your Eyes on another Picture, you behold the dreadful and fatal Consequence. I almost dare affirm that those two Works of his, which he calls the *Rake's* and the *Harlot's Progress,* are calculated more to serve the Cause of Virtue, and for the Preservation of Mankind, than all the *Folio's* of Morality which have been ever written; and a sober Family should no more be without them, than without the *Whole Duty of Man* in their house."[3] How far is the full "Force of Humour" compatible with the primary intention to instruct? The difficulty with the criticism of Hogarth in his own time, and so with the contemporary criticism of the comic writing of Cervantes, Fielding, and Smollett is that the parts of the artist's work not obviously instructive are often taken to be irresponsibly "burlesque" or "grotesque." It is for this reason perhaps that in the Preface to *Joseph Andrews,* Fielding tries to limit the burlesque in his work to mere matter of style. Thus the *Universal Spectator* had said of the Dutch grotesque: "In this Species we have at present a Gentleman of our own Country very excellent, I mean the ingenious Mr. *Hogarth,* who has given the Town a new Piece of Humour in his *Harlot's Progress,* and in that of a *Rake,* which will shortly appear. These Grotesque Painters I take to be exactly the same with the Burlesque Poets, the Design of both being to please, and move Laughter. But they are both too apt to give up Decency for a Joke: The Poet would leave Modesty for a merry Rhyme or a Clench; as the Painter would good Manners for an arch Conceit."[4] Charles Lamotte's *Essay upon Poetry and Painting* (1730) distinguished clearly between the legitimate low humor of the Flemish painters (Teniers, "Brewer," "Hemskirk," "Bruchels") and the distortions of Italian caricature, which is identified with the burlesque vein of Scarron and Cotton and strongly censured.

The whole discussion is deeply affected by the extravagant faith in cautionary examples and overt moral lessons which was common to the age. Pope is reported to have said of *Pamela,* "It will do more good than many volumes of sermons," and Fielding himself had seen the absurdity and caught up this remark in a burlesque prefatory letter to *Shamela,* "It will do more good than the C[lerg]y have done harm in the world." But what Fielding really finds lacking in *Pamela* is not only the provision of good examples and the antiseptic and astringent effect of bad examples, but the free play of the comic spirit. The comic intention is justified by the serious moral purpose, but the two modify each other. Didactic purpose should bridle the license found in an Aristophanes or a Joyce, and the comic spirit can best attain true freedom and serve its purpose when it is allowed to "sport with human follies, not with crimes." Its theme is social maladjustment caused by the deviations of individuals from a norm of rational morality. According to official doctrine the social maladjustments were to be presented as matter for reproof and correction; according to comic practice, they might afford sheer amusement. Such deviations had long been called "humors." Though the distinction is not explicitly made by Fielding, it is important to keep in mind the twofold conception of humor inherited from the seventeenth century, as (*a*) powerful and basic individual inclination, or (*b*) mere whim, or superficial affectation.[5] When Fielding tells us in the Preface to *Joseph Andrews* that "the only source of the true Ridiculous (as it appears to me) is affectation," and that "affectation proceeds from one of these two causes, vanity or hypocrisy," he is evidently combining the idea of humor as a superficially assumed role with the corrective tradition of comedy. The "ridiculous" in Fielding's sense does not cover the whole field of the comic, but that part which is socially and morally disapproved. This tradition imposed content as well as method of approach; the novelist as satirist inherited a stock collection of themes from the various modes of satire. Hooker's analysis brings out the importance of the different meanings of "humor" in this connection: "Humour as imitation or affectation was still ridiculous, while humour as particular inclination, individual uniqueness, or even individual eccentricity should be held above ridicule."

It is enlightening to consider these distinctions in relation to a rational observer. Confronted with various humors, he may be concerned with pronouncing moral judgments (even to the point of being moved by fierce indignation), or he may tolerate and enjoy the pageant of humors, the display of diversities, at the same time perhaps feeling superior because he is exercising control by placing or classifying people.[6] This acceptance of basic variations in human nature had been building up since the late seventeenth century. The humorist, Corbyn Morris pointed out in 1744, is free of ostentation and affectation (Fielding's source of the ridiculous), for he is "obstinately attached to sensible peculiar Oddities of his own genuine Growth."[7] Humor is interesting and natural, Morris continues, and despite its foibles "frequently exhibits very *generous benevolent* Sentiments of Heart; And these, tho' exerted in a particular odd Manner, justly command our Fondness and Love."[8] It had been orthodox doctrine ever since Sir William Temple that England was preëminently the country of humorous characters, and this was consistent with its being also a country of good-natured people.[9] Morris claims superiority for the presentation of humors over the flashes, strokes, and allusions of wit.[10] To use Shenstone's later phrasing, it was "humour and Vanbrugh" against "wit and Congreve." The critical opposition between humor and wit as ingredients of comedy helps us to realize the direction in which Fielding was moving—from wit to humor, uncertainly and tentatively in his comedies, definitely in *Joseph Andrews*.

Morris's *Essay* gives us a fuller view of the theories underlying the creation of Parson Adams than we can find in Fielding's own Preface, or in his later Jonsonian definition of humor as "a violent Impulse of the Mind, determining it to some one peculiar Point, by which a Man becomes ridiculously distinguished from all other Men."[11] For drama and fiction, the tolerant and sympathetic treatment of humors offered a middle way between the hard-boiled attitude and libertinage of Restoration comedy, and uncritical submissiveness to a supposed ideal in the presentation of virtuous characters. The new view of humor gave novelist and reader a good opportunity to be both inside and outside the character at the same time. One could participate sympathetically in eccentricities which had good intentions and generosity at their very center, and at the same time recognize tolerantly that the humorist displayed a relatively harmless kind of vanity or pride, for so his attachment to his own bent or peculiar point might be called. "He is excessively *proud*," says Morris, "and yet without knowing or suspecting it" (p. 17). One could never change Parson Adams's opinions, or shake his confidence in his own sermons and his Greek scholarship.

Instead of talking about pride, affectation, and vanity, we may view the situation in terms of a contrast or an attempted adjustment between a rigid or static system on the one hand, and on the other the flexible and shifting actualities of the mind and the world. We may think of the humorous character as rigid and unadapted in a world that requires flexibility; but we may also think of the humorous character as complex and flexible in its encounter with the rigid formulas of society and received opinion. The humor of the situation does not always lie in the incongruity between a fixed humor in the comic character and a shifting world; it may lie in the incongruity between the world's stereotypes and the unpredictable variety of the comic character's attitudes. Cervantes plays this double game, and so does Fielding. Don Quixote and Parson Adams combine a primal innocence and direct simplicity of judgment with dignity and learning, and with what we may call a rich inner resourcefulness. Who can deny that Don Quixote is a true knight, and Adams a true priest? And too much should not be made of their disqualifications for coping with this wicked world; though they are both unworldly, they do get along in their fashion with keen relish and interest. The reader is rewarded by the attainment of an imaginative vision which goes beyond mere social and moral correctness and sagacity. Lionel Trilling has recently written, in speaking of the Cervantic tradition: "The characteristic work of the novel is to record the illusion that snobbery generates and to try to penetrate to the truth which, as the novel assumes, lies hidden beneath all the false appearances."[12] This well describes the special form that Aristotelian recognition takes in modern fiction, the transmutation of the Quixote theme in the novel of manners, though such a theory, like Fielding's own Preface, lays excessive emphasis on the analytical and the satirical. "Snobbery" must be extended to mean any set of mechanically applied or conventional values by which the individual is to be judged and with which he therefore comes into conflict. If the situation is pushed to the limit, the introversion of the central character carries us beyond the bounds of comedy. But comedy avoids excessive introversion, and sets up a kind of unstable equilibrium between the rule and the case. After all that can be said about pressures and social contexts the great comic characters—Don Quixote, Falstaff, Alceste, Parson Adams —remain unadapted and unreconstructed. Falstaff will never purge and live cleanly; Don Quixote and Parson Adams never really learn by experience. We must go to them; they will not come to us. "Would I were with him, wheresome'er he is, either in heaven or in hell!" An illuminating statement of the social effect of great comedy is to be found in a recent sociological study: "Great comic art deals with contradictions arising in the individual when he tries to resolve the variant roles offered him by competing institutions. It is never otherworldly, does not seek to mystify us (like the tale of wonder), nor does it give our lusts free rein through the vicarious abasement of others (as in lewd comic art), . . . or transcend contradictions in social action by appeal to extra-social symbols of divine ends, cosmic purpose, or laws of nature. . . . The moment of transcendence in great comic art is a social moment, born out of the conviction that we are human after all, even though we try to be gods."[13]

The theory that the ridiculous character is exhibited for purposes of correction hardly holds even for secondary figures. The supporting cast is presented with a dash of exaggeration and gusto that puts out of the question the possibility of their being examples by which readers might correct themselves. No one is going to take warning by the lustful Lady Booby, the ineffable Slipslop, with her strange words, the porcine Parson Trulliber, the illiterate and sycophantic justice of the peace, the silly lord who tries to abduct Fanny, the puny Beau Didapper, the notable inn-keeping Tow-wowse couple. In this comic masterpiece Fielding's reiterated moral judgments actually result in heightening the rich incongruity of the spectacle, and Fielding is more uniformly successful than Richardson in fortifying our assurance that we are not merely being regaled with a cautionary tale. For example, in the passage introducing Lady Booby we read: "My lady was a woman of gaiety, who had been blessed with a town education, and never spoke of her country neighbours by any other appellation than that of the Brutes" (I, iii). When she visits the Adamses, all she can say in response to their greetings is, "Quelle bête! quel animal!" (IV, ix) Simple as these touches are, we have to read the whole of *Joseph Andrews,* and *Tom Jones* and *Amelia* too, to realize the full significance of the town-and-country theme thus lightly presented. The enlightenment comes not in the mere exhibition of examples—this is just a convenient and conventional formula to get things going—but in the incomparable rendering of the way Fielding's own world feels to a man of fair intelligence and genuine good will who is innocently going about his business. The bad people are interesting and often amusing examples in themselves, but taken together they add up to a powerful representation of a world of corrupt and inert institutions, riddled with stupid convention and snobbery. The pageant of town and country, road and inn, is thus shifted to a different level from the casual escapades and adventures of the picaresque tradition in its simplest form.

Obvious instances will suffice: anyone who has read twelve chapters of *Joseph Andrews* is likely to remember that when Joseph is found by a passing stagecoach in a pitiable condition, beaten, robbed, and naked, little or nothing would have been done for him "unless the postillion (a lad who hath been since transported for robbing a henroost) had voluntarily stripped off a great-coat, his only garment, at the same time swearing a great oath (for which he was rebuked by the passengers), 'that he would rather ride in his shirt all his life, than suffer a fellow-creature to lie in so miserable a condition' " (I, xii). This brilliant episode, which hinges on the legal possibility that the passengers in the coach might be indicted as accessories after the fact if Joseph should die, is but the first of a pungent series of incidents on the road and in the country parish, all turning on the perversion of the law in the hands of the malicious, the stupid, the inhumane, and the corrupt. In the last Book the characters are shown in a pattern exactly determined by points of law. Lady Booby's attempt to forbid the banns for Joseph and Fanny and Parson Adams's attitude raise familiar issues:

Some Parish Officers have presum'd to forbid Banns, because the Parties have been Poor, and like to create Charge to the Parish, or because the Man has not been an Inhabitant, according to the Laws made *for the Settlement of the Poor.* But,

No Person has Authority to forbid the Minister to proceed in pub-lishing the Banns, but the *Ordinary only* [Judge Ecclesiastical]. If in-deed the Minister be fully satisfy'd, that there be any of the three *Im-pediments* above-mention'd, [Pre-Contract, Consanguinity, Want of Con-sent, if either party is under twenty-one] he ought in reason to forbear Publication, and is liable to Censure, if he proceed to Marry them; if it can be proved, that he knew the Impediment: But the Curate is not to stop his proceeding, because any peevish, or pragmatical Person, with-out just Reason or Authority, pretends to forbid him. Poverty is no more an Impediment of Marriage, than Riches, and the Kingdom can no more subsist without Poor, than without Rich. And I see no Reason to doubt, but that Banns may be publish'd, and Marriage be solemn-iz'd betwixt two Persons that do at present *abide*, or *sojourn* within a Parish, tho' they be not fix'd Inhabitants, according to *the Acts for Set-tling the Poor*.[14]

The whole economy of presentation in Fielding's great novels is due to the presence of the narrator himself. This sub-ject has recently been carefully studied by Professor Wayne C. Booth, who points out that in *Joseph Andrews* "the intrusions of the narrator, his characterization, and his discussion with his 'reader' are carried far beyond anything in Cervantes," and are only to be matched among Fielding's predecessors by Mari-vaux.[15] The appearance of such a narrator is closely connected with the assumption of the *persona* or mask for satirical pur-poses by the great Augustans, Swift and Pope, and also of course with the emergence of the essayist in the *Spectator* tradition.[16] Fielding does not merely comment on his characters and their actions; he refers explicitly to his plans and methods as the writer of the story, and to the reader's possible reactions. Since the traditional or conventional assumption was that a piece of prose fiction was an objective report of fact, the view of the author at work had a more striking effect in prose fiction than in satire or essay. Fielding's characteristic intrusion is to comment on the method he is following in telling the story. Thus, when Mrs. Slipslop snubs Fanny, he writes an essay on "high" people and "low" people, and continues: "And now, reader, I hope thou wilt pardon this long digression, which seemed to me necessary to vindicate the great character of Mrs. Slipslop, from what low people, who have never seen high people, might think an ab-surdity" (II, xiii) . The main line of the narrative is never seri-

108 THE EARLY MASTERS OF ENGLISH FICTION

ously deranged, and the defense of digression or interpolation is really playful. Thus the chapter in which Fanny is abducted is followed by "a discourse between the poet and the player; of no other use in this history but to divert the reader" (III, x), and "the exhortations of Parson Adams to his friend in affliction; calculated for the instruction and improvement of the reader" (III, xi). Fielding then continues: "Neither the facetious dialogue which passed between the poet and the player, nor the grave and truly solemn discourse of Mr. Adams, will, we conceive, make the reader sufficient amends for the anxiety which he must have felt on the account of poor Fanny, whom we left in so deplorable a condition" (III, xii). In general Fielding the narrator is sincere when he says that he does not wish to disappoint or baffle the expectations of the reader. In this respect his intrusions differ radically from those of Sterne, as we shall see, and it should also be noticed that neither Fielding nor Sterne ever claims that he has complete control over characters and plot, that he can determine what his people say and do or that he is making up the story. At most the intrusive narrator claims only that he has absolute power to decide what to do next in the process of telling the story; telling the story is a game, but fabricating the story is not overtly recognized as part of the game.

3) The narrator imparts to the story a higher unity than is derived from the mechanism of the plot. Technically the discovery that Joseph is Wilson's son, and so not of mean birth, is the "recognition" that produces the final "reversal," but a hundred deservedly forgotten storytellers could have used this device for resolving the plot. It may even be taken as a burlesque of the stock recognition ending of romance, an instance in which Fielding extends the burlesque method from form to content. On the same level are the numerous coincidences and accidental meetings in the book. But it is the narrator who really holds the story together and gives it genuine significance. He keeps the coarser and more extravagant scenes from being taken too seriously; he keeps us amused, not merely disgusted, with Lady

Booby, Mrs. Slipslop, and the others. Since he is superior, self-controlled, and playfully ironical, he works and makes for coherence; in this respect he differs from the whimsical narrator who professes to be making a topsy-turvy game of the story, as in Marivaux's *Pharsamon* and Sterne's *Tristram Shandy,* or from one of Richardson's correspondents in playful mood, wondering whither her impulsive pen will carry her next. Though Fielding the narrator may seem to be playful or mock-serious in his profession of a well-wrought and sensible plan, he never absolves himself from responsibility. "We hope, therefore, a judicious reader will give himself some pains to observe, what we have so greatly laboured to describe, the different operations of this passion of love in the gentle and cultivated mind of the Lady Booby, from those which it effected in the less polished and coarser disposition of Mrs. Slipslop" (I, vii). What Fielding really says here is that in the first place, he is following the psychology of the passions faithfully, and, secondly, in his ironic way, that "the Colonel's lady and Judy O'Grady are sisters under the skin." He plants such a barb with the precision of a picador, and invites your attention to his accuracy. This is after all the basic intellectual and moral responsibility which neoclassical criticism enjoins.

But the precedents offered by the broad comedy and realistic narrative of Cervantes and Scarron warranted the introduction of physical humor and farcical episode, and this vein of realism was traditionally combined with burlesque or mock-heroic style. The narrator enters here to validate the burlesque style, and to make it plain that he is using this device deliberately and keeping it within limits. As Fielding says guardedly in his Preface: "In the diction, I think, burlesque itself may be sometimes admitted. . . . But though we have sometimes admitted this in our diction, we have carefully excluded it from our sentiments and characters; for there it is never properly introduced." Byron, commenting upon vulgarity in literature, comes close to this point: "It [vulgarity] does not depend upon low themes, or even low language, for Fielding revels in both;—but is he ever vulgar? No. You see the man of education, the gentleman, and the scholar, sporting with his subject—its master, not its slave."[17] There is a broad vein of caricature in the presentation of many of the secondary characters which is closely related to burlesque, and it has already been suggested that the "recognition" at the end can be taken as an extension of the burlesque method to the plot; but in general it is correct to say that the burlesque devices in Fielding's novel simply emphasize the fact that the narrator is in complete control. He is in such complete control, in fact, that the effect is one of detached interest; the term "intrusion" is unfortunate if it suggests fussiness or intermeddling, the kind of petty involvement in the affairs of the story for which Thackeray and Trollope were later censured.

The mock-heroic or burlesque method may also appear in his imputing elevated, rhetorical, formal, or sententious language to his characters with special intent. He touches on this matter in *Jonathan Wild*, without going fully into his motives for embellishing diction: "If it should be observed, that the style of this letter doth not exactly correspond with that of our hero's speeches, which we have here recorded, we answer, it is sufficient if in these the historian adheres faithfully to the matter, though he embellishes the diction with some flourishes of his own eloquence, without which, the excellent speeches recorded in ancient historians (particularly in Sallust,) would have scarce been found in their writings" (III, vi). When Lady Booby tempts Joseph and calls him a boy, " 'Madam,' says Joseph, 'that boy is the brother of Pamela, and would be ashamed that the chastity of his family, which is preserved in her, should be stained in him.' " And when Joseph leaves she exclaims: "Whither doth this violent passion hurry us! What meanness do we submit to from its impulse! Wisely we resist its first and least approaches; for it is then only we can assure ourselves the victory. No woman could ever safely say, so far only will I go" (I, viii). As the *New Yorker* would say, this may be put under the head of "exclamations we doubt ever got exclaimed," but it is not just stilted writing. Joseph's speech suggests innocently priggish virtue; Lady Booby's style is that of a battered harridan playing the tragedy queen. Fielding makes capital of his very clichés. The interpolated tale of Leonora is deliberately filled with the stock formulas of the current love tale or "novel."

In one important passage in the Preface Fielding treats burlesque as a way of presenting a tolerant and comic view of the human spectacle:

And I apprehend my Lord Shaftesbury's opinion of mere burlesque agrees with mine, when he asserts, There is no such thing to be found in the writings of the ancients. But perhaps I have less abhorrence than he professes for it; and that, not because I have had some little success on the stage this way, but rather as it contributes more to exquisite mirth and laughter than any other; and these are probably more wholesome physic for the mind, and conduce better to purge away spleen, melancholy, and ill affections, than is generally imagined. Nay, I will appeal to common observation, whether the same companies are not found more full of good-humour and benevolence, after they have been sweetened for two or three hours with entertainments of this kind, than when soured by a tragedy or a grave lecture.[18]

This seems to be Fielding's most complete recognition of humor as an aesthetic experience rather than as a tool of didacticism, his theoretical recognition of a genial tolerance that could cover Parson Adams, Tom Jones, and Squire Western. The more even diffusion of humor in *Joseph Andrews* as compared with *Tom Jones* may be described by saying that Fielding's genius here exercises just the degree of control which keeps a sense of ethical direction but at the same time affords easy play for intrinsically humorous episode. He still has the fluidity of the old picaresque or Cervantic model of adventures on the road, but keeps all matters in hand; and in the last part the presentation of the action within the framework of the parish holds individual character and social milieu in equilibrium. The sequence of life in town, life on the road, and life in the country parish was to be given in reverse order in *Tom Jones*. The parish and the road proved to be a better vehicle for Fielding's humor than the town, where he was too much preoccupied with the shortcomings and vices of high life. The center of action on the road is often the inn-kitchen, where travelers of all sorts gathered to eat, drink, and talk, unless those of the better class wished to withdraw to private rooms. As the German traveler Moritz wrote later: "They showed me into the kitchen, and set me down to sup at the same table with some soldiers and the servants. I now for the first time, found myself in one of those kitchens which I had so often read of in Fielding's fine novels. The chimney in this kitchen, where they were roasting and boiling, seemed to be taken off from the rest of the room and enclosed by a wooden partition. The rest of the apartment was made use of as a sitting and eating room. All round on the shelves there were pewter dishes and plates, and the ceiling was well stored with provisions of various kinds, such as sugar loaves, black puddings, hams, sausages, flitches of bacon, etc."[19]

Yet Fielding is interested in the action rather than the setting, and it is a striking fact that there are no elaborately described interiors in his work—whether inn, cottage, or manor house. The concluding action in the home parish has much comic gusto in the continuation of the Adams comedy and in the further satire of the operations of the law. It is somewhat weakened by the appearance of Mr. B— and Pamela, conceived of as snobs who object to the marriage of Joseph and Fanny, but not fully realized as characters. One feels that Fielding now finds the intended satire of Richardson hanging heavy on his hands. The despicable Beau Didapper, introduced as a libertine suitor to Fanny, brings inferior city comedy into the country. The burlesque recognition of Joseph as Wilson's son has nothing to do with *Pamela,* where Richardson departed from the common pattern of the *roman de mésalliance* by deliberately keeping Pamela's birth obscure. Fielding had already used the burlesque recognition in *The Author's Farce* (1730). The news that Fanny is really an Andrews child, with the result that Joseph and Fanny are thought for a short time to be brother and sister, is a superficial use of the "false alarm" incest device which reappears near the end of *Tom Jones.* But the prosperity of true comedy lies not in the ending. This point should be kept in mind for *Tom Jones* also, different as the two books are in structure. The final synthesis in *Joseph Andrews,* though not technically the dramatic conclusion, is made in the series of night adventures in Booby Hall involving all the principal characters in the book.[20] On the surface this might appear to be a rough-and-tumble traditional inn scene transplanted to a country house, with Didapper getting into the wrong bed once (with Mrs. Slipslop), and Adams blundering into the same situation twice (with Mrs. Slipslop and then with Fanny herself). The spirit of the scene is that of the comedy of the road, the central part of the story; the treatment of ugly and promiscuous lust on a comic level carries us back to the earliest chapters, with the amorous Slipslop as the connecting link. Adams for the last time passes innocent and unscathed through a physical ordeal, and Joseph and Fanny are as usual innocently passive. The method of the scene is essentially that which Cervantes uses in his important inn scenes, with various characters and themes converging. *Tom Jones* comes to mind here also, with the mode of Cervantes and this comparatively playful study in *Joseph Andrews* leading in one way or another to the famous night in the inn at Upton.

Joseph Andrews won moderate critical and marked popular approval despite the fact that it labored under the stigma of being low and burlesque. Under the circumstances, one could hardly expect full and formal approval for either *Pamela* or *Joseph Andrews*. An unusually favorable statement of the case, which enables us to see the new work overcoming opposition, is to be found in the *Museum*: "The *Travels of Joseph Andrews* have been admitted into the best Company, been read and admired by the most elegant Judges, for the just Representation of certain Characters, tho' they are chiefly taken from the lowest Life. We are content to follow Parson *Trulliber* into his Hog-Sty, or Mrs. *Tow-wowse* into her Ale-house, and think ourselves sufficiently repaid for our Condescension, if we are made to laugh by a just Description of these dirty Scenes."[21]

Fielding's *Life of Mr. Jonathan Wild the Great* was published in Volume III of the *Miscellanies* of 1743, and appeared in an extensively revised version in 1754, the only early separate edition in the period.[22] Wild, a notorious criminal of the 1720's, was an organizer of theft and robbery, whose racket was to return stolen goods on commission. He had been the subject of criminal biographies by Defoe and others.[23] Fielding develops a sustained ironical burlesque of the criminal biography on the thesis that true and consistent greatness must be clear of any taint of goodness, witness the great conquerors and kings of history, Alexander the Great, Julius Caesar, Jonathan Wild himself, and of course Sir Robert Walpole. In a thoroughgoing way which invites comparison with Swift, the narrative ironically sets forth inverted standards of honor and magnanimity. It was a moral commonplace that the poor man who robs and steals is sent to the gallows, while the man who robs and kills on the grand scale is a hero. Fielding uses variations on this theme: "How easy is the reflection of having taken a few shillings and pounds from a stranger, without any breach of confidence, or perhaps any great harm to the person who loses it, compared to that of having betrayed a public trust, and ruined the fortunes of thousands, perhaps of a great nation?" (I, v) A later soliloquy of Wild's elaborates the theme: "What is the life of a single man? have not whole armies and nations been sacrificed to the honour of ONE GREAT MAN? nay, to omit that first class of greatness, the conquerors of mankind, how often have numbers fallen by a fictitious plot, only to satisfy the spleen, or perhaps exercise the ingenuity, of a member of that second order of greatness, the Ministerial? What have I done, then? Why, I have ruined a family, and brought an innocent man to the gallows. I ought rather to weep with Alexander, that I have ruined no more, than to regret the little I have done" (IV, iv) . These familiar ideas reappear in mock-heroic comments by Lovelace: "Learn of the *Royal Butchers;* who for sport (an hundred times worse men than thy Lovelace) widow ten thousand at a brush, and make twice as many fatherless—Learn of *them,* I say, how to support a *single* death."—"Are not you and I, Jack, innocent men, and babes in swadling-cloths, compared to Caesar, and to his predecessor in heroism Alexander, dubbed for murders and depredation *Magnus?*"[24] But usually Fielding, in the vein of *The Beggar's Opera,* ironically presents public and private crime on the same level as instances of true greatness. It is all the same whether a man suffers as a traitor on Tower Hill or as a thief at Tyburn (I, v). Newgate "is a castle very far from being an improper, or misbecoming habitation for any Great Man whatever" (III, xiv). This leveling is carried out so thoroughly that the surface incongruity between low matter and high style is not emphasized; the characteristic effect is not that of burlesque epic, and few of Fielding's epic similes appear.

The satirical method Fielding takes from Swift is to set up and isolate an absolute standard denoted by noble words which are then deprived of content or taken to mean the opposite of themselves. Honor, for example, cannot depend on Good Nature, Humanity, Honesty, or Truth. "In what then doth the word honour consist? Why in itself alone. A man of honour is he that is called a man of honour" (I, xiii). Inhumanity is set forth as high humanity: "Is it not more generous, nay, more good-natured, to send a man to his rest; than after having plundered him of all he hath, or from malice or malevolence depriving him of his character, to punish him with a languishing death, or what is worse, a languishing life?" (III, iii) Similarly, in the opening chapter Fielding undermines the term "perfection" by playing on its ethical and aesthetic meanings. Greatness "marred by goodness" works "to the disadvantage of that great perfection, uniformity of character." The portrayal of Jonathan Wild is a triumph of art, it is implied, as it approaches the heroic standards of the "perfection of daemonism." The principle of uniformity becomes with marvellous cogency the stoic principle of majestic constancy, and the great man can always wrap himself in his virtue. " 'Tis the inward glory, the secret consciousness of doing great and wonderful actions, which can alone support the truly great man, whether he be a *Conqueror,* a *Tyrant,* a *Statesman,* or a *Prig"* (II, iv).

It is in circumstances of distress that true greatness appears most wonderful. For, that a prince in the midst of his courtiers, all ready to compliment him with his favourite character or title, and, indeed, with every thing else; or that a conqueror, at the head of an hundred thousand men, all prepared to execute his will, how ambitious, wanton, or cruel soever, should, in the giddiness of their pride, elevate themselves many degrees above those their tools, seems not difficult to be imagined or indeed accounted for. But that a man in chains, in prison, nay, in the vilest dungeon, should, with persevering pride, and obstinate dignity, discover that vast superiority in his own nature over the rest of mankind, who, to a vulgar eye, seem much happier than himself; nay, that he should discover Heaven and Providence (whose peculiar care, it seems, he is) at that very time at work for him; this is among the arcana of greatness, to be perfectly understood only by an adept in that science. (II, xi)

Here Fielding is dealing with the theme that always recurs in the eighteenth century novelists and satirists, the mutations of pride, vanity, and egoism. He is cutting below the surface to the roots of human nature. His fierce oversimplification is modified only slightly by another device he has also learned from Swift, the intermingling of ironical understatement with ironical exaggeration. His exalted hero, he tells us at the outset, is not a consummate pattern of virtue; little imperfections darken his good qualities, or in other words he is not absolutely free from moral compunctions. But there is no actual softening or realistic complication of the character.

The evident intention to satirize Walpole and the sustained burlesque suggest the tone of the late 1730's, and such considerations might be used to date the work before *Joseph Andrews* Digeon and Baker are for the earlier date; Cross would associate the whole work with the fall of Walpole in 1742, and Dr. Dudden has recently offered a compromise by suggesting that the opening sketch of Wild may be early, the extended narrative contrasting Wild and the virtuous Heartfree having been added later. If this is so, Fielding did not take full advantage of his newly acquired experience in prose fiction: the colorlessly virtuous citizen Heartfree, the diametrical opposite of Wild, does not inspire the incisive ethical analysis of Fielding's best work. The story is to be judged as a satire rather than a novel. As with Swift, the question can be raised, How far is the satire intended to cover the actual complexities of life in eighteenth century England? Are not Wild, Heartfree, and the rest abstractions pointed up to enforce an antithesis, and as such are they not, like the Houyhnhnms and the Yahoos, hard to fit into the real world we are supposed to be talking about? A Houyhnhnm or a Heartfree must surely be an inadequate symbol of Swift's complete man, or Fielding's. And as with the pride of the Yahoo, the villainy of a Wild precludes enjoyment of the ludicrous spectacle of criminals on their dignity, as in *The Beggar's Opera* a few years before, or later in Burns's *Jolly Beggars*. The sustained bitter irony in *Wild* keeps Fielding from exercising the vein of free humorous comment which had appeared in *Joseph Andrews* and was to be further developed in *Tom Jones*. The playful use of detail is checked, and the city subject excludes the life of the countryside and the varied incidents of the road. Thackeray's imitation of this work, *Barry Lyndon,* occupies a similar position in his career as a novelist; it shows his power without giving him a chance to do his most characteristic work.

II

The publication of *The History of Tom Jones, A Foundling* in 1749, after the completion of *Clarissa* in 1748, places the high point of eighteenth century fiction almost exactly midway in the century. Of *Tom Jones* the historian of the subject may say in all sincerity what Dr. Johnson said ironically of Gray's *Odes:* "My process has now brought me to the *Wonderful Wonder of Wonders."* The closest analysis of this story can only heighten our admiration of the master. *Tom Jones* builds on all Fielding's acquired skills and accumulated experiences—his early dramatic work, his experiments in satire and burlesque, his fruitful work with the theory and practice of prose fiction, and the hard-earned wisdom of middle age. The theory of the comic epic in prose is to be taken in this broad context; Fielding now calls his work "this heroic, historical, prosaic poem" (IV, i). The narrator is completely in control: he devises a cunning plot; he defines and elaborates more systematically his underlying psychology and ethics; his command of style is so

THE EARLY MASTERS OF ENGLISH FICTION

complete and is exercised with so much skill and charm that one thinks of Max Beerbohm's figure of Thackeray piping and the words trooping at his call.

In an effective essay Professor Crane has questioned the traditional praise of the plot of *Tom Jones,* not because it is undeserved but because it tends to detach the plot as a mechanism from the qualities and ideas of the characters and from the thought and style of the narrator.[25] The point is well made. But why is it particularly necessary to urge that in *Tom Jones* the plot is an integral part of a larger structure? No critic has yet felt called upon to plead that the plot of *Clarissa* is inseparably linked with theme and character. The answer must be that in *Tom Jones* the ingenious mechanism of hidden and overt action, hidden and overt motives, does after all solicit attention as a mechanism. Fielding's method involves a free use of external and accidental circumstances and of the conventional situations of romance and drama in order to elicit those illustrative acts and attitudes which are his theme. The motto on the title-page is Horace's line about Ulysses, *Mores hominum multorum vidit;* and whether this is interpreted to refer to the novelist's inclusive view of manners or to the hero's range of experience, it points to a critical comedy of manners rather than to intrigue and adventure. The adventure sequence is to be interpreted in terms of an ethical view of life. The plot is not merely the delayed revelation of the secret of Tom's birth and his attainment of final success, but the ordering of events in cause-effect sequence so as to display character in action. Our admiration of the contrivance of the plot should not be directed chiefly toward the planting and concealing of clues about the secret of Tom's birth, and the steps by which the secret is finally revealed, but rather toward the way in which the whole tissue of circumstance operates to produce Tom's ordeal. In this system the minor detail may be of importance not so much for its symbolic or illustrative use, as in Richardson and Sterne, but rather for its place in the cause-effect sequence that leads to great events. Thus when Jones learns that Sophia treasures her old muff because he had once put his hands in it, Fielding comments:

Though this incident will probably appear of little consequence to many of our readers, yet, trifling as it was, it had so violent an effect on poor Jones, that we thought it our duty to relate it. In reality, there are many little circumstances too often omitted by injudicious historians, from which events of the utmost importance arise. The world may indeed be considered as a vast machine, in which the great wheels are originally set in motion by those which are very minute, and almost imperceptible to any but the strongest eyes. (V,iv)

If the reader will please to refresh his memory, by turning to the scene at Upton, in the Ninth Book, he will be apt to admire the many strange accidents which unfortunately prevented any interview between Partridge and Mrs. Waters, when she spent a whole day there with Mr. Jones. Instances of this kind we may frequently observe in life, where the greatest events are produced by a nice train of little circumstances; and more than one example of this may be discovered by the accurate eye, in this our history. (XVIII, ii)

But it is only in retrospect that the importance of certain details and situations appears. Bridget's favorable attitude toward Tom is explained when we know that he is her son; Blifil's interview with the lawyer Dowling when Allworthy is supposed to be on his deathbed is of crucial importance in postponing the revelation about Tom's birth. These devices involve a slighting and oblique treatment of character and circumstance: the novelist deliberately calls attention to some details and not to others, and when he does not dwell on the circumstance, his treatment of character in action is accordingly circumscribed. To refer to the instances just cited, we cannot be admitted to Bridget's mind, or to Dowling's character and motives, or, in this connection, even to Blifil's. For the work taken as a whole, circumstance must bring out character, must illustrate as we go along what really happens in the world when morally responsible agents live and move. The result is a comic externalization of character in action. Even the principal characters are seldom if ever left alone with their thoughts and feelings; this is especially true of Tom, of course, who is an extrovert if there ever was one. Here we have the great achievement but also the limitation of Fielding's art; the beautiful network of circumstance does not blur into the mysterious penumbra enveloping human action and human life. The right-minded man has a chance to order his world, though "not without dust and heat."

Fortune favors the brave and the benevolent, and Tom Jones has a lot of good luck as well as a lot of bad luck. The novelist himself was aware of the difficulty of planning natural incidents in confirmation of "the great, useful, and uncommon doctrine which it is the purpose of this whole work to inculcate, and which we must not fill up our pages by frequently repeating, as an ordinary parson fills his sermon by repeating his text at the end of every paragraph" (XII, viii). He here faces the fundamental difficulty of didactic fiction, and as a great critic as well as a great artist asserts in the same passage: "I am not writing a system, but a history, and I am not obliged to reconcile every matter to the received notions concerning truth and nature." Facts are stubborn, but principles are valid, and facts and principles conflict. The attitude the novelist takes toward this conflict determines whether he is to write tragedy or comedy. Cervantes alone wrote both.

The action begins with the discovery of the foundling in Squire Allworthy's bed. The central theme is immediately set by the attitude of the benevolent Allworthy toward little Tom. Characters are introduced when and as their attitudes bear on Tom's fortunes; the emphasis is not on the picture of the household and the Somersetshire parish, but on the presentation and evaluation of the characters as they meet this test—Deborah Wilkins the housekeeper, Allworthy's sister Bridget (really Tom's mother), Jenny Jones, Tom's supposed mother, Partridge, Tom's supposed father, Bridget's son Blifil, whose father Captain Blifil has recently died, the tutors Thwackum and Square, the gamekeeper George Seagrim and his family, and then Squire Western and his family. The marshalling of this cast of characters is completed by the introduction of Sophia Western in Book IV. The rich and varied action is controlled by sharp, even abstract, ethical oppositions. Allworthy, the rational benevolist, is supposed to be in control, but he has remarkably bad luck in his ménage— his hypocritical sister, the two Blifil brothers, the Doctor and the Captain, who quarter themselves upon him, the latter marrying Bridget and begetting Allworthy's black-hearted nephew. Moreover, to educate Tom and Blifil he engages the pedant Thwackum, representing the authority of the Church and a harsh application of the doctrine of original sin, and his colleague Square, who represents a heterodox rationalism, the application of an abstract formula of "the fitness of things." Both have "utterly discarded all natural goodness of heart" (III, iv). Allworthy, Tom, and the heroine Sophia all have this natural goodness, and in the long run like will to like. They are free from the "vast quick-sightedness into evil" which Fielding condemns as "a vicious excess," "a very pernicious evil in itself," and a sure sign of a bad heart (XI, x). "There is a kind of sympathy in honest minds, by means of which they give an easy credit to each other" (XIV, v), and also to the misrepresentations of evil-doers, as Heartfree does in *Jonathan Wild* (II, iii). This is what the eighteenth century called "candor." Tom has this quality too, and shares with Allworthy what the novelist playfully calls "a blameable want of caution and diffidence in the veracity of others" (VIII, vii); in Tom's career this is one aspect of his invariable display of natural goodness in the form of spontaneous impulse. He has the "sanguine disposition of mind," combined with high vitality and candor, which is the key to happiness, but which often gets him into trouble in this gross and wicked world. The alignment of characters, and the set moral discourses attributed in the early books to Allworthy, Thwackum, Square, and even Captain Blifil, might make the book excessively didactic, were it not for the pungent though not copious use of detail, the application of hearty burlesque, and the rich commentary of the narrator. The only characters who do not fall precisely into the ethical scheme are the earthy ones, notably Squire Western, secondarily the Seagrims, and the unfortunate Partridge, who is to reënter as a comic character.

As the two boys grow up, it is evident that Tom is generous, loyal, impulsive, and highly sexed; Blifil is selfish, hypocritical, and coldly deliberate. Tom's indiscretions make him the easy victim of the formalistic self-interested hypocrites, Blifil, Thwackum, and Square. The discovery of his parentage, almost as near the surface as in *Oedipus the King,* is averted and post-poned until the end of the story, though both the lawyer Dowling and the servant girl Jenny Jones have the secret. But in the *Oedipus* we think of the hero's very existence as involved in the awful secret, whereas when we think of Tom we dwell on his impulsive acts and varying fortunes, and only incidentally on his pedigree. His errors have some points of contact with the series of events in which the revelation is approached and then avoided, but the real story is his career, no matter who his parents may be. He falls completely out of Allworthy's favor, seems to have lost all hope of winning Sophia Western, and at the end of the great opening section of the story he takes to the open road. Even though all the prizes seem to have escaped him, he still has his good nature and vitality and the under-lying advantages which they must eventually secure for him.

The general impression made by the early part of the story is that the novelist himself has the vitality and goodness of heart which he imputes to Jones, and that when he marshals the re-sources of his style he is more than a match for any of his situa-tions or characters. He is superior to his subject without being contemptuous of it. He ranges from the vernacular speeches of Squire Western to carefully applied passages of elevated rhetoric, largely though not exclusively mock-heroic. These variations from the sound middle style which he uses for analysis, discussion, and narrative summary extend the range of his imagination, feeling, and humor far beyond his formal ethical preoccupations. Such flights as the introduction of Sophia Western (IV, ii) and the battle in the churchyard (IV, viii) come as a release from the study of good and evil hearts; and Tom's love-soliloquy (V, x) just after he has come from All-worthy's bedside and before he retires into the grove with Molly Seagrim is one of the most remarkable examples we have of the function of this elevated style in Fielding's narrative.

Fielding cannot treat Tom's journey from Somersetshire to London as he had treated the journey of Parson Adams and Joseph from London to the West. It is not merely a matter of incidental adventure, though we now get long self-characterizing speeches from the people met on the way (e.g., the landlady, the physician, and the lieutenant in VII, xiii), and other incidents are purely episodic—Sophia's being taken for the Chevalier's mistress, and the encounters of Tom and Partridge with the puppet-master and the gypsies. The narratives of Mrs. Fitzpatrick and the Man of the Hill, interpolated "novels" in the tradition of Cervantes, break continuity in a way that Fielding would not have admitted in the first part of the story, but may possibly be defended as providing social background for the coming action in London. During the famous night in the inn at Upton, what might at first seem to be incidental adventure is turned into an elaborate system of encounters that bring together the lines of the plot. Jones is virtually discovered by Sophia while he is in bed with Mrs. Waters, and more than this, the loose talk of Partridge as reported by other servants leads Sophia to believe that Tom is really faithless. The enforced separation now becomes an estrangement. Once more Tom loses by a narrow margin, partly by his own fault and partly by bad luck. Other characters involved in the plot make their entrances and exits during the night. Fielding's model here is probably the last long inn-sequence in *Don Quixote I,* where various themes and characters in Cervantes' extended narrative converge, although of course Cervantes does not weave so close a texture. At Upton Fielding prolongs and elaborates the parish plot, while the affair of Jenny Waters and the entry of the Fitzpatricks point forward to London. Upton gives us the longest continuous series of incidents in the book, and the sequence is strongly colored, though not dominated, by the mock-heroic style (see especially IX, iii, v) , while the action is sustained in the manner of drama by rapid entrances and exits and a drumfire of dialogue. The situations set up by the external action are not thinly or superficially conceived; on the contrary, the events are used to evoke one of the richest comedies in literature, but it is still possible to distinguish between the mechanism of events and the use Fielding makes of it.

The humor thins out in the London part of the story. When the principal characters are transferred from country to town, they appear in what Fielding himself considered a disadvantageous medium. Characters in high life, he complained, are dull and affected (XIV, i). Evidently he believes that the beaus and ladies differ from the fine folk of the Restoration only in having the vice without the wit. He does suggest that the modern fine gentleman goes in for politics, connoisseurship, and gambling (XIII, v), but he gives us no such character at length. Largely in accordance with this change in social setting, Fielding now depends on dialogue rapidly interchanged in set scenes; there are fewer long self-characterizing speeches than he had used in presenting the humors of the road, and fewer leisurely discussions of general principles than in the first part. This change can also be described by saying that the later books cover shorter and shorter periods of time and become more and more crowded with incident. Moreover, Fielding does not now indulge in his characteristic mock-heroic flights; practically all the mock-heroic passages come before Book XIII.[26] At the same time, a device used by the novelist with special frequency in the later books is the statement that he is omitting something for one reason or another. "A very mournful scene now passed between the prisoner and his friends, at which, as few readers would have been pleased to be present, so few, I believe, will desire to hear it particularly related" (XVII, ix). And later in the chapter, in the conversation between Mrs. Waters and Jones: "Many more things of this kind she uttered, some of which it would do her no great honour, in the opinion of some readers, to remember; nor are we quite certain but that the answers made by Jones would be treated with ridicule by others. We shall therefore suppress the rest of this conversation, and only observe that it ended at last with perfect innocence, and much more to the satisfaction of Jones than of the lady."[27]

Through most of the London action, the moral atmosphere grows more corrupt; illicit love in high or fashionable life (the affairs of Mrs. Fitzpatrick, Tom and Lady Bellaston) and in middle life (young Nightingale and Nancy Miller), the plot against Sophia's honor in which Lady Bellaston tries to use the vicious Lord Fellamar, the use of new agents to entrap and ruin Tom, even the inferior sensational touch of the false alarm about incest, the vestige of the Oedipus theme—all these circumstances darken the picture until a remarkable and artificial series of discoveries and reversals brings Tom off triumphant. In a couple of days his fortunes right themselves so rapidly that, as Dudden points out, it is impossible to tell exactly in what order the events occur, and indications are that Fielding hastened things along because he wanted to finish his work. Here again, a certain disparity appears between the intrigue and the total intention of the book. Fielding's famous farewell to the reader should be reviewed at this point as a classic statement of the genial and rational attitude of the narrator, and perhaps as a half rueful admission that he feels that he ᐧmust now lay aside pleasantry and get down to plain narrative (XVIII, i).

The plot structure is connected with the formal moral alignment of the characters which we have already noted. As far as the characters are good they are actual or potential helpers of Tom's cause; as far as the characters are basically vicious or insincere they oppose or thwart Tom's cause. What had been in Defoe a simple use of the "helper" is richly elaborated in Fielding. The structure of the book admits from time to time the introduction of new characters who take one side or the other. The complications of the plot, the frauds foisted on the world by social pretense and convention and by selfish evil-doers, widen the gap between appearance and reality; the characters are largely engaged in revealing or concealing the truth about Tom. He is the victim of their designs and prejudices, and the subject of their judgments; more or less formal verdicts are always being pronounced on his case. The mixed quality of human nature is often indicated by the way in which some characters now help, now hinder, e.g., Partridge, Mrs. Honour, Black George, Mrs. Fitzpatrick; clear and consistent allies of Tom, such as Mrs. Miller and the repentant highwayman, are hard to find, but as virtue and truth assert themselves all but the incorrigible are won over.

Recent critics have rightly emphasized the role of the narrator in keeping the whole story on the comic level, in making certain that we shall not be too tragically concerned for Tom even when his fortunes are at their lowest. It is hard to improve on Henry James's statement of the case:

> It is very true that Fielding's hero in *Tom Jones* is but as "finely," that is but as intimately, bewildered, as a young man of great health and spirits may be when he hasn't a grain of imagination; the point to be made is, at all events, that his sense of bewilderment obtains altogether on the comic, never on the tragic plane. He has so much "life" that it amounts, for the effect of comedy and application of satire, almost to his having a mind, that is to his having reactions and a full consciousness; besides which his author—*he* handsomely possessed of a mind—has such an amplitude of reflexion for him and round him that we see him through the mellow air of Fielding's fine old moralism, fine old humour and fine old style, which somehow really enlarge, make every one and every thing important.[28]

The steadying influence and broad views of the narrator are intended to insure that individual acts and episodes shall be viewed in the light of a basic toleration of human nature. In Tom's case this toleration is variously modulated into active sympathy and amusement, and, when he is in serious trouble, into what Crane has well called "a kind of faint alarm which is the comic analogue of fear."[29] There is a touch of absurdity about Tom's misfortunes, especially about his affairs with women. In considering Tom's amours it should be borne in mind that Molly Seagrim, Mrs. Waters, and Lady Bellaston all make the advances to him, and that he might well have been in danger from Mrs. Fitzpatrick also (XVI, ix). Current mores allowed the young unmarried man a fairly wide range of sexual freedom provided that he did not seduce the innocent virgin or the virtuous wife. But it remained uncertain how far he could go, and many thought even in his own day that in taking money from Lady Bellaston our hero went too far. Sensitive souls even in a supposedly robust age might wonder too just how a man might make the transition from Molly Seagrim to Sophia Western: "There is something extremely indelicate in professing a

Passion for a virtuous Woman before we have undergone a sufficient Quarantine after the Contagion of an abandoned one, and Man in such a Situation resembles a Centaur, half human, half brute.''[30] It is the maintenance of the comic level that must sustain Fielding here; one of the conventions of comedy is that, unlike tragedy, it permits an escape from the past.

Fielding's genius is so completely in control and his humor so pervasive that our attention is caught at once by his withholding comic or ironic treatment. Sophia is delightfully and sympathetically but not profoundly presented in terms of the magnificent compliments of the narrator. Like Clarissa she takes flight from her father's house to avoid a forced marriage; the alternatives here are very lightly touched, in comic rather than serious vein; she had a choice between "Cupid, who lay hid in her muff," and the "extreme piety," nay, the vanity of martyrdom (VII, ix). Like Clarissa too, she takes filial duty very seriously, and even toward the end of the story her attitude is described thus: "Had her honour, given to Jones, and something else, perhaps, in which he was concerned, been removed, I much doubt whether she would not have sacrificed herself to a man she did not like, to have obliged her father" (XVIII, ii). But there is no emphasis on the divided mind here, and Sophia is never enveloped in an atmosphere of tragic melancholy, even though at the beginning of the attempted rape by Lord Fellamar she is found reading Southerne's *Fatal Marriage* (XV, v).

Blifil, Tom's villainous half-brother, does not lend himself either to a comic or a tragic scheme, presented as he is without any admixture of virtuous or even natural impulse. Like Lovelace, he engineers a conspiracy which is technically the mainspring of the plot, but unlike Lovelace he is not betrayed from within. At the other extreme, Allworthy of Paradise Hall is presented as a straight and rather gullible benevolist; his name and residence suggest that he is too good for this intriguing world. It has already been remarked that Fielding's good characters carry unsuspecting candor to an extreme degree. Since Fielding seems to have encouraged the identification of

Allworthy with his friends and patrons, Ralph Allen and George Lyttelton, he could not very well have intended to make Allworthy's credulity matter of comedy. Allworthy does not play the Orgon to the hypocrites in his household. He is a homiletic character; he utters and inspires set moral discourses, and there is no intimation that Fielding finds these discourses tedious or expects the unregenerate reader to find them so. Yet Fielding's Good Man differs from Richardson's in being more tolerant and easy-going, "for men of true wisdom and goodness are contented to take persons and things as they are, without complaining of their imperfections or attempting to amend them" (II, vii). He did not fail to see the faults of Thwackum and Square, but it could not be expected that he should take drastic action about them (III, v).

The limitations imposed by Fielding's plan upon the presentation of Tom's character are of considerable interest. Tom is an adequate central figure in a comedy, but we are not admitted to intimacy with him; he does not take root in our imagination as an individual; his love for Sophia is not felt from within as a unique experience; we see him in a profoundly respectful and passionately admiring attitude toward the heroine, which we may take as a well-executed illustration in a novel of the period. When Fielding is not engaged in exploring current manners, he is likely to use the stereotyped rhetoric of speech and gesture for the expression of serious feelings. When such expressions are insincere, the effect is comic; and even with sincere feeling the formal rhetoric may give a mock-heroic and playful effect. We may be expected to smile at Tom's love-speeches; this is not always clear (see V, vi), but there can be no doubt about one of his apostrophes to the absent Sophia—"How contemptible would the brightest Circassian beauty, dressed in all the jewels of the Indies, appear to my eyes!"—followed as it is by the emergence of Molly Seagrim, by no means clad like a Circassian beauty (V, x). The rhetoric is very important here; it helps to solve the problem of presenting comically Tom's concurrent attachments to Molly and Sophia. The difficulty is that we feel we must impute the rhetoric to the narrator; the style does not obviously inhere in the character, like the speeches of Don Quixote and Parson Adams.

Tom's acts of benevolence, especially in the city, his generosity to the good-hearted highwayman, his good offices in arranging the marriage between young Nightingale and the betrayed Nancy, are without an infusion of humor, and seem to be arranged by the author as a timely demonstration of his goodness of heart. We are certainly expected to take Tom's formal statements of the doctrine of benevolism at face value: "If there are men who cannot feel the delight of giving happiness to others, I sincerely pity them, as they are incapable of tasting what is, in my opinion, a greater honour, a higher interest, and a sweeter pleasure than the ambitious, the avaricious, or the voluptuous man can ever obtain" (XIII, x). "And do not the warm, rapturous sensations which we feel from the consciousness of an honest, noble, generous, benevolent action, convey more delight to the mind than the undeserved praise of millions?" (XIV, vii) This exaltation of the good heart, the benevolent intention and act, on which Allworthy, Sophia, Tom, Mrs. Miller, and Fielding would all agree, reflects contemporary ethical theory. It can be connected with Shaftesbury, but Shaftesbury makes benevolence a component of a moral, religious, and aesthetic complex which might seem to Fielding to be needlessly elaborate for the ordinary man's plain path, and decidedly heterodox as well. Square's views on virtue and religion have something in common with Shaftesbury, and his elaborate speculative construction may be said to combine Shaftesbury's "natural beauty of virtue," "the eternal fitness of things" expounded as an absolute rational standard by Samuel Clarke, and possibly Wollaston's "unalterable rule of right."[31] Both Square and his orthodox opponent Thwackum, as has been remarked, discard "all natural goodness of heart" (III, iv), and this can be reconciled with the statement that Square "held human nature to be the perfection of all virtue" (III, iii) when we consider that for Square that is only an *a priori* formula which cannot serve as

THE EARLY MASTERS OF ENGLISH FICTION

a touchstone to identify in ordinary experience the degree of goodness (not of course perfect goodness) actually to be found in human behavior.

Fielding himself, of course, relies heavily on ethical formulas, and yet his highest praise is reserved for those "who, as Prior excellently well remarks, direct their conduct by something

> Beyond the fix'd and settled rules
> Of vice and virtue in the schools,
> Beyond the letter of the law." (XV, x)

The novelist's moral estimate of his characters rests on pairs of oppositions: benevolence versus envy (see especially *Tom Jones,* XVII, v), candor versus a suspicious and self-regarding prudence, and spontaneity versus formalism. Thus there arises a tendency to exalt virtuous impulse as against the set codes of schools, societies, and states, corrupted as they are by pedagogues, snobs, venal politicians, and sage exponents of the "profit motive." Fielding's sentimentalism consists in this shift of emphasis from public to private virtue rather than in any formal doctrine of the goodness or badness of human nature conceived in theological terms. Fielding, if he had ever read the passage, would have endorsed the exposition of Mark the Lombard to Dante:

> Your first impulses are by heaven aroused—
> I mean not all but granted that I did,—
> Yet light is given you for good or ill. . . .
> Well may you see that wicked leadership
> Is the true origin of the world's guilt,
> And not that human nature is corrupt.[32]

As in the education of Tom, Fielding is an ethical empiricist, working in concrete situations. He is the very opposite of the supposed sentimentalist who contents himself with mere feeling or fine sentiments. Both Square and Tom find themselves in Molly's bedroom, but Fielding and Tom can cope with this situation and Square cannot. An error derived from the misuse of the idea of natural goodness is found in the Man of the Hill, that tedious person whose long story discourages the reader. He represents the extreme position taken by those who expect to find the ideal of "philanthropy" (a disposition to expect men to be perfectly good) realized in the life of the world and so pass easily from "philanthropy" to "misanthropy": "However it may seem a parodox, or even a contradiction, certain it is that great philanthropy chiefly inclines us to avoid and detest mankind; not on account so much of their private and selfish vices, but for those of a relative kind; such as envy, malice, treachery, cruelty, with every other species of malevolence. These are the vices which true philanthropy abhors, and which rather than see or converse with, she avoids society itself" (VIII, x). Gulliver's identification of his fellow-men as Yahoos immediately comes to mind. Sarah Fielding, no doubt under her brother's influence, had set up a somewhat similar ethical opposition in *David Simple*. Here Mr. Orgueil represents the Stoic pride, and holds that human nature reaches full dignity by subduing the passions; at the opposite pole are those who give up human nature as necessarily a "sink of iniquity." The true intermediate position is the one recommended to the writer of sentimental drama, "to affect the Passions in such a manner, as that the *Distresses* of the Good should move Compassion, and the Amiableness of their Actions incite Men to imitate them; and the *Vices* of the Bad stir up Indignation and Rage, and make Men fly their Footsteps."[33] Fielding undertook to animate the dry bones of such theories.

Sophia's father, the immortal Squire Western, is not so much a responsible being whose actions are brought before an ethical tribunal, as a spontaneous manifestation of humors. Fielding enjoys the sight and sound of him, and he likes to see Partridge and other characters in action too, without being too judicial about it, but this interest in the spectacle is not so fully indulged as in *Joseph Andrews*. In the scene with gypsies and the puppet-master, or Partridge at the play, we feel that the novelist is enjoying a holiday. Partridge's role may be compared with Sancho Panza's, but it is not invested with a significance comparable with Sancho's; there is no real interaction between Partridge and Tom as there is between Sancho and the Don. The presentation of humors for their own sake is limited, and so is the presentation of manners and local or temporal color. It is a mistake to overemphasize, on the strength of a few lusty scenes, Fielding's portrayal of a good gross merry England, a country filled with robust and brutal creatures nurtured on roast beef and ale. To be sure, he can be vividly specific, like Cervantes, rather than gravely philosophic and analytical, like Molière at his best. His décor suggests Cervantes; his formal emphasis on basic ethical issues suggests Molière. He does not fill in with as much description of landscapes and interiors as some of his contemporaries. At the same time, his easy handling of story and commentary gives a profoundly humorous and richly varied effect. There is an effortless mastery about the presentation; it is weighty and full without being pretentious; everything takes its due place and yet there is no straining for points, no hysterical emphasis. It is this freedom from strain that makes Fielding an easier novelist to live with than Richardson.

Tom Jones bears frequent rereading as few other novels do because of the unfailing adequacy and resourcefulness of the style and because of the wit and wisdom often conveyed by a casual phrase, or the perspective opened by an incidental passage. Minor examples will illustrate. The following may seem to be just a casual flourish in the manner of Swift's "Description of the Morning," yet it shows a perfect blending of social comedy and mock-heroic: "Those members of society who are born to furnish the blessings of life, now began to light their candles, in order to pursue their daily labours for the use of those who are born to enjoy these blessings. The sturdy hind now attends the levee of his fellow-labourer the ox; the cunning artificer, the diligent mechanic, spring from their hard mattress; and now the bonny house-maid begins to repair the disordered drum-room, while the riotous authors of that disorder, in broken interrupted slumbers, tumble and toss, as if the hardness of down disquieted their repose" (XI, ix). Or consider the glimpse we get of the Irish gentleman, Mr. Macklachlan, in the inn at Upton: "This young fellow lay in bed reading one of Mrs. Behn's novels; for he had been instructed by a friend, that he would find no more effectual method of recommending himself to the ladies than the improving his understanding, and filling his mind with good literature" (X, ii) . Accept this passage in place of a scene in a comedy, with Macklachlan in the stock role of a "Witwoud," a foolish pretender to gallantry and wit.   Or note the introduction of Mrs. Miller, "who was the widow of a clergyman, and was left by him, at his decease, in possession of two daughters, and of a complete set of manuscript sermons" (XIII, v). Mrs. Miller's plight would be good for a circumstantial chapter in the work of a mediocre sentimentalist. Or the case of poor Partridge at the beginning of the story, who "left the country, where he was in danger of starving with the universal compassion of all his neighbours" (II, vi). Or the skilful and economical way in which a London street scene is blended with the disreputable affair of Tom and Lady Bellaston:

The lady presently after quitted the masquerade, and Jones, notwithstanding the severe prohibition he had received, presumed to attend her. He was now reduced to the same dilemma we have mentioned before, namely, the want of a shilling, and could not relieve it by borrowing as before. He therefore walked boldly on after the chair in which his lady rode, pursued by a grand huzza from all the chairmen present, who wisely take the best care they can to discountenance all walking afoot by their betters. Luckily, however, the gentry who attend at the Opera-house were too busy to quit their stations, and as the lateness of the hour prevented him from meeting many of their brethren in the street, he proceeded without molestation in a dress which, at another season, would have certainly raised a mob at his heels. (XIII, vii)

Or observe the stroke by which Squire Western in town is instantaneously presented: "The squire sat down to regale himself over a bottle of wine, with his parson and the landlord of the Hercules Pillars, who, as the squire said, would make an excellent third man, and could inform them of the news of the town, and how affairs went; for, to be sure, says he, he knows a great deal, since the horses of a many of the quality stand at his house" (XVI, ii). Could more be done with Fielding's town and country theme in a single sentence?

The subject of the early reception of *Tom Jones* has been carefully studied by Cross and Blanchard, though they exaggerate the early exaltation of *Clarissa* and denigration of *Tom*

Jones.[34] We now know from an interesting letter of Joseph Spence's that an edition of 2,500 copies was sold before the announced publication date, "perhaps an unheard-of case."[35] If *Clarissa* was often read for facile pathos and edification, *Tom Jones* was often read for facile humor. William Shenstone, a discriminating reader in his way, seems to prefer the humor for its own sake to the structure of the whole:

> I think as you do that ye Plan is by no means easy, but must own at the same time y^t several *Parts* have afforded me much Amusement. There is a good deal of wit dispers'd thro'out, or rather ty'd up in Bundles at ye beginning of every *Book*. You will conclude my Taste to be not extremely *delicate,* when I say I am cheifly pleas'd with ye striking Lines of Mr *Western's* Character. It is I fancy a natural Picture of thousands of his Majesty's rural subjects; at least it has been *my* Fortune to see ye original pretty frequently. Tis perhaps a likeness y^t is easily taken, & moreover he seems to apply it too indiscriminately to Country-gentlemen in general. But it is ye only Character y^t made me *laugh:* & y^t is a great point gain'd, when one is in danger of losing y^t *Faculty* thro' Disuse. Tis moreover a Character better worth exposing than his Landlords and Landladys wth which he seems so delighted—his Serjeants & his Abigails, &c. [36]

As a humorous novel, *Tom Jones* was often considered "low"; from Hogarth to Goldsmith the humorists of the period had to face this charge, and Fielding had already satirized such criticism in his account of the puppet-master who threw out Punch and Judy and all such stuff and offered only grave and improving entertainment (*Tom Jones,* XII, v). But Cross goes too far when he concludes that the eighteenth century did serious injustice to the book. Many a reader must have brushed aside objections made in the name of prudery and delicacy, or colored by personal prejudice, to reach a position which may be illustrated from two minor writers of the next generation:

> When the rigid and fastidious vent their spleen against the labours of the novelist, they ought to recollect that there are compositions of this nature, which, in almost every country, have raised their authors to the pinnacle of fame.—A *Rousseau* will ever be esteemed in France—a *Goethe* in Germany—and a *Fielding* and a *McKenzie* will be admired whilst the English language is understood.—The efforts of the former indeed have been carried as far as the human genius can extend—his *Tom Jones,* the first work of the kind in our own, or perhaps in any language, evinces such a strength and profundity of understanding, such an intimate knowledge of men and manners, such a flow of wit and

perpetual spring of humour, as Nature in the same person rarely chuses to combine. Its morality, notwithstanding the foolish cavils of ignorance and prudery, is ever obvious and striking; and the entertainment which it is capable of affording has been participated [sic], not only by all who have the smallest pretensions to taste, but by almost all who can read.[37]

Perhaps of all men none ever saw deeper into the human mind than Shakespear and Fielding; that the former was the greater genius will not bear the shadow of a dispute; but that immortal poet is not greater in the superior walks of tragedy and comedy, than this inimitable writer is in comic romance. His characters are not only true to nature, they are nature itself; pourtrayed in colours whose brilliancy almost dazzles the eye without ever offending the most scrupulous judge. His humour is incomparable; his plots excellent, and his incidents superior to those of any writer the world ever produced; every little accident of his drama develops character in a manner that can never be sufficiently admired. Never lived a man that saw in a quicker manner the foibles, vices, and wrong side of a character with such keenness. Which however did not arise from a misanthropy in his disposition, for he could paint the best, but from a strength of ridicule that exhibited in a moment all he saw.[38]

III

On October 25, 1748, Fielding took the oaths as justice of the peace for Westminster, presiding at the Bow Street Court, and in January, 1749, his jurisdiction was extended over Middlesex. Hereafter his literary work was deeply colored by his immediate concern with the state of public morals. He published pamphlets on the current crime wave, the liquor problem, poor relief, and legal aid for the poor, and took austere views of public amusements, the growth of luxury among the middle and lower classes, and such stock topics of the censors. With his brother John he reformed the London police force, and put heavy emphasis on law enforcement, accepting almost without question the fearfully severe criminal code of the time. In the early 1750's his health failed rapidly, he suffered terribly from the gout, and finally in the vain hope of recovery set sail for Lisbon, where he died in October, 1754.

His last novel *Amelia* must be read partly in the light of his increasing preoccupation with the morals of contemporary society. Perhaps, as one who was both a novelist and a reformer, Fielding was especially sensitive to the swelling chorus of complaints about the popularity of immoral and ephemeral fiction in the years 1750 and 1751. His novels, as well as Smollett's, were in danger of being confounded with the current trash about beggars, foundlings, and ladies of pleasure, "that vast inundation of histories, memoirs, adventures, &c. &c. &c. &c."[39] The *Magazine of Magazines,* mentioning *Tom Jones* and *Peregrine Pickle,* calls on Justice Fielding, perhaps ironically and satirically, to stem the tide:

The squire's daughter will talk to the parson of nothing else but the last new songs at *Vauxhall,* the plays that were acted at both houses, and the novels that were published last month; on the whole, it would not be unworthy the genius of a Fielding to draw up *An enquiry into the causes of the late great encrease of magazines and other pamphlets,* occasional and periodical, with some proposals for remedying the growing evils. In this capacity Mr. *Fielding* may act as an enquirer, as a justice, as a law-giver, and executioner; for whoever is acquainted with his writings must confess, that there is no body so well acquainted with human nature, so capable of representing virtue in its own amiable dress, or vice in its natural deformity, that has such a thorough insight into the causes and effects of things, is such a master of character, and so able to draw the picture of an author, and a reader of every kind.[40]

But fortunately Fielding continued to write fiction instead of moralizing about it, even though such comments put him on the defensive. His claims as a serious novelist were, with hostile intent, contrasted with his humble duties as a working magistrate:

The Judge looked exactly like the celebrated Mr. *F---g.* I do not mean the humorous Mr. *F---g,* he who is so intimate with the Doorkeepers of the great Stage of Nature, that, whenever he pleases, he can step, with the Authority of a *Beau,* behind the Scenes, sit down in the *Green Room* to observe the Actors, and afterwards publish his Discoveries to the World, in the Histories of *Jonathan Wild, Joseph Andrews,* and *Tom Jones;* but the same Gentleman, when quitting the *Tripod of Apollo,* he assumes a becoming Gravity of Countenance, and utters an elaborate *Charge* to a *Grand Jury,* or seated in the Chair of his worthy Predecessor, the never-to-be-forgotten Sir*T....s D....l,* he grants out Warrants for the battered Drabs of his Neighbourhood, and magisterially decides the Quarrels of *"Linkboys vile, and Watermen obscene."*[41]

Amelia was published on December 19, 1751. Andrew Millar is said to have paid Fielding a large sum, eight hundred or a thousand pounds, for the copyright; the first printing was five thousand copies, and the second, in January, 1752, three thousand.[42] As with *Tom Jones,* there must have been a large prepublication sale; these figures show not only what was expected of *Amelia* but how successful *Tom Jones* had been. But *Amelia* was not the book Fielding's readers were looking for. Sarah Fielding and Jane Collier may have had this situation in mind when they wrote soon afterward that the public wanted nothing from comic writers but "risible figures" and broad jests. "Otherwise, let them paint the most agreeable images of human nature, let them ever so accurately search the inmost recesses of the human heart, there is a general outcry set up against them, that they are spiritless and dull."[43] Yet there is some truth in Lady Mary Wortley Montagu's inscription on the flyleaf of her copy, "Inferior to himself, Superior to most others."[44]

The narrator is much less prominent in *Amelia,* so that we do not get the pervasive ironical commentary of *Joseph Andrews* and *Tom Jones.* The misfortunes of Amelia and her husband Booth are intended to make a direct impact on our moral sentiments, and to illustrate the vicious state of English society. The moral is given largely by exhibition rather than analysis, and this involves a change in literary form. The epic convention here subsides into the style of a grave history or realistic tale.[45] In the Preface to *The Journal of a Voyage to Lisbon,* Fielding confirms our impression that he now preferred the history to the epic: "I must confess I should have honoured and loved Homer more had he written a true history of his own times in humble prose, than those noble poems that have so justly collected the praise of all ages; for though I read these with more admiration and astonishment; I still read Herodotus, Thucydides and Xenophon with more amusement and more satisfaction."[46] Grave history in *Amelia* tends to suppress both the epic style and the more extravagant and grotesque forms of the comedy of humors. The shift in method is spontaneous rather than deliberate. An early chapter (I, vi) gives the adventuress Miss Matthews a tragedy speech, compares her to a list of tragic heroines, elevates her mood with epic similes, and debases it by comparison with the tricks of a woman of the town. But thereafter the novelist does not use much elevated rhetoric; the epic similes, which had already become infrequent in the last part of

THE EARLY MASTERS OF ENGLISH FICTION

Tom Jones, now disappear almost entirely. The brief but important introductory chapter shows that Fielding conceives of the novel as an elaborate structure showing the causes and effects of action. Such a structure is a work of art, but at the same time, by virtue of its very organization, it teaches a morality of consequences:

Life may as properly be called an art as any other; and the great incidents in it are no more to be considered as mere accidents, than the several members of a fine statue, or a noble poem. The critics in all these are not content with seeing any thing to be great, without knowing why and how it came to be so. By examining carefully the several gradations which conduce to bring every model to perfection, we learn truly to know that science in which the model is formed: as histories of this kind, therefore, may properly be called models of HUMAN LIFE, so by observing minutely the several incidents which tend to the catastrophe or completion of the whole, and the minute causes whence those incidents are produced, we shall best be instructed in this most useful of all arts, which I call the ART OF LIFE. (I, i)

The role of the heroine, and the naming of the book for her, suggest that Fielding was not averse to writing for a public that interested itself in Richardson's heroines. Amelia's sufferings are due to a hostile family and to a woman's position in a predatory masculine world; in a critical situation she is, like Pamela and Clarissa, hard put to it for help. Strange as it may seem, except for the continuation of *Pamela,* she is the first respectable married heroine in English fiction; and this is the first English novel to deal fully with the family life of a young married couple with small children, again with the exception of the *Pamela* sequel. We have to take the point of view of the 1750's to appreciate fully the novelty of such a passage as this:

When these offices were performed, she employed herself another hour in cooking up a little supper for her husband, this being, as we have already observed, his favourite meal, as indeed it was hers; and in a most pleasant and delightful manner they generally passed their time at this season, though their fare was very seldom of the sumptuous kind.

It now grew dark, and her hashed mutton was ready for the table; but no Booth appeared. Having waited, therefore, for him a full hour, she gave him over for that evening; nor was she much alarmed at his absence, as she knew he was, in a night or two, to be at the tavern with some brother officers; she concluded, therefore, that they had met in the Park, and had agreed to spend this evening together.

At ten, then, she sat down to supper by herself, for Mrs. Atkinson was then abroad; and here we cannot help relating a little incident, however trivial it may appear to some. Having sat some time alone reflecting on their distressed situation, her spirits grew very low, and she was once or twice going to ring the bell, to send her maid for half a pint of white wine; but checked her inclination, in order to save the little sum of sixpence, which she did the more resolutely, as she had before refused to gratify her children with tarts for their supper, from the said motive; and this self-denial she was very probably practising to save sixpence, while her husband was paying a debt of several guineas, incurred by the ace of trumps being in the hands of his adversary. (X,v)

Fielding's reference to this "little incident" shows that he was conscious of innovation here.

Amelia's happiness and fortunes are of course bound up with those of her husband, Billy Booth, only we never speak familiarly of "Billy" as we speak of "Joseph" or "Tom." He is represented as a worthy army officer for whom those in authority should, it is assumed, do something good. He has retired from the army at the time of the action of the story, but he is now in straits for money, and is trying to get another commission by the influence of supposed friends or the favor of the great. The only way to get a commission, of course, was by purchase at a very high price, ranging from about £400 for a commission as ensign (second lieutenant) to £1500 for a captaincy. The assumption is that the hero deserves all he wants, and that a society that does not immediately oblige him is perforce corrupt. Booth is too genteel to seek his fortune in rough and tumble adventure, like the elevated picaro who is the center of Smollett's stories, and marriage precludes such a career for him. Both Tom Jones and Booth confront the world's conspiracy under a natural handicap, as Fielding presents the situation, of corrigible and venial faults. Tom gets by with his boyishness and his simple but sound ethics; Booth is old enough to know better, and Fielding's measured intentions impute to him specific theories in psychology, ethics, and natural theology, more fully worked out than Tom's, and farther from the truth. "The doctrine of the passions had been always his favourite study; . . . he was convinced every man acted entirely from that passion which was uppermost" (III, iv). This familiar doctrine is sometimes associated with reckless abandonment to impulse: thus Lovelace says, "Some one passion

THE EARLY MASTERS OF ENGLISH FICTION

predominating, in every human breast, breaks thro' principle, and controuls us all."[47] Orthodox moralists would say that it is realistic to recognize the ruling passion, build upon it, and try to turn it to good; the error consists in accepting it passively or letting it run wild. Booth's error, then, is partly "accidia," or sloth, and partly too narrow a view of the range and possibilities of the passions, which keeps him from realizing how they may be turned to active good. When he is converted at the end of the story by reading Barrow's sermons, he says to Dr. Harrison: "Indeed, I never was a rash disbeliever; my chief doubt was founded on this, that as men appeared to me to act entirely from their passions, their actions could have neither merit nor demerit." Dr. Harrison replies with the Christian version of the appeal to the passions: "A very worthy conclusion truly, but if men act, as I believe they do, from their passions, it would be fair to conclude that religion to be true, which applies immediately to the strongest of these passions, hope and fear, chusing rather to rely on its rewards and punishments than on that native beauty of virtue which some of the ancient philosophers thought proper to recommend to their disciples" (XII, v). Harrison's piety and scholarship contribute comments which lack the power of Fielding's own essays, but there is no reason to doubt that they represent Fielding's views in 1750. The corruption of character presented in the story points to original sin, but when the designs of Colonel James make Amelia almost despair of humanity, Harrison answers: "Do not make a conclusion so much to the dishonour of the great Creator. The nature of man is far from being in itself evil; it abounds with benevolence, charity, and pity, coveting praise and honour, and shunning shame and disgrace. Bad education, bad habits, and bad customs, debauch our nature, and drive it headlong, as it were, into vice. The governors of the world, and I am afraid the priesthood, are answerable for the badness of it" (IX, v). This is not far from the melioristic doctrine of *Grandison;*[48] the difference in emphasis is that Richardson in his last novel dwells on the good that can be done by those who have the power,

Fielding in his last novel on the evil wrought by the bad practices of society and on the ensuing martyrdom of virtue.

The characterization of Amelia suffers less from this preoccupation with formal doctrine than the characterization of Booth. He is a man of sturdy physique, "with the shoulders of a porter and the legs of a chairman" (XI, i), but he shows little energy or vitality; he is not a hearty genial youth like Tom, and he seems to be the victim of chance impulses rather than strong drives. It is almost as hard to believe in his serious interest in ethics as it is to believe in Tom Jones's classical scholarship. In general, eighteenth century fiction had a hard time concentrating attention and interest on young men; Tom Jones and Lovelace are the greatest successes in this field, and it is well known that Smollett had considerable difficulty just here. Fielding does concentrate on Booth, but ends by making him an unattractive variant of the type of credulous good man who figures largely in Fielding's other novels. With some further variation and shifting of emphasis Booth could have been brought close to being the defeated and insignificant man, the "little man, what now?" of the eighteenth century. Amelia herself, though beautifully presented, is viewed externally as a member of society rather than as a vital center of experience. We may say that the externalization of Sophia is brilliant, the externalization of Amelia delicate. The pathos of her situation, and her unvarying devotion to an unworthy husband and innocent children, remind us of her namesake in *Vanity Fair*. But Fielding's theme is the relation of this couple to society and particularly to the London milieu, and he does not tell the story as a record of Amelia's inner life.

The book starts well with the arrest of Booth and the prison scenes (established as a stock theme in English fiction from Defoe to Dickens). The accounts of earlier action given by Booth and Miss Matthews, a former friend who becomes his mistress in prison, do not heighten the interest. Professor Gerould rightly remarks that the flashbacks in *Amelia* tend to make the story prolix and slow.[49] The same objection can be made to the block of chapters devoted to Mrs. Bennet's story in Book VIII. If we ask why Fielding does not succeed in these departures from chronological order, a procedure often used with success by Richardson and Sterne, the answer may be partly that by having previous action told by the characters themselves he loses the advantage of his own presence as critical and humorous narrator (thus the irony of Booth's telling the story of his courtship of Amelia to the amorous Miss Matthews is largely lost); or we may also say that Fielding tells his stories in the hard clear light of overt social relationships, and is not eminently qualified to render the halflights and overtones of reminiscence. The past in Fielding's novels is something to be got over with, or lived down, not to be lived with or longingly recovered. His flashbacks, however relevant, strike us as interpolations.

To return to *Amelia*, the record of Booth's service abroad and the residence of the couple in France is not noteworthy. The most significant part of the story begins with the residence of Booth and Amelia in London and the gathering of a group of characters who help or hinder them, and who are thus to be judged like the helpers and hinderers in *Tom Jones*. The action is more exclusively in middle or low life than in the city chapters of *Tom Jones*, but Fielding is not entirely at home in such a milieu, even though he does important pioneering work here. Amelia's virtue is somewhat remotely threatened by a licentious lord and by Booth's pretended friend Captain or Colonel James, but their contrivances are not carried to the point of imminent danger. The licentious lord, indeed, had succeeded in seducing Mrs. Bennet, as she tells Amelia, by exactly the same devices he is using with Amelia and Booth—a meeting in disguise at an oratorio, professed fondness for the children, tickets for a masquerade, professed eagerness to serve the duped husband. Here Fielding approaches cautiously the repulsive situation presented outright in his early comedy, *The Modern Husband* (1732), where the plot turns on a husband's sale of his wife's virtue; but he finds some difficulty in adapting this intrigue and the social criticism of the 1730's to the social criticism and ethical interests of the 1750's and to the new humanism of the novel. Sex, treated in this way, is now no theme for comedy.

As has been said above, it is assumed in this story, as generally in eighteenth century literature and life, that the great and powerful should help people of merit, particularly gentlefolk in reduced circumstances, or professional men and scholars, and that it is comparatively easy to tell where merit lies. The constant complaint is that the great fail in compassion and benevolence. In the case of the veteran soldier Bob Bound, Booth explains that

he was one of the scandals of his country. That the Duke of Marlborough had, about thirty years before, made him an ensign from a private man, for very particular merit; and that he had not long since gone out of the army with a broken heart, upon having several boys put over his head. He then gave her an account of his family. . . .
"Good Heavens!" cries Amelia, "what are our great men made of! are they in reality a distinct species from the rest of mankind? are they born without hearts?"
"One would indeed, sometimes," cries Booth, "be inclined to think so. In truth, they have no perfect idea of those common distresses of mankind which are far removed from their own sphere. Compassion, if thoroughly examined, will, I believe, appear to be the fellow-feeling only of men of the same rank and degree of life for one another, on account of the evils to which they themselves are liable. Our sensations are, I am afraid, very cold towards those who are at a great distance from us, and whose calamities can consequently never reach us" (X, ix).

As Booth remarks later, "You can receive favours only from the generous, and, to be plain with you, there are very few who are generous that are not poor" (XII, viii). The story contains no benevolent and powerful gentleman like Allworthy or Sir Charles Grandison. Fielding's indictment of society now moves him slightly in the direction of sentimental democracy. He can entertain the idea, again in the words of Booth, that "love, benevolence, or what you will please to call it, may be the reigning passion in a beggar as well as in a prince; and wherever it is, its energies will be the same" (III, vii). In a long conversation about unchristian pride, Amelia goes so far as to say to Mrs. Bennet that she "should not be ashamed of being the wife of an honest man in any station" (VII, x). Yet Fielding would not think of writing a story of *mésalliance,* or of centering his story about a character like Bob Bound. The sergeant Joe Atkinson, though he inspires sentimentally democratic utterances, is kept in his place. The middle-class characters, Mrs. Ellison and Mrs. Bennet, qualify respectively as hinderer and helper, and are not given full characterization in their own right. Concentration on the social and moral aspects of the affairs of Booth and Amelia limits the development of humble characters, and also of humorous characters in the old tradition. The only true eccentric in the book, Major or Colonel Bath, is marginal for the action. There are hints that Fielding might have developed Dr. Harrison as a learned and virtuous humorist, but the novelist did not indulge himself in this way.

Amelia's faith and virtue remain unshaken, and she forgives her husband his errors and infidelities; Booth himself, as has been noted, is at last converted out of hand. Their other difficulties are cleared up, like Tom Jones's, in the last chapter.

We can share some of the disappointment of contemporary readers with *Amelia,* though we should not neglect this remarkably original work, but we are in a better position than Fielding's own generation to appreciate the importance of *Joseph Andrews* and *Tom Jones.* It is the task of the literary historian somehow to work his way beyond the events of authorship, publication, and reception to some estimate of fundamental values. Such an estimate, it is hoped that our discussion has shown, confirms the preëminent place their contemporaries assigned to Richardson and Fielding in the fiction of the century, accepts without exaggeration the differences between the two as artists and moralists, and will probably end by viewing both not merely as worthy pioneers but as consummate masters of their craft. The niceties of reputation and influence cannot be recorded here. Despite the personal opposition to Fielding and the cries about indecorum in his own day, discriminating readers and critics were always disposed to think of that age in prose fiction as the consulship of Richardson and Fielding. Both novelists suffered in due course from changing tastes and especially from the prudery of the nineteenth century. Fielding appears to lose more ground than Richardson here because in a sense he had more ground to lose; but when all gains and losses have been reckoned it no doubt remains true that Fielding has given more entertainment and delight to later readers than has Richardson. Among secondary novelists of the late eighteenth and early nineteenth centuries the more imitable and less valuable features of the work of Richardson and Fielding were endlessly repeated, though genial repetition of Fielding's character-types and situations was wholesome and harmless, and "documentation" of humors in the manner of Smollett and Sterne inevitably blended with Fielding here. Among critics particularly interested in the technique of fiction, Fielding's skills, at least until recently, have been more adequately and generally appreciated than Richardson's. Both novelists at their best show that technique is inseparable from theme and intention: both are seriously concerned with the moral issues of character as raised within their own society, displayed by Richardson in prolonged and intensive analysis, by Fielding in the light of a broad and humane humor unmatched in its toleration of man's limitations and possibilities save in Shakespeare and Cervantes.

IV

Tobias Smollett

I

The young heroes of Fielding and Smollett and their experiences in English society invite autobiographical interpretation all too easily. Fielding criticism, as scholars since Dobson have shown, has suffered from the tendency to identify Jones and Booth, the novelist's two principal heroes, with the novelist himself. Fielding, however, depends on firm plot construction and on a consistent application of theories of human nature; borrowed episodes, anecdotes, transcribed pieces of local color, personal reminiscences and mannerisms are clearly secondary to his main purpose. One is not tempted to spend too much time ticketing episodes and inquiring about originals. In Smollett we find a more obvious use of personal experience, of specific detail picked up along the road of life, though the *caveat* against simple autobiographical interpretation still holds. Smollett was, we may say, a compiler of episodes and snapper-up of incidents and images; he got his material both from books and from life. His general scheme invites comparison with Fielding and the picaresque tradition; his indefatigable compilation and the relation between his fiction and the great mass of his miscellaneous prose invite a closely guarded comparison with Defoe. All this is not to deny the substantial nature of his own contribution.

Richardson was fifty-one when he published *Pamela,* Fielding thirty-five when he published *Joseph Andrews,* Smollett two months short of twenty-seven when he published *Roderick Random* in January, 1748. *Random* may fairly be called a young man's book; Smollett was the only one of the major British novelists of the century who published an important novel at such an early age. This makes it easier to understand the obvious use of personal experience in this first story, and the harsh and violent accumulation of humorously savage episodes may be analogous to the way young men in our own time set about writing war novels. But Smollett is not the coming young man of his century: he uses the old-fashioned formula of the modified picaresque novel, not a "confessions of" or "education of" or "sorrows of" formula. In fact one of his difficulties, as we shall see, is that when he comes to feel that he should use newer modes he does not take to them naturally.

Smollett was born of a good family in Dumbartonshire, and after studying medicine at Glasgow came up to London with literary ambitions, but was glad to get a post as surgeon's mate aboard the *Chichester*, and took part in the disastrous Carthagena expedition. He returned to Jamaica and married an heiress there; then he undertook to practise medicine in London, at the same time publishing unimportant satires and trying to get a play produced, until he scored his success with *Roderick Random*. He tells us that he wrote the story within eight months, and that there were intervals of several weeks during that period when he did not work steadily at the book. *Random* preceded *Tom Jones* by a year, and has suffered somewhat by the comparison, though of course it should be judged as a different kind of work. By what is no doubt merely a natural parallel, both books give us the sequence of life in the home parish, life on a journey or journeys, and high life in town. "Rory" is the generic young man in a somewhat different sense from Tom. Fielding's young hero learns something from life, and can even be called in some respects docile; Smollett's hero learns little or nothing. "Random" is apparently a nickname, but fits the character very well. His early life suggests Smollett's; Roderick studied medicine at Glasgow, showing a turn for literature as well, and then made his way to London, where he endured the scorn of the English for the beggarly Scot, was kidnapped and made surgeon's assistant aboard the man-of-war *Thunder*, and saw service at Carthagena. The graphic naval scenes, the first of importance in English fiction, must in some sense be transcriptions.[1] There had been hints of this kind of work in the rough and hearty writing of Ned Ward, whose *Wooden World Dissected, in the Character of a Ship of War* (1706; 3rd ed., 1744) gives us perhaps the most vivid picture of life aboard a man-of-war that we have before Smollett.[2] The following series of adventures in France, in London, and at Bath shows Roderick as a commonplace and somewhat unscrupulous adventurer. Professor Kahrl has pointed out that the picaresque formula had long been extended, with due modifications, from the rogue-servant to the young man of good family who has set out on his wanderings. The young adventurer might be only a temporary exile from the upper or middle classes. Roderick is of good family, but his grandfather has disinherited him and he is none too scrupulous about how he gets money. He is accompanied by a comic servant named Strap, and Smollett complained unreasonably that Fielding copied Tom Jones's Partridge from this character. The presence of the servant helps to bring out the assumption that the young gentleman cannot really lose his status; this cycle from gentility to vagabondage and return may be compared and contrasted with Defoe's cycle from the middle class to criminal adventure to more or less convincing repentance. But the central character is kept none too steadily in view, and the outcast Roderick, a rawboned young Scot with lank red hair, appears later as a man about town, a wit, and a fortune hunter.

First and last, the autobiographical theme in *Random* and the supposed introduction of real people gave Smollett considerable trouble. Later he wrote to an American admirer: "The only similitude between the circumstances of my own Fortune, and those I have attributed to Roderick Random, consists in my being of a reputable Family in Scotland, in my being bred a Surgeon, and having served as a Surgeon's mate on board of a man of war, during the Expedition to Carthagena. The low situations in which I have exhibited Roderick, I never experienced in my own Person."[3]   But his fullest statement on the subject is in an early and characteristic letter to Alexander Carlyle:

> I am not a little mortified to find the characters strangely misapplied to particular men whom I never had the least intention to ridicule—by which means I have suffered very much in my Moral Capacity; Some persons to whom I have been extremely obliged being weak enough to take umbrage at many passages of the Work, on the supposition that I myself am the Hero of the Book, and they of consequence concerned in the History—
> I have heard of Love's indignation from many hands, and you may be sure treat it with the contempt it deserves; the more so as I am informed that he has by way of revenge propagated many lies to my disadvantage—
> I shall take this opportunity therefore of declaring to you, in all the sincerity of unreserved Friendship that no person living is aimed at in all the first part of the Book; that is while the scene lies in Scotland and that (the account of the Expedition to Carthagene excepted) the *Whole* is not so much a representation of my life as that of many other needy Scotch Surgeons whom I have known either personally or by Report— The character of Strap (who I find is a favourite among the Ladies every where) is partly taken from the life; but the circumstances of his attachment to Random entirely feigned—[4]

It is characteristic too, as we shall see, that Smollett should work by types and make the Roderick of the early part of the story into the familiar figure of the "needy Scotch Surgeon." The theme was familiar, and the youthful James Thomson had written from London concerning the choice of "surgery" as a profession: " 'Tis, as you can't but know, the merest drug here in the world. Scotland is really fruitful of Surgeons, they come here like flocks of Vultures every day, and by a merciful providential kind of instinct transport themselves to foreign countries. The Change is quite full of them. They peruse the shipbills and meet the Sea Captains."[5] John Armstrong, later a good friend of Smollett's, was another Scottish physician who applied for an appointment to the West Indies in 1741.[6]

Somewhat on the model of the Preface to *Joseph Andrews,* Smollett provides an important Preface to *Roderick Random.* A story, he begins by saying, is the best way to convey satire; the fortunes of the hero involve sympathy for virtue and indignation at vice. Though he recognizes the supreme position of

Cervantes, he takes the *Gil Blas* of Le Sage as his immediate model, but finds this admired author too much given to mirth and to easy transitions from distress to happiness. "This conduct, in my opinion, not only deviates from probability but prevents that generous indignation which ought to animate the reader against the sordid and vicious disposition of the world." The theme is repeated in the motto on the title-page of the first edition:

Et genus, et virtus, nisi cum re, vilior alga est.
[Horace, *Satires*, II, v, 8.]

We may translate freely, "Family and character don't amount to anything, unless you've got the money." Smollett expects the reader to sympathize with his hero, who is supposed to represent "modest merit struggling with every difficulty to which a friendless orphan is exposed, from his own want of experience, as well as from the selfishness, envy, malice, and base indifference of mankind." But the emphasis shifts from the alleged merit of the struggling orphan to the view of undisguised human nature· "I persuade myself the judicious will not only perceive the necessity of describing those situations to which he must of course be confined in his low estate, but also find entertainment in viewing those parts of life, where the humours and passions are undisguised by affectation, ceremony, or education; and the whimsical peculiarities of disposition appear as nature has implanted them." Deep-rooted hostility to high life as the zone of affectation and basic insincerity runs through all the novelists of the time, but it is characteristic of the attitude of Smollett and Hogarth that the spontaneous revelations of low life are taken to be in large part a revelation of evil. Smollett professes to adopt the *saeva indignatio* of Juvenal rather than the laughing satire of Horace, or Cervantes' humane and thoughtful view of man in action. Here he shows some resemblance to Defoe, whose fixed attitude is that one should take a severe view of the facts.

But the theory of indignant satire is inadequate for the novelist's practice; it is not flexible enough for the exigencies of life and will not see the novelist through his variegated tour of the world. Smollett really uses it as an ethical short-cut, a kind of inverted sentimentalism, with spontaneous indignation instead of spontaneous benevolence as the test of virtue, though the two may well be combined. No doubt he had personal reasons for this attitude; we find that he is likely to be mortified in the manner of his own heroes when he finds that his candid intentions are misunderstood or when he encounters contempt or neglect. Though the theory is inadequate, there is real personal power behind it. Yet Roderick is not an interesting enough individual to convey Smollett's criticism of life, though he has of course all the advantages of Smollett's brilliant, graphic, and varied style. The story is not controlled throughout by an effective commentator, a voice of reason.[7] For example, the narrator in Fielding could take a playful attitude toward his own rhetoric, or the rhetoric of his characters, e.g., the love-making of Tom Jones. When Roderick expresses his passion for the beauteous Narcissa in similar style, there is no such depth of implication, no running irony, and the rhetoric rings hollow. In his most characteristic work, Smollett visualizes gross humanity in action, but he does not push his analysis of the action very far, and he can be defended and explained as the exponent of a kind of story in which the immediate quality of the action outweighs its ultimate significance.

The career of Smollett's hero is strikingly punctuated by the introduction of a series of intensely visualized grotesques. Though these figures may be technically helpers or hinderers of the hero, they do not invite analysis from that point of view, as do the auxiliary characters of Defoe, Fielding, and Richardson. We may restate and follow up the account of the comedy of humors already given in the discussion of Fielding by noting four possible ways of viewing these characters:

(*a*) As fantastic and monstrous creatures, living in a world conditioned only by their own obsessions and manias. From Jonson to Dickens the comedy of humors may eventually land us in a world of fantasy and nightmare. This vein of character-

THE EARLY MASTERS OF ENGLISH FICTION

ization is sometimes connected with the device of animal caricature, and men become apes, asses, owls, bears, foxes, and vultures (note the cast of characters in *Volpone* and the Apologue to *Roderick Random*). Along with the animal symbols there may be symbols of mechanism; men become grotesque puppets or automata. Baker is probably right in finding a distinctively Scottish quality in Smollett's caricatures; this tendency can be noted in Scottish literature from Dunbar to Carlyle.

(b) As more or less corrigible members of society, who may here see their errors as in a glass. This is the stock theme of the corrective force of satire, endlessly repeated by poets, essayists, novelists, and dramatists. Satire professedly corrective may deal in the grotesque, and use the animal and mechanical symbols mentioned under (a), but if it goes very far in this direction the intention of the satirist becomes doubtful (compare Swift and Smollett).

(c) As natural variations of the human stock, to be viewed with sympathy and toleration, a position already described at length in our discussion of Parson Adams.

(d) As documentation, as representatives of race, nationality, social class, vocation, and milieu. But in Smollett's early work this documentation is almost always connected with satire. Though the action of *Random* begins "in the northern part of this united kingdom," there is no attempt to give the Scottish chapters a national coloring; we are conscious of nationality only when we see Roderick and his fellow Scots in London, where they are objects of derision.

The divergence of (a) and (b) is important. The humorous character may be detached so completely from society at large that he is of little or no force as an example. As Read puts it, Smollett's "caricatures of humanity . . . are too extravagant to affect the conscience of a public; yet that is the function of satire."[8] On the other hand, (a), (c), and (d) can march together, and this, it will be seen, is a restatement of the quixotic theme. The sketch of Roderick's uncle Tom Bowling presents a humorous monomaniac with underlying naïve good intentions and in some sense representative of a class.

In *Random* and the other novels the grotesque characters and the actual physical situations in which they are involved stand out in bold relief and detach themselves. Systematic social satire and the running account of the fortunes of the hero also involve a large group of less intensely visualized characters, mostly given to plotting and cheating—corrupt officials, amorous beaus, and dishonest tradesmen. Here Smollett owes much to Elizabethan and Jacobean drama.[9] But he fills in the scene in his own way. Roderick's first visit to an ordinary will illustrate:

[I] found myself in the middle of a cook's shop, almost suffocated with the steams of boiled beef, and surrounded by a company of hackney coachmen, chairmen, draymen, and a few footmen out of place or on board wages, who sat eating shin of beef, tripe, cow-heel, or sausages, at separate boards, covered with cloths which turned my stomach. While I stood in amaze, undetermined whether to sit down or walk upwards again, Strap, in his descent, missing one of the steps, tumbled headlong into this infernal ordinary, and overturned the cook as she carried a porringer of soup to one of the guests. In her fall, she dashed the whole mess against the legs of a drummer belonging to the foot-guards, who happened to be in her way, and scalded him so miserably that he started up, and danced up and down, uttering a volley of execrations that made my hair stand on end. While he entertained the company in this manner, with an eloquence peculiar to himself, the cook got up, and, after a hearty curse on the poor author of this mischance, who lay under the table, scratching his rump with a woeful countenance, emptied a salt-cellar in her hand, and stripping down the patient's stocking, which brought the skin along with it, applied the contents to the sore. This poultice was scarce laid on, when the drummer, who had begun to abate of his exclamation, broke forth into such a hideous yell, as made the whole company tremble; then, seizing a pewter pint-pot that stood by him, squeezed the sides of it together, as if it had been made of pliant leather, grinding his teeth at the same time with a most horrible grin. (chap. xiii)

This comes closer to the harsh writing of modern naturalism than to the ethical symbolism of the physically repulsive as we find it in Swift and Hogarth. The humorous vision becomes so violent and so extreme as to verge on nightmare, yet the imagery never goes over into blurred discontinuity, but remains sharp and massive, sometimes attaining the extreme of incongruity, as in the appearance of Melopoyn in the Marshalsea:

We had not been here many minutes, when a figure appeared, wrapt in a dirty rug, tied about his loins with two pieces of list, of different

THE EARLY MASTERS OF ENGLISH FICTION

colours, knotted together; having a black bushy beard, and his head covered with a huge mass of brown periwig, which seemed to have been ravished from the crown of some scarecrow. This apparition, stalking in with great solemnity, made a profound bow to the audience, who signified their approbation by a general response of "How d'ye do, doctor?" He then turned towards us, and honoured Jackson with a particular salutation: Upon which my friend, in a formal manner, introduced him to me, by the name of Mr. Melopoyn. This ceremony being over, he advanced into the middle of the congregation, which crowded around him, and hemming three times, to my utter astonishment, pronounced with great significance of voice and gesture, a very elegant and ingenious discourse upon the difference between genius and taste, illustrating his assertions with apt quotations from the best authors, ancient as well as modern. (chap. lxi)

When Smollett pushes his effects to the limit, as in the passage about the ordinary, man's plight in this curious world passes the bounds of derision; thus the Welsh humors of Morgan in the naval chapters scarcely counterbalance the fearful savagery of Mackshane and Captain Oakum. In another direction, as in the description of Melopoyn, we may have incidental description on the level of sheer irrelevant improvisation, and the scene yields absurd rather than cruel surprises. There is still a basis in the manners of the time: with Melopoyn we may compare the case of Usher Gahagan, whose Latin translation of Pope's *Messiah* and *Temple of Fame* was appropriately published on the day he was to be executed at Tyburn for filing guineas.[10] Sterne might have handled such a subject, but his Melopoyn would have displayed more fantastic gesture and his erudition would have been aired at whimsical length. Smollett is massive and energetic, but the expense of energy seems disproportionate to the occasion, and the alleged ethical purpose (as sometimes in Swift and Hogarth) seems comparatively pallid. In Roderick's experiences in the ordinary, Defoe would have specified what there was to eat, making an inventory rather than a pantomime of it; and though Fielding is not always averse to the breaking of heads and shins, such a scene in his work would more clearly have had a place in the development of the history. Smollett feels a certain obligation to profess a plan, but it does not fully control his story. Of course this does not mean that Smollett is a cynic or a skeptic; he is too much a man of his time to hold formal views that would keep him in chaos, but he cannot make a genial game of an analysis of man's place in the world, as Fielding and Sterne do in their different ways. Yet by falling short of a complete plan Smollett renders with unsurpassed immediacy that side of his age which has been well described by Professor Plumb: "There was an edge to life in the eighteenth century which is hard for us to recapture. In every class there is the same taut neurotic quality—the fantastic gambling and drinking, the riots, brutality and violence, and everywhere and always a constant sense of death."[11]

In fairness to Smollett, the tone of his work when he is not at the extremes of fantasy, caricature, and violence should also be marked. He owes much, as has been said, to dramatic tradition, and in particular to the stock devices and characters of city comedy—gulls, chuckle-headed young roués, and braggarts. He is not notably successful with silly talk on the level of the comedy of manners, as in the following speech by Captain Weazel's wife, a vein of gabble which he passed on to Dickens: " 'The last affair happened that very day on which I received a love-letter from Squire Gobble; and don't you remember, my dear, I was prodigiously sick that very night with eating ortolans, when my Lord Diddle took note of my complexion's being altered, and my lady was so alarmed that she had well-nigh fainted.' 'Yes, my dear,' replied the captain, 'you know, my lord said to me with a sneer, "Billy, Mrs. Weazel is certainly breeding." And I answered cavalierly, "My lord, I wish I could return the compliment." Upon which the whole company broke out into an immoderate fit of laughter; and my lord, who loves a repartee dearly, came round and bussed me' " (chap. xii). And the grotesque comedy of gesture also has its lighter moments, which we may illustrate from *Peregrine Pickle:*

He promoted such a quick circulation of the bottle, that their mirth grew noisy and obstreperous; they broke forth with repeated peals of laughter, without any previous incitement, except that of claret. These explosions were succeeded by Bacchanalian songs, in which the old gentleman himself attempted to bear a share; the sedate governor snapped time with his fingers, and the parish priest assisted in the chorus with a most expressive nakedness of countenance. Before midnight, they were almost all pinned to their chairs, as if they had been fixed by the power of inchantment; and what rendered the confinement still more unfortunate, every servant in the house was in the same situation; so that they were fain to take their repose as they sat, and nodded at each other like a congregation of anabaptists. (chap. lxvi)

And in *Random* there is sometimes a lighter kind of episode, based on human rascality and credulity, with which Smollett scores a marked success, such as the encounter of Roderick and Strap with the cheating schoolmaster-innkeeper who quotes Horace and presents them with an outrageous bill (chap. x), or the adventure with the "dropper" who pretends to find half a crown and share it with them, and then cheats them at cards (chap. xiv). These brilliant lighter scenes, it is interesting to notice, are closely paralleled in Goldsmith's *Vicar of Wakefield*.

Peregrine Pickle (1751) repeats and extends the effects of *Roderick Random*. The two heroes are much alike, outcasts of good family who are unscrupulous in their quarrels, their practical jokes, and their amours, but who are duly rewarded with a beautiful girl and a fortune at last. The early part of *Peregrine Pickle* is dominated by the great Hawser Trunnion, a monomaniac nautical humorist who with his retainers Jack Hatchway and Tom Pipes maintains his garrison on land as if it were a ship at sea. Professor Kahrl has called attention to a probable original for Trunnion in Admiral Hore, prominent at Carthagena, who later kept a country house in Cheshire in this way.[12] Trunnion comes to have the gigantic quality of some of Ben Jonson's creations. His obsessions follow him everywhere, as when he tacks elaborately across country on horseback and keeps his bride waiting at the church because the wind is wrong. The oddity must be its own excuse for being; nothing is too monstrous or too trifling. When Gamaliel Pickle's wife is pregnant she longs for a pineapple, three black hairs from Trunnion's beard, and a certain lady's "porcelain chamber-pot of admirable workmanship" (chap. vi). This is perfectly gratuitous; Smollett has his version of *Vive la bagatelle*. The excessively specific may be in itself comic, and Smollett likes to base his fantasies on a device in comedy that suddenly produces precise details from the magazines of human activity. Thus Ben Jonson:

Or were you enamour'd on his copper rings,
His saffron jewel, with the toad-stone in 't,
Or his embroider'd suit, with the cope-stitch,
Made of a hearse cloth, or his old tilt-feather,
Or his starch'd beard? (*Volpone,* II, v.)

Or bits of Lady Wishfort's denunciation of Foible, in Congreve's *Way of the World:* "Go, hang out an old Frisoneer gorget, with a yard of yellow colberteen again! Do; an old gnawed mask, two rows of pins, and a child's fiddle; a glass necklace with the beads broken, and a quilted nightcap with one ear!" (V, i) The comic use of such groups in Smollett and Sterne is quite different from the business-like inventories of Defoe and Richardson.

Without fully visualizing his settings, Smollett loves to introduce suddenly the palpable details of circumstance and action. Such a passage as the following is intended to startle the reader as Pipes startled his hearers: "Pipes was a natural genius in the composition of discords; he could imitate the sound produced by the winding of a jack, the filing of a saw, and the swinging of a malefactor hanging in chains; he could counterfeit the braying of an ass, the screeching of a night-owl, the caterwauling of cats, the howling of a dog, the squeaking of a pig; the crowing of a cock; and he had learned the war [w]hoop, uttered by the Indians in North America. These talents were exerted successively at different times and places, to the terror of Mrs. Trunnion, the discomposure of the commodore himself, and the consternation of all the servants in the castle" (chap. xiii). When Tom attended Peregrine at Winchester, he became "master of revels" to the boys: "He regulated their motions by his whistle, instructed the young boys in the games of hustle-cap, leap-frog, and chuck-farthing; imparted to those of a more advanced age the sciences of cribbage and all-fours, together with the method of storming the castle, acting the comedy of Prince Arthur, and other pantomimes, as they are commonly exhibited at sea; and instructed the seniors, who were distinguished by the appellation of bloods, in cudgel-playing, dancing the St. Giles's hornpipe, drinking flip, and smoking tobacco" (chap. xvi). Hatchway, Pipes, and Peregrine plan to improve on nature by frightening Trunnion with an apparition, and construct a fantastic "prop": "To the hide of a large ox, Pipes fitted a leathern vizor of a most terrible appearance, stretched on the jaws of a shark, which he had brought from sea, and accommodated with a couple of broad glasses instead of eyes. On the inside of these he placed two rush-lights, and, with a composition of sulphur and saltpetre, made a pretty large fuse, which he fixed between two rows of the teeth" (chap. xiii). This grotesque monster becomes more than incidental detail, and represents the limit toward which Smollett's animal-caricatures move. The animal theme occurs in the record of Pipes's ventriloquism, it will be noted, and in other connections: "Trunnion's subjection was like that of a bear, checquered with fits of surliness and rage; whereas Pickle bore the yoke like an ox, without repining" (chap. xx); and later a baboon is dressed in hunting costume, put on horseback, and easily mistaken for young Gam Pickle (chap. lxxxvi). In another of Smollett's elaborate nightmares, the grotesque painter Pallet rides "a jack-ass adorned with bells" down the corridor of an inn and creates a series of bedroom scenes (chap. lvi). Pallet's cries in a following night scene are taken to be the howling of a dog, and interpreted as signs of hydrophobia (chap. lvii).

Trunnion's crew are Peregrine's allies, and Pipes is his attendant during much of his career, though Pipes does not acquire the importance of Strap or Partridge as a comic servant. It is by no means obvious at first that Trunnion has a heart of gold, but with him, as with Roderick's Tom Bowling, underlying goodness asserts itself. His famous epitaph fitly rounds out the extravaganza (chap. lxxix). The exit of Trunnion halfway through the book is surprising; one would not expect a star character like Western, Parson Adams, or Micawber to be disposed of in this way. The loss of Trunnion is comparable to the loss of Falstaff. In such cases the author "lights on" the character, as Scott says, and then the character takes over the author; but Smollett does not go all the way with Trunnion and live with him as Fielding does with Parson Adams or Sterne with Uncle Toby. We are likely to think that Smollett wrote his novels by improvising incidents, and we may infer that he welcomed humorous characters particularly because they produced incidents; but he seems to have felt that the major characters realized themselves fully in his densely packed fantastic scenes, rather than in long modulated sequences of events.

Though Smollett's best vein is original, he is disposed in *Peregrine Pickle* to vary the plan he followed in *Roderick Random* by moving somewhat in the direction of Fielding and Richardson. The shift from the first-person point of view in *Random* to the third-person point of view in *Pickle* may well have been made under the influence of Fielding's great success as semidetached narrator. Yet it is impossible to take the graceless Pickle as seriously as we take Tom Jones, or his attempted seduction of the heroine Emilia with even a shadow of the seriousness with which we take Lovelace's attempted seduction of Clarissa. In an able article Professor Putney makes out the best case possible for the moral history of Pickle as the unifying theme of the book.[13] But while Richardson and Fielding reach the height of their architectonic power in a second novel, there is no comparable technical advance in *Pickle,* no real balance between the serious and the humorous plots. Smollett's heroines count for little or nothing as characters; the girls Roderick and Peregrine marry can be disposed of in the words newspapers used to use in announcing such matches—"an agreeable lady with a fortune of 30.000 *l.*"

Perry continues his rough-and-tumble career at Winchester and Oxford and then on the Continent. Now that he has left the garrison behind, much of the action is carried by a second group of humorists including the painter Pallet, Peregrine's tutor, Jolter, and the classical republican doctor evidently intended as a caricature of Dr. Mark Akenside. These humors include the famous banquet in the manner of the ancients, which Professor Kahrl has discovered was worked up from a Latin cookbook attributed to Apicius.[14] Smollett often presents the characters' views and attitudes in long monologues and expositions. The combination of pedantry, low comedy, and caricature is massive, but less attractive than the jack-tar doings of the garrison. In the summer or early autumn of 1749 the novelist had taken a tour through parts of France, Flanders, and Holland,[15] and had visited Paris the following summer, and no doubt he used his observations on these two trips for the Continental scenes in *Pickle*. But though his details for a place like Brussels are specific, he does not elaborate settings and local color, except for a grotesque account of Dutch manners. In the further history of the eighteenth century novel Continental travel narrative is often associated with serious, dramatic, and melodramatic stories, as, in diverse ways, in Smollett's *Ferdinand Count Fathom*, Richardson's *Grandison*, and later in the Gothic novels. More brilliant variations of the humorous travel narrative were to appear in Book VII of *Tristram Shandy*, *A Sentimental Journey*, and Smollett's own *Travels* and *Humphry Clinker*.

In the later part of *Pickle*, Smollett makes considerable play with the Welshman Sir Cadwallader Crabtree, whom Scott later copies as Sir Mungo Malagrowther in *The Fortunes of Nigel*. One principal humorist follows another in this long story; Crabtree takes his turn as a substitute for the humorists of the garrison and the traveling group of pedants. He is the malcontent and misanthrope of post-1600 English comedy, and the sequence in which he sets up as a necromancer and derides and gulls those who expose themselves by consulting him is thoroughly Jonsonian. "By these means, the whole variety of characters, undisguised, passed as it were in review before the confederates, who, by divers ingenious contrivances, punished the most flagrant offenders with as much severity as the nature of their plan would allow" (chap lxxxiv). Smollett thus tries to dramatize the humorist as satirist, a plan to which he was to return with greater success in *Humphry Clinker*.

There is a certain monotony in Perry's career in London and at Bath: he "performed innumerable exploits among whores, bullies, rooks, constables and justices of the peace" (chap. lxxxviii). The biographical novel of our own day which sees a young man through several crops of wild oats does much the same thing with more exotic material, a lush vocabulary, and made-to-order romanticism. One of the more interesting episodes turns on the situation which Shaw parallels in the plot of *Pygmalion* (chap. lxxxvii). Peregrine ventures disastrously into politics and finance, and is then reduced to associating with wits and critics. Toward the end of the story, just as Roderick had been imprisoned in the Marshalsea, Peregrine finds himself in the Fleet as an insolvent debtor, and the faithful Pipes and Hatchway follow him there as Sam Weller was to follow Mr. Pickwick. Though the prison theme had appeared in Defoe and was being used by Fielding, Smollett made it his special property and handed it on. Perry's fortunes mend rapidly, and we leave him in possession of his father's fortune and the beautiful Emilia.

This novel is marked by Smollett's personal attacks on Akenside, Quin, Garrick, Lyttelton, and Fielding. He had already begun this practice of personal satire in *Random*. The personal references are interesting to a biographer or a general student of the period, but the material is intractable, and does not fit so well into Smollett's general scheme as, say, the dunces fit into the *Dunciad*. Even more awkward is the interpolation of the "Memoirs of a Lady of Quality," an account of the career of the notorious Lady Vane put into this book under circumstances which are not at all clear; of the same sort is the insertion of the accounts of Daniel MacKercher's career and the Annesley case in the prison scenes. One suspects Smollett of being ready "to eke out the volume." Perhaps his literary conscience hurt him when he paused to comment adversely on Fielding's use of the narrator's essay-comment: "I might here, in imitation of some celebrated writers, furnish out a page or two, with the reflections he made upon the instability of human affairs, the treachery of the world, and the temerity of youth; and endeavour to decoy the reader into a smile, by some quaint observation of my own, touching the sagacious moralizer: but, besides that I look upon this practice as an impertinent anticipation of the peruser's thoughts, I have too much matter of importance upon my hands, to give the reader the least reason to believe that I am driven to such paltry shifts, in order to eke out the volume" (chap. xcvi).

As has been suggested, Smollett makes a serious attempt to give his central figure due importance in this long story, but has difficulty in adjusting humor and satire to Peregrine's personality. Peregrine is driven by pride and passion; at times he uses the conventional rhetoric of honor, candor, and vengefulness, and at other times shows himself susceptible to the claims of simple humanity. His reactions are conventionally violent, whether he faints as a lover or rages as a bravo. The course of events only heightens the "agreeable ferocity" with which he enters upon life at Winchester (chap. xvii), and his "natural haughtiness of disposition" (chap. xxxv). In adversity he is moved by "that self-tormenting indignation which is inspired by the prosperity of folly, ignorance, and vice" (chap. xcv), an expression which takes us back to the Introduction to *Roderick Random*. But we can hardly take Peregrine's soliloquy in imprisonment as an intimation of dawning philosophy. " 'If I must be prisoner for life,' said he to himself, 'if I must relinquish all my gay expectations, let me at least have the satisfaction of clanking my chains so as to interrupt the repose of my adversary; and let me search in my own breast for that peace and contentment, which I have not been able to find in all the scenes of my success. In being detached from the world, I shall be delivered from folly and ingratitude, as well as exempted from an expence, which I should have found it very difficult, if not impracticable, to support; I shall have little or no temptation to misspend my time, and more undisturbed opportunity to earn my subsistence, and prosecute my revenge. After all, a jail is the best tub to which a cynic philosopher can retire' " (chap. xcvi). What runs through all this is a certain harsh tenacity. In his misfortune he unsentimentally rejects the devoted friendship of Hatchway and Pipes, and even refuses the hand of Emilia until his status is changed by the recovery of his father's fortune. Even when the happy ending was arranged, "he took the road to the garrison in the most elevated transports of joy, unallayed with the least mixture of grief at the death of a parent whose paternal tenderness he had never known. His breast was absolutely a stranger to that boasted *storge* or instinct of affection, by which the charities are supposed to subsist" (chap. ciii). This marks perhaps the extreme limit of Smollett's tough-mindedness.

Smollett had now committed himself to miscellaneous literary labors. He translated Le Sage, his important version of *Gil Blas* appearing in October, 1748, and *The Devil upon Crutches* (probably his) in February, 1750; by 1748 he had already agreed to translate *Don Quixote,* and was paid for this work in 1749, though his version did not appear until 1755, and he evidently had to get up his Spanish to carry it out. Though he was giving up the practice of medicine, his work as compiler and editorial supervisor of large-scale works launched by the booksellers diverted his energies from prose fiction in the 1750's. After the great success of *Roderick Random, Peregrine Pickle* was a relative failure; early readers seem to have been chiefly interested in the scandals of the Lady of Quality.

Ferdinand Count Fathom (1753) is much shorter than the first two novels and marks a change of direction. The Dedication contains Smollett's definition of the novel: "A novel is a large diffused picture, comprehending the characters of life, disposed in different groups, and exhibited in various attitudes, for the purposes of an uniform plan, and general occurrence, to which every individual figure is subservient. But this plan cannot be executed with propriety, probability, or success, without a principal personage to attract the attention, unite the incidents, unwind the clue of the labyrinth, and at last close the scene, by virtue of his own importance." The first sentence uses the analogy of painting, the second the analogy of dramatic plotting. It is worth remembering that "group" was still largely a painter's term. In practice Smollett paid more attention to the "groups" and the "various attitudes" of his "diffused picture" than to the rigorous organizing of his story around a "principal personage" and the unwinding of a plot. The opening chapter of *Fathom* contains Smollett's most elaborate defense of his use of scenes from low life: if the critics accept Petronius, Ovid, Juvenal, Persius, and Lucian among the ancients, Rabelais, Swift, and Pope among the moderns, and in particular such works of fiction as *Don Quixote, Guzman d'Alfarache,* the *Roman Comique,* and *Gil Blas,* why should they be severe on an English novelist who deals with low themes? Perhaps this statement means little more than that Smollett, like the other novelists of his age, is somewhat on the defensive and seeks high literary precedents for his work, as Fielding comprehensively invokes the muse of Aristophanes, Lucian, Cervantes, Rabelais, Molière, Shakespeare, Swift, and Marivaux (*Tom Jones,* XIII, i). Richardson stood apart from Fielding, Smollett, and Sterne in refusing to defend the new novel by citing precedents in Spanish or French fiction.

The hero of *Fathom* wins even less sympathy than Pickle; he has "an amazing fund of villainy and ingratitude." We may say of him what Smollett himself says of the women in Goldoni's comedies: "Indeed their resentments are so cruelly implacable, and contain such a mixture of perfidy, that, in my opinion, they are very unfit subjects for comedy, whose province it is, rather to ridicule folly than to stigmatize such atrocious vice."[16] Smollett may be none too certain of his own purpose in *Fathom,* but he is experimenting with new effects. Instead of the comedy of humors, personal and social satire, and journalistic use of the travel theme, we find Fathom's international career connected with a series of sensational romantic or melodramatic episodes. Later critics noticed that Smollett here anticipates the effects of Gothic romance, particularly in two striking episodes, the night scene in the lonely cabin, with a dead body still warm and bandits nearby (chaps. xx, xxi), and the midnight visit to the tomb of the wronged Monimia, with the appearance of her phantom, which is of course "no phantom" (chap. lxiii). The use of a false alarm by night to produce terror is familiar from Cervantes and Le Sage, and appears in the sheep-stealing episode in *Joseph Andrews* (III, ii), the episode of the idiotic old man and the raven "Ralpho" in *Roderick Random* (chap. xiii), and the episode of Trunnion and the jackdaw in *Peregrine Pickle* (chap. ii), but in all these cases the grotesque outweighs the terrifying. Folklore or popular superstition hardly appears in the realistic fiction of the period except as a minor part of the comedy of manners, or very occasionally for a touch of atmosphere.[17] Smollett does not move far in either direction, but shows some inclination to experiment with a debased and facile romanticism, as in the scene of the seduction of Celinda to the accompaniment of mysterious groans and the music of an Aeolian harp (chap. xxxiv). In spite of Smollett's well-established reputation as a novelist, *Fathom* did not attract much notice and apparently had little success. Though the *Monthly Review* remarked that the story was "a compound of all that is detestable" in the romances of roguery, it found that the book had varied though uneven merits.[18]

II

We must leave it to Smollett's biographer, Professor Knapp, and to the excellent special study of Professor Martz, *The Later Career of Tobias Smollett* (1942), to give a full interpretation of the significance of his Grub Street labors for his personal history and his literary art. It was known that he had a main hand in the *Critical Review* from its beginning in 1756, and in the minor *British Magazine* (1760), and his career as editor and reviewer was acrimonious. He was unfortunately involved in politics, and published the *Briton* (1762-63) in support of Bute's administration. Perhaps, however, the greater part of his energy during these years went into the writing, compiling, and editing of large-scale historical and travel collections, which were evidently among the most profitable of the projects undertaken by eighteenth-century booksellers. Such works are *A Complete His-*

THE EARLY MASTERS OF ENGLISH FICTION

tory of England and its *Continuation* (1757-65), *Compendium of Voyages* (1756), *The Modern Part of the Universal History* (1759-66), *The Present State of All Nations* (1768-69). He also had a hand in a huge translation of Voltaire's works. These labors paid well, and Smollett made more than a good living with his pen. In *Peregrine Pickle* he speaks slightingly of this kind of work.

He had, in his affluence, heard of several authors, who, without any pretensions to genius, or human [?] literature, earned a very genteel subsistence, by undertaking work for booksellers, in which reputation was not at all concerned. One (for example) professed all manner of translation, at so much *per* sheet, and actually kept five or six amanuenses continually employed, like so many clerks in a compting-house; by which means, he was enabled to live at his ease, and enjoy his food and his bottle, ambitious of no other character than that of an honest man, and a good neighbour. Another projected a variety of plans for new dictionaries, which were executed under his eye by day-labourers, and the province of a third was history and voyages, collected or abridged by understrappers of the same class. (chap. xcii)[19]

We may deplore what seems to us a waste of energy, but Professor Martz has shown that it was not a total loss, that the period of "compilation" affected *Humphry Clinker* in important ways. The effect of these prolonged editorial labors on Smollett's vigorous personality was not entirely happy. We cannot improve on his own statement of the case in a letter to Dr. John Moore, August 19, 1762:

Dear Sir

Your last found me in the Country to which I had repaired for the Benefit of purer Air; but, whether it was too keen for my Lungs, or the change of Bed produced a fresh Cold; I was driven home by the asthma; and Soon after, I went to Dover with a View to bathe in the Sea, & to use the Exercise of riding on Horseback, & sailing in a Vessel alternately. There too I was disappointed. Immediately after my Arrival, the weather broke; my asthma returned; my flesh fell away; & my spirits failed; So that I returned very disconsolate, & almost despairing of Releif. The Journey, however, did me Service. I have been at home these Eight days, and find myself better than I have been these three years. Indeed I am at present perfectly well, but, how long I shall enjoy this Respite I cannot foresee. The Civilities you have shewn to the three Foreigners on my account, I shall never forget. They are very full of your Praise; & talk much of the Hospitality and Industry of the People of Glasgow. I am much obliged to you for your kind Expressions of Concern about my Health & Fortune—with respect to the last, I have no Cause to complain of want of Encouragement. The Public has been always a liberal Patron to me since I commenced Author. My Difficulties have arisen from my own Indiscretion; from a warm temper easily provoked to Rashness; from a want of Courage to refuse what I could not grant without doing injustice to my own Family; from Indolence, Bashfullness & want of Oeconomy. I am Sensible of all my weaknesses: I have suffered by them Severely: but I have not Vigour of Mind Sufficient to reform: & So I must go on at the old rate to the end of the Chapter.

Your Conjecture is right in Supposing I still write some articles in the Critical Review. As I am Proprietor of that work, I should be a Fool to give it up; at a Time when it begins to indemnify me for all the Vexation & Loss I have Sustained by it, but, the Laborious Part of authorship I have long resigned. My Constitution will no longer allow me to toil as formerly. I am now so thin you would hardly know me. My Face is shrivelled up by the asthma, like an ill dried Pippin; & my Legs are as thick at the Ancle as at the Calf—if we have a Peace this Season, and I live till the spring, I will endeavour to manage matters so as to be able to make an Excursion to the South of France. I made a push to go Physician to our Army in Portugal; but miscarried. The Secretary of war professed great Friendship, and assured me I might command his best offices. I asked the Place: he expressed great Concern that I had not applied a week before. He said both the Physicians were appointed: This was true; but two other Physicians have been appointed since. You see how much I may depend upon the Friendship of this Gentleman. If my Health had held out, I would have buffeted the storms of Life, without having Recourse to the Protection of any man—as it is, I hope no misfortune shall ever be able to tame the Freeborn spirit of Dear Sir,
Your affectionate, humble Servant—
Ts Smollett[20]

In the Dedication of *Ferdinand Count Fathom* to himself, Smollett had already shown a power of self-analysis which transcended the attitude of indignant virtue and candor prescribed for the satirist.

Know, then, I can despise your pride while I honour your integrity; and applaud your taste, while I am shocked at your ostentation. I have known you trifling, superficial and obstinate in dispute; meanly jealous, and awkwardly reserved; rash and haughty in your resentments and coarse and lowly in your connections. I have blushed at the weakness of your conversation, and trembled at the errors of your conduct. Yet as I own you possess certain good qualities, which overbalance these defects, and distinguish you on this occasion as a person for whom I have the most perfect attachment and esteem, you have no cause to complain of the indelicacy with which your faults are reprehended: and as they are chiefly the excesses of a sanguine disposition and looseness of thought, impatient of caution or controul, you may, thus stimulated, watch over your own intemperance and infirmity with redoubled vigilance and consideration, and for the future profit by the severity of my reproof.

THE EARLY MASTERS OF ENGLISH FICTION

The Adventures of Sir Launcelot Greaves is an oddity; it was written by Smollett to promote his new project, the *British Magazine,* where it appeared in monthly installments from January, 1760, to December, 1761. At the opening of the story Smollett anticipates an objection to his plan: "What! (said Ferret) you set up for a modern Don Quixote?—The scheme is rather too stale and extravagant.—What was an humorous romance, and well-timed satire in Spain, near two hundred years ago, will make but a sorry jest, and appear equally insipid and absurd when really acted from affectation, at this time of day, in a country like England" (chap. ii). It seems as if these words were addressed to the author rather than to Sir Launcelot, and Smollett is handicapped by an uncertain or irresolute conception of the central figure; he still finds it difficult to build his story around a humorous character. In an attempt to adjust Sir Launcelot's mania to English society, his quixotism is much attenuated: "Even in his maddest hours he never adopted those maxims of knight-errantry which related to challenges" (chap. xviii). Though actually equipped with armor, he is a half-sympathetic study of a philanthropist, a fantastic variant of the good man or benevolist exalted in current popular ethics. Though the book is not well organized, it has some fine sketches of humorous characters and some remarkable genre pieces, notably the inn interior, a high visualization of a type of scene much used from Fielding to Dickens. Smollett was largely responsible for handing on such situations and devices, so that Scott could write at the beginning of *Kenilworth:* "It is the privilege of taletellers to open their story at an inn, the free rendezvous of all travellers, and where the humour of each displays itself, without ceremony or restraint." Other tableaux in *Sir Launcelot Greaves*—the prison, the madhouse, the hearing before the foolish Justice Gobble, and the election scenes—make the story at least superficially Hogarthian. Almost all these stock situations reappear long afterwards in *The Pickwick Papers.* Together with the direct connection with Cervantes there is marked influence from Fielding here, especially from the journeys in

Joseph Andrews and *Tom Jones;* Fielding imparts to Smollett at this point a closer concern with the structure of English society (country gentry, tenants, justices of the peace, lawyers, soldiers) and occasionally a touch of the mock-epic style: "The reader may have seen the physiognomy of a stockholder at Jonathan's when the rebels were at Derby, or the features of a bard when accosted by a bailiff, or the countenance of an alderman when his banker stops payment; if he has seen either of these phaenomena, he may conceive the appearance that was now exhibited by the visage of the ferocious captain, when the naked sword of Sir Launcelot glanced before his eyes" (chap. xiii) .[21]

The Adventures of an Atom (1769) is a coarse *roman à clef* whose only point is political satire. Smollett's ordeal in literary and political controversy had now lasted twenty years, from *Random* to the *Atom,* and may be compared and contrasted with Fielding's twenty years from the attacks of the *Grub-street Journal* in the early 1730's to the times of *Amelia* and the Justice in Bow Street. Smollett's most vital work in the 1760's is the *Travels through France and Italy.* Locality in the first two novels had been subordinated to adventure and episode: *Fathom,* as has been noted, moves at times toward an imaginative correlation of setting and action. The next step would be the interaction of setting and character. Smollett's young heroes could hardly become either humorous or sentimental travelers, but Smollett himself had possibilities. In the *Travels,* though he takes much material from the guidebooks, the account is colored by his own reactions; and from his letters (such as the one transcribed above) and from this travel narrative we can make out the origins of Matthew Bramble, the central character in *Humphry Clinker.* In the *Travels* and in *Clinker* the traveler reports by letter to a medical adviser, dwelling most emphatically on bad symptoms, inconveniences, and unpleasant experiences. We see the rough world of the early novels from a different point of view: "Through the whole south of France, except in large cities, the inns are cold, damp, dark, dismal, and dirty; the landlords equally disobliging and rapacious; the servants aukward, sluttish, and slothful; and the postilions lazy, lounging, greedy, and impertinent. If you chide them for lingering, they will continue to delay you the longer: if you chastise them with sword, cane, cudgel, or horse-whip, they will either disappear entirely, and leave you without resource; or they will find means to take vengeance by overturning your carriage" (Letter xli).

Sterne's references to Smollett the traveler as the peevish "Smelfungus" in *A Sentimental Journey* no doubt encouraged a sentimental generation to underrate the *Travels*. But Smollett can view inconveniences and sufferings, his own and others, with a kind of humorous gusto. He makes such reports as the following with decided relish: "Mr. M---e has been long afflicted with violent spasms, colliquative sweats, prostration of appetite, and a disorder in his bowels. He is likewise jaundiced, all over, and I am confident his liver is unsound. He tried the tortoise soup, which he said in a fortnight stuffed him up with phlegm. This gentleman has got a smattering of physic, and I am afraid tampers with his own constitution, by means of Brookes's Practice of Physic, and some dispensatories, which he is continually poring over" (Letter xii). The traveler can make a good story of his own discomfiture, as in the long account of his painful efforts to reach the gates of Florence by walking through a dark wet night (Letter xxxiv), or in the superbly told episode in which he mistakes a French nobleman for the fellow who has charge of the post horses, and bullies him elaborately (Letter viii). Underneath all the grumbling and scolding there is keen observation and even a fine detachment, and it took humorous self-knowledge to write: "The truth is, I was that day more than usually peevish, from the bad weather, as well as from the dread of a fit of the asthma, with which I was threatened: and I dare say my appearance seemed as uncouth to him, as his travelling dress appeared to me. I had a gray mourning frock under a wide great coat, a bob wig without powder, a very large laced hat, and a meagre, wrinkled, discontented countenance." The humane side of life is recognized but not emphasized. The loyal servitor beloved of the eighteenth century appears only for a moment: "Our old driver Joseph . . . no sooner recognized my servant at a distance, by his musquetoon, than he came running towards our carriage, and seizing my hand, even shed tears of joy. Joseph had been travelling through Spain, and was so imbrowned by the sun, that he might have passed for an Iroquois. I was much pleased with the marks of gratitude which the poor fellow expressed towards his benefactors" (Letter xl).

A helpful account of the relation between the *Travels* and *Clinker* has been given by Martz. The novelist is disposed to rely on compiled material or "general history," and *Clinker* shows the effect of his literary labors in the preceding period. The travel episode becomes brief and specifically localized; the style becomes more simple and precise. At the same time, it should be noted, compilation as such cannot center or color the story. How interesting after all are the details from guidebooks which Smollett gathers in the *Travels?* There is a gap between mere appropriation of material and the expression of an individual's attitude or humor. But the term "compilation" may serve to indicate the way in which Smollett gets material for the quick sketch or incisively told incident, less objective than Defoe, more objective than the vignette of Sterne, far less circumstantial and leisurely than Richardson, not so expansive and heavy as the elaboration of incident in *Peregrine Pickle*.

Smollett centers *Clinker* about the irascible and elderly valetudinarian Matthew Bramble, a peppery Welsh squire who, in quest of health and comfort and also out of curiosity and restlessness, travels through England and Scotland with an odd family group. Thus, for the first time in Smollett's career, the story is successfully centered about a humorous character who with all his peculiarities is rational and pungent and can convey the satire that Smollett always wants to write. The young observer-adventurer who formerly occupied the central position fades out and becomes Bramble's intelligent and conventional nephew Jery Melford. The story is in letter form, but instead of shadings of feelings and inner hesitancies we have quick notations and vigorous reactions. The comic letters are virtually humorous monologues that display characteristic oddities, but they are not so massive as some of the monologues in *Pickle*. The device of contrasting points of view is well used in the early part of the book, but it is not carried through; the later letters, especially those from Scotland, are sometimes filled out with travel material not thoroughly assimilated to the character. Smollett is not much concerned with epistolary machinery, and the method is in danger of becoming routine: "Once more, dear doctor, I resume the pen for your amusement"[22] (Bramble, October 11). Sometimes the letter-writer addressing his correspondent is obviously the novelist addressing his reader: "In my last I treated you with a high flavoured dish, in the character of the Scotch lieutenant, and I must present him once more for your entertainment" (Jery, July 13). But the short and varied letters with their abrupt openings and transitions sustain a quick and spirited movement. It has long been known that Smollett must have taken the idea of having various members of a household report experiences in parallel from Christopher Anstey's *New Bath Guide* (1766), and more generally the combination of travel observations, social satire, and playful domestic humors appears in Anstey's popular work.[23] Bath had already inspired relatively colorless satire of fashionable follies in *Roderick Random*, and innumerable references in current literature show how this field for satire might be widened: "There is at *Bath*, during the Season for drinking the Waters, a Concourse of People of all Ranks and Conditions: Men of Quality, mixed with Sharpers, Adventurers, and Fortune-hunters; Persons in a weak and languishing Condition, who repair thither for the Recovery of their Health, and others, who by their Debaucheries seem bent upon impairing their Constitutions, and reducing themselves to the same State with the former; People of Fortune, who, weakly devoted to the Mode, venture Estates upon a Card or a Die, and Sharpers who acquire Estates by taking Advantage of the Weakness of these Fools of Quality; so that a Spectator who has any turn to Observation, cannot fail to be amused by such a Groupe of Characters."[24] But Smollett's sharpened sense of the local and specific and the humors of the family group now transform the theme. Probably the success of the Bath letters early in his new story revealed to him the full possibilities of his plan.

Professor Knapp points out that about 40 per cent of the novel is made up of Bramble's letters, about 50 per cent of Jery Melford's.[25] Thus two prevailing points of view are offered, the humors of Bramble and the semidetached comments of Jery. Though the pleasant young niece Lydia is not particularly interesting, yet the novel is based, as Smollett's other stories are not, on a humane and relatively sensible family group. In *Random* and *Pickle* Smollett had represented his young hero as bitterly estranged from parents or grandparents, but protected by a violently humorous kinsman (Bowling or Trunnion) who acts *in loco parentis*. In *Clinker*, Smollett reorganized his group by abandoning the family feud, a harsh and unrewarding theme, and concentrating on the less exacting relationships between the quizzical old uncle and his wards. These relationships keep clear of pathos and tragedy, and it may be noted that there is an analogous humorous distancing in the relations between little Tristram and his father and uncle. Within the family scheme of *Clinker* we still have a superb gallery of grotesques— Matthew's sister Tabitha, a querulous old maid who reminds us of Grizzle Pickle, Winifred Jenkins, the coarse and selfish serving-woman of the school of Slipslop, and above all the violently grotesque Lieutenant Lismahago, a pragmatical humorist who displays pedantry as one of Scotland's principal exports. It is surprising to find that Tabitha writes only six letters,—she is presented largely and Lismahago entirely in the letters of other correspondents—and Winifred writes only ten; nevertheless their brief contributions, full of inspired misspellings and misuses of words, add a racy flavor that pervades the whole book.

The world of *Clinker* is still Smollett's world, a jungle in which amazing fauna are to be found, a region of endless absurdities, but there is no longer so much talk about fierce indignation. There is a general parallel with Sterne here: while the great world may rage without, the obliquities of these originals are harmless, and manifest themselves in a well-grounded order of things. Bramble and Jery as chief reporters exercise a degree of humane control over the whole spectacle. Smollett, as has been suggested in the discussion of the *Travels,* is very close to Bramble—in his health and medical lore, his temperament, his likes and dislikes, his set opinions, the places and people he knows, and the style of his letters. Smollett to Dr. John Hunter in 1771 might pass for a report from Bramble to Dr. Lewis, except for the reference to his wife: "With respect to myself, I have nothing to say, but that if I can prevail upon my wife to execute my last will, you shall receive my poor carcase in a box, after I am dead, to be placed among your rarities. I am already so dry and emaciated, that I may pass for an Egyptian mummy, without any other preparation than some pitch and painted linen; unless you think I may deserve the denomination of a curiosity in my own character."[26] This grim humor has a flavor which can be immediately appreciated. Smollett's humorous characters never require long study. Jery, who had never observed his uncle at close range before, almost immediately reaches a just estimate: "His singularities afford a rich mine of entertainment; his understanding, so far as I can judge, is well cultivated; his observations on life are equally just, pertinent, and uncommon. He affects misanthropy, in order to conceal the sensibility of a heart, which is tender, even to a degree of weakness. This delicacy of feeling, or soreness of the mind, makes him timorous and fearful; but then he is afraid of nothing so much as of dishonour; and although he is exceedingly cautious of giving offence, he will fire at the least hint of insolence or ill-breeding" (April 24).

Bramble is Smollett, but he is also a type which can be recognized in the mirror of contemporary literature. The sympathetic treatment of humors in the Quixote tradition, already discussed in connection with Parson Adams, had helped to clear the way for the free imputation of benevolism and sensibility to harsh and grotesque characters. The course of popular ethics had carried this so far that sensibility and harshness might even appear together without the fusing power of humor, as in Smollett's young heroes. Roderick Random thus reports his experience at a moving play: "My attention was engaged in spite of myself, and I could not help weeping with the heroine of the stage; though I practiced a great many shifts to conceal this piece of unpolite weakness" (chap. xlv). Even that hard young fellow Peregrine Pickle was a philanthropist in spite of himself: "Numberless were the objects to which he extended his charity in private. Indeed, he exerted this virtue in secret, not only on account of avoiding the charge of ostentation, but also because he was ashamed of being detected in such an awkward unfashionable practice, by the censorious observers of this humane generation. In this particular, he seemed to confound the ideas of virtue and vice; for he did good as other people do evil, by stealth; and was so capricious in point of behaviour, that frequently, in public, he wagged his tongue in satirical animadversions upon that poverty which his hand had, in private, relieved" (chap. lxxxix). Between the earlier and the later Smollett comes Goldsmith's Man in Black:

His manners, it is true, are tinctured with some strange inconsistencies; and he may be justly termed an humourist in a nation of humourists. Though he is generous even to profusion, he affects to be thought a prodigy of parsimony and prudence; though his conversation be replete with the most sordid and selfish maxims, his heart is dilated with the most unbounded love. I have known him profess himself a man-hater, while his cheek was glowing with compassion; and while his looks were softened into pity, I have heard him use the language of unbounded ill-nature. Some affect humanity and tenderness, others boast of having such dispositions from Nature; but he is the only man I ever knew who seemed ashamed of his natural benevolence. He takes as much pains to hide his feelings as any hypocrite would to conceal his indifference; but on every unguarded moment the mask drops off, and reveals him to the most superficial observer.[27]

Bramble is like the Man in Black; his misanthropy is partly a device to conceal his sensibility, as Jery says. In this respect he differs from Smollett's other more savagely sardonic Welshman, Cadwallader Crabtree in *Peregrine Pickle*. But Bramble is not merely a sentimentalist in masquerade; like Molière's Alceste, he can be diagnosed as a neurotic, and at the same time admired for the pride and honesty that lead him to talk harsh sense about the world. The humorous malcontent, like the quixotic enthusiast, can win our admiration as he exposes the human predicament.

The sincere humanity of Smollett-Bramble appears to best advantage when it flavors the satirical and grotesque parts without impairing their vividness and force. There are occasional purely pathetic incidents, one of them particularly admired by Carlyle: "Nothing by Dante or anyone else surpasses in pathos the scene where Humphry goes into the smithy made for him in the old house, and whilst he is heating the iron, the poor woman who has lost her husband, and is deranged. comes and talks to him as to her husband. 'John, they told me you were dead. How glad I am you have come!' And Humphry's tears fall down and bubble on the hot iron."[28] We are likely to be thankful that Smollett is sparing with such scenes of calculated pathos, but it remains true that his humane approach largely determines his treatment of the comic servant Humphry, a guileless grotesque and simple-hearted Methodist who turns out to be the natural son of Matthew Bramble and is married off to Winifred Jenkins. This seems puzzling; the uncertain status of Humphry and the naming of the book for him probably indicate that Smollett was greatly interested in his new experiment of compounding comedy by mixing sympathy and humor in novel proportions.

We are on certain ground when we find Smollett giving us fresh versions of many of his old devices. The book is full of bizarre inventories and lists, spirited and surprising. Take Humphry's account of his accomplishments:

"An please your honour . . . I can read and write, and do the business of the stable indifferent well—I can dress a horse, and shoe him, and bleed and rowel him; and as for the practice of sow-gelding, I won't turn my back on e'er a he in the county of Wilts—Then I can make hog's puddings and hob-nails, mend kettles and tin sauce-pans."—Here uncle burst out a-laughing; and inquired what other accomplishments he was master of—"I know something of single-stick, and psalmody; . . . I can play upon the Jew's-harp, sing Black-ey'd Susan, Arthur-o'Bradley, and divers other songs; I can dance a Welsh jig, and Nancy Dawson; wrestle a fall with any lad of my inches, when I'm in heart; and, under correction, I can find a hare when your honour wants a bit of game. (Jery, May 24)

Is it fanciful to detect, in this fine piece of inspired clowning with its natural rhythm, a softened version of Smollett's savage animal and mechanical symbols? Another excellent passage of this kind is Dennison's account of his friend Wilson's accomplishments (Bramble, October 11), which invites comparison with the doings of Pipes in *Pickle.*

As the novelist approaches the end of his story, he does not feel obliged to give a full account of serious transactions, but improvises a brilliant afterpiece containing his most characteristic comic effects. The severely grotesque is still here, as when Lismahago plays Pierrot in *Harlequin Skeleton:* "His long lank sides, and strong marked features, were all peculiarly adapted to his part.—He appeared with a ludicrous stare, from which he had discharged all meaning; he adopted the impressions of fear and amazement so naturally, that many of the audience were infected by his looks; but when the skeleton held him in chace his horror became most divertingly picturesque, and seemed to endow him with such preternatural agility as confounded all the spectators. It was a lively representation of Death in pursuit of Consumption, and had such an effect upon the commonalty, that some of them shrieked aloud, and others ran out of the hall in the utmost consternation" (Jery, November 18). The account of the three concluding marriages shows the novelist's persistent love of robust high jinks, and the cats shod with walnut shells that frighten Humphry and Winifred in their nuptial couch walk into the story from the early pages of *Peregrine Pickle,* and give us a last glimpse of the animal-machine symbol. Winifred's memorable words in the concluding letter, "Our satiety is to suppurate," assure us that Smollett's humor is inveterate and incorrigible.

In *Clinker* too Smollett had a last free fling at the word-game that he invariably enjoyed. His exuberance had always found some expression in gratuitous play on words as well as gratuitous absurdity of episode, as in the braggart lieutenant's song in *Roderick Random*, a burlesque of a song in Thomas Arne's *Comus*:

> Would you task the moon-ty'd hair,
> To yon flagrant beau repair;
> Where waving with the popling vow,
> The bantling fine will shelter you. (chap. liii)

The word-game as played in the letters of Tabitha and Winifred has affinities with the verbal bagatelles of Swift and Fielding, and was traditionally connected with the role of the comic servant; it also points forward to the far more elaborate and pretentious game played by James Joyce.[29]

The relating of his comedy of humors to his travel itinerary imposed special problems on Smollett. The English letters are given over to a humorous and satirical report of a familiar social scene, and, as has been said, make effective use of the device of contrasting points of view. But evidently Smollett did not think of Scotland as a familiar scene to be satirized; his prospective readers were for the most part English, and they knew little about Scotland and were notoriously prejudiced. Lismahago, as Martz has suggested, may in some sense be considered the spokesman for and defender of Scotland;[30] but he does not accompany the travelers through Scotland, and his pedantry does not represent the picturesque Scotland which is described as Bramble's party moves across the Border, any more than do the crabbed humors of the Scottish lawyer Micklewhimmen. Under the influence of national pride and with the obvious motives of the picturesque traveler, Smollett gives long descriptions of Edinburgh and its surroundings, Leith, the Firth of Fife, then Glasgow, his native vale of Leven, and the West Highlands. His enthusiasm for the "hills of Morven" and Ossian and for the picturesque in general remains somewhat extraneous; it is not blended with humor, and Smollett does not allow Bramble to play his salutary role of quizzical and adverse commentator. Yet the ingredients here are the ingredients of the early Scott— humorous realism, precise topographical and social detail about remote and interesting places with a romantic context. And

Smollett on occasion has a sense of the humorous aspect of the romantic which he passes on to Scott. Thus he describes the office of Dougal Campbell's hereditary piper with great gusto, but adds that Campbell himself cannot endure the sound of the pipes; and since the honor of the clan does not allow him to dispense with this service he is "fain to stop his ears with cotton" and "to fortify his head with three or four night-caps" (Jery, September 3). Here we are close to the shrewd humorous twist that Scott could give to his romance:

[Waverley] had now time to give himself up to the full romance of his situation. Here he sat on the banks of an unknown lake, under the guidance of a wild native, whose language was unknown to him, on a visit to the den of some renowned outlaw, a second Robin Hood, perhaps, or Adam o'Gordon, and that at deep midnight, through scenes of difficulty and toil, separated from his attendant, left by his guide. What a variety of incidents for the exercise of a romantic imagination, and all enhanced by the solemn feeling of uncertainty at least, if not of danger! The only circumstance which assorted ill with the rest was the cause of his journey—the Baron's milk-cows! this degrading incident he kept in the background. (*Waverley*, chap. xvi)

Though *Random* long continued to be ranked as the best of Smollett's novels, *Clinker* has always held a special place in the affections of British readers. Apart from its intrinsic merit, it is most clearly representative of the standard cast of characters and the special modifications of the comedy of humors which Smollett passed on to Scott and Dickens. The serious depreciation of Smollett as a novelist was very largely the work of the mid-nineteenth century.[31] Scott's putting him on a level with Fielding has been ascribed to national sentiment and prejudice, and so might Carlyle's high estimate be, but these views are more nearly representative of the age than later readers find it easy to believe. Perhaps Dickens' memorable references, deeply colored by early reminiscence, are the best record we have of a spontaneous delight in Smollett that has been largely lost.[32] The critical balance that was so badly deranged in the Victorian period has been more tardily readjusted for Smollett than for Richardson, Fielding, and Sterne. It can be said of criticism of Smollett in our own day, as of current criticism of eighteenth century fiction in general, that its tendency is to substantiate by

THE EARLY MASTERS OF ENGLISH FICTION

closer analysis the judgment of discriminating eighteenth century readers on the fiction of their own age.

Trunnion's ride on his wedding day. George Cruikshank.

Laurence Sterne

I

The preëminence of Richardson and Fielding in the generation after 1750 gave currency to a superficial distinction between the serious and the humorous novelist. The serious novelist was didactic, and was concerned with wickedness and suffering, heroism and virtue; the humorous novelist, though also concerned with moral standards, dealt with folly rather than wickedness, could enjoy a moral holiday and present manners in a robust and even outrageous way, could take advantage of the distinction between what virtuous people could say and do and what virtuous people could see and hear. This is to be taken as a statement of readers' expectations, not as an accurate description of the novelists themselves. Continuing with this oversimple contrast, we may say that variations on the model of the humorous novel had great success in the third quarter of the century, and that variations on the model of the serious novel had great success in the last quarter. Smollett and Sterne, in different ways, won success by variations on the humorous novel. The serious novel often came to be nicknamed "sentimental"; Sterne was the first to offer a humorous novel which could also be nicknamed "sentimental."

Until recently the English-speaking world has been for the most part merely tolerant of Sterne's humorous and sentimental effects. He has often been taken to be a "Mr. Oddity," and somehow at the same time the arch-sentimentalist. German criticism evolved philosophical conclusions from his combination of humor and pathos, and Coleridge's memorable comments belong here; but in general it has remained for post-Victorian criticism to do justice to Sterne's original genius, and the present generation is showing intense interest in his oblique and complex methods. Here, even more than with the other novelists, we gain much from an adequate biography—the late Governor Cross has done this great service for both Fielding and Sterne— and we also have the advantage of our own persistent interest in the technique of prose fiction. The age of Joyce, Proust, and Kafka tolerates deviations from plain objective narrative as never before, and this accrues somewhat to the advantage of Richardson and greatly to the advantage of Sterne.

Sterne's work is so highly individual that one is tempted to linger over what Gamaliel Bradford used to call "psychography." The solid English eighteenth century tolerated eccentricity and oddity; it took the stability of institutions for granted, and assumed that the whole system was so well established that it could put up with extreme mannerism in its representatives— the don, the lawyer, the clergyman, the squire, and even the author himself. It was an age of good sense, but it was also an age of harmless play, and in Great Britain at least comedy and satire were not taken to be dangerously subversive. This point is connected with what has been said about the development of a sympathetic attitude toward the humorous character—Sir Roger de Coverley, Parson Adams, Doctor Primrose, Goldsmith's Man in Black, Smollett's Matthew Bramble. In real life Dr. Johnson stood as the incarnation of the idea that a humorist could be a pillar of society; his fundamental views were steady and predictable, his reactions highly unpredictable. It was humor that helped to keep Johnson's Toryism from being "monolithic," as we like to say nowadays. Johnson would not have been flattered by the comparison with Sterne—"nothing odd will last"—but admirers of Johnson's humor, or Goldsmith's, cannot be blind to the side of life Sterne represents. In Sterne the novelist himself becomes the humorist, writing about humorists; the actions of the novelist become unpredictable for the immediate future, like the actions of the characters; whim or impulse is thus raised to the second power, since we must reckon with the unforeseen both in form and content; the novel seems to become disorganized and irresponsible, though this disorganization is apparent rather than real.

We are tempted to find the explanation in the temperament and experiences of Sterne himself: the son of an army officer, he was taken in charge by members of his family, educated at Cambridge, given church livings and eventually a place in the Cathedral Chapter at York. In all this there appears little discipline, no real professional training or steady effort of any kind, no striking down of deep roots. Sterne appears as a clever minor clergyman, depending, like so many people in the eighteenth century, on the good graces of patrons, but not deeply involved or seriously concerned with the quest for favor. He liked to read, write, paint, converse, hunt a little, farm a little. Dilettante, humorist, virtuoso—all are words that might apply. He had written some political pieces for the York newspapers,[1] and developed his informal and flexible style in letters and sermons; as a member of the "Demoniacs" who met at John Hall Stevenson's "Crazy Castle" at Sutton-on-the-Sea, he participated in facetious talk and scribbling inspired by the reading of odd and useless works, and also, it must be added, by the sophomoric aspiration of the members to be considered devilishly witty and reckless. The local success of *A Political Romance*, later called *The History of a Good Warm Watchcoat* (1759), led to the rapid writing of the first two volumes of *The Life and Opinions of Tristram Shandy*, published at York by Hinxman in December, 1759, and in London by Dodsley at the beginning of 1760.[2] The immediate and prodigious success of this work made Sterne a literary lion, and he came up to town in March, 1760, and exploited his popularity by publishing two volumes of sermons in May. *Tristram Shandy* absorbed much of the rest of his life: Volumes III and IV appeared in January, 1761, V and VI in December, 1761, dated 1762, VII and VIII not until January, 1765, after a long sojourn in France in quest of health. Volume IX, in fact and probably in intention the last, appeared in January, 1767; meanwhile Sterne had again traveled extensively on the Continent, and the special outgrowth of this tour was *A Sentimental Journey through France and Italy,* "by Mr. Yorick," brought out in February, 1768, the sixth and last New Year season marked by one of Sterne's important publications. Two more volumes of the *Journey* were promised, but Sterne died a few weeks later.

Sterne's apparently whimsical and erratic ways in *Tristram Shandy* gave contemporary readers a delightful but not entirely unprecedented surprise. No one could take literally those famous remarks, "Ask my pen,—it governs me,—I govern not it" (VI, vi), or, "I begin with writing the first sentence—and trusting to Almighty God for the second" (VIII, ii), or the novelist's report that when he is at a loss what to do next a pinch of snuff, a shave, or a clean shirt will help him out (IX, xiii). "A sudden impulse comes across me—drop the curtain, *Shandy*—I drop it —Strike a line here across the paper, *Tristram*—I strike it—and hey for a new chapter!" (IV, x) He can deliberately propose to insert "a good quantity of heterogeneous matter," so as to "keep up that just balance betwixt wisdom and folly, without which a book would not hold together a single year" (IX, xii) ; he can assert that he has attained "that necessary equipoise and balance, (whether of good or bad) betwixt chapter and chapter, from whence the just proportions and harmony of the whole work results" (IV, xxv). Effects are carefully calculated, and Sterne looks at his scenes and characters with an artist's eye.

Obviously the work is in part a burlesque, yet it is not the mere mimicking of a serious literary form, with the new novel of Richardson and Fielding being rallied out of its dignity. What happens is that homely and trivial detail as found in the new novel is used in a manner which partakes of the mock-heroic or burlesque tradition and the related tradition of "learned wit."[3] Cervantes had so used the material detail of picaresque episode and the matter picked up by Don Quixote in his reading; Sterne makes similar use of the everyday circumstances of English domestic life, material newly exploited in the developing novel of manners, combining this with details acquired by himself and his characters in reading and in the pursuit of hobbies. Sterne says in one of his letters, referring to a ludicrous episode involving Dr. Slop: "I will reconsider Slops fall & my too Minute Account of it—but in general I am perswaded that the happiness of the Cervantic humour arises from this very thing—of describing silly and trifling Events, with the Circumstantial Pomp of great Ones—perhaps this is Overloaded —& I can soon ease it."[4] But Sterne's real point is that the events are not "silly and trifling." The petty realistic details and the claims of the old learning, the old pompous rhetoric, and the new science are taken to be ludicrous and important at the same time. They can be absurd and significant. The same can be said of feeling or "sentiment"; it is inevitable and admirable, the glory of human nature, but at the same time ludicrous. Remarkable results follow when such attitudes are put into the framework of the didactic novel. *Shandy,* Sterne remarks in reporting one of his sermons, is "a moral work more read than understood."[5]

The straight moralist uses his symbols in a serious and systematic way, and he may believe that his moralizing depends on his pattern and his intention being easily recognized. An impoverished imagination may reduce his symbols to mere signs; Clarissa's coffin, brought into the lodgings where she spends her last days, is as obvious as a skull and crossbones. The satirist like Swift, on the other hand, may intend to degrade or deride the thing symbolized by the use of the symbol. Sterne's mock-serious use of detail or episode departs from the facile code of the didactic novelist and also avoids savage satire; he blends the use of a symbol that might be taken as degrading or ludicrous with the assertion of its dignity and significance, the implication that the low things of the earth may surpass the great, and the humble things confound the mighty. Here he takes over and alters the device in Swift which Professor Pons calls "the animal myth,"[6] with which we may also associate the scheme of the macrocosm and the microcosm. Initial attention centers on the physical detail or object nearest at hand, which may be absurd, homely, trivial, or ignoble, and yet have great referential value.

Hence Sterne's constant attention to gestures, which he takes to be the psycho-physical crossroads of life. Here he elaborates a technique already developed by Defoe and Richardson, and at the same time reminds us, in a variation of the manner of Swift, that man is grotesquely involved with a body. Both Defoe and Richardson had gone some distance in substituting spontaneous gesture for the formal grammar of attitude, and Sterne bases his pantomime on this new realism and enhances its significance. In such a passage as the following we see exactly what Richardson passed on to Sterne: "Mr. Grandison was in the midst of a fine speech, and was not well pleased. He sat down, threw one leg over the knee of the other, hemmed three or four times, took out his snuffbox, tapped it, let the snuff drop thro' his fingers, then broke the lumps, then shut it, and twirled it round with the fore-finger of his right-hand, as he held it between the thumb and fore-finger of the other, and was quite like a sullen boy: Yet, after a while, tried to recover himself, by forcing a laugh at a slight thing or two said in company, that was not intended to raise one" (*Grandison*, II, 2). Richardson realizes the principle stated by Sterne in one of his sermons: "I would sooner form a judgment of a man's temper from his behaviour on such little occurrences of life, as these, than from the more weighed and important actions, where a man is more upon his guard:—has more preparation to disguise the true disposition of his heart."[7] And in *Shandy:* "A man of sense does not lay down his hat in coming into a room,—or take it up in going out of it, but something escapes, which discovers him" (VI, v). As already appears in Richardson, the minutiae of gesture are built up into action and characterization:

My father thrust back his chair,—rose up,—put on his hat,—took four long strides to the door,—jerked it open,—thrust his head half way out, —shut the door again,—took no notice of the bad hinge,—returned to the table,—plucked my mother's thread-paper out of *Slawkenbergius's* book,—went hastily to his bureau,—walked slowly back, twisting my mother's thread-paper about his thumb,—unbuttoned his waistcoat,— threw my mother's thread-paper into the fire,—bit her satin pin-cushion in two, filled his mouth with bran,—confounded it;—but mark!—the oath of confusion was levelled at my uncle *Toby's* brain,—which was e'en confused enough already,—the curse came charged only with the bran,—

the bran, may it please your honours,—was no more than powder to the ball. (III, xli)

Gestures and reactions are intimately associated with unconsidered and trivial objects, the snuffbox, the pincushion, the thread-paper, and it turns out that such details are not trivial after all. You can pick them up everywhere, they offer short cuts to reality, and their abundance mocks the set and formal proceedings of mankind:

I hate set dissertations,—and above all things in the world, 'tis one of the silliest things in one of them, to darken your hypothesis by placing a number of tall, opaque words, one before another, in a right line, betwixt your own and your reader's conception,—when in all likelihood, if you had looked about, you might have seen something standing, or hanging up, which would have cleared the point at once—"for what hindrance, hurt, or harm, doth the laudable desire of knowledge bring to any man, if even from a sot, a pot, a fool, a stool, a winter-mittain, a truckle for a pully, the lid of a goldsmith's crucible, an oil bottle, an old slipper, or a cane chair,"—I am this moment sitting upon one. Will you give me leave to illustrate this affair of wit and judgment, by the two knobs on the top of the back of it. (III, xx)

This catalogue from Rabelais (III, xvi) savors of random, homely, even gross experience, and of the possibilities of order Sterne finds in such experience. He plays with the idea of random chapters on any topics or objects that may offer,— chapters on chapters, on sleep, on whiskers, on chambermaids and buttonholes, green gowns and old hats.[8] Finding topics or objects is a game, like riding a hobbyhorse, "the sporting little filly-folly which carries you out for the present hour—a maggot, a butterfly, a picture, a fiddle-stick—an uncle Toby's siege— or an *any thing*, which a man makes a shift to get a-stride on, to canter it away from the cares and solicitudes of life" (VIII, xxxi).

Before we go on to consider the bearing of Sterne's apparently random notations and collectanea on the general plan of his book, we may notice how this method applies to the novel of manners and to his notorious sentimentalism. Some trifling situation or object may be invested with moral and metaphysical meaning, and it is asserted, at least half seriously, that the discovery of such significance is the test of virtue as well as of in-

THE EARLY MASTERS OF ENGLISH FICTION

telligence. This gives us the context of Corporal Trim's hat or Uncle Toby's fly. An obvious illustration is the familiar passage in the letters (of doubtful date and provenience, but undoubtedly genuine), often used to illustrate the appearance of the term "sentimental": "One solitary plate, one knife, one fork, one glass!—I gave a thousand pensive, penetrating looks at the chair thou hadst so often graced, in those quiet, and sentimental repasts—then laid down my knife, and fork, and took out my handkerchief, and clapped it across my face, and wept like a child."[9] Here we should notice not only the flood of tears (everybody in the eighteenth century who sheds a tear is called sentimental), but the series of gestures correlated with the physical props—knife, fork, glass, chair, handkerchief—and the importance with which this little system of acts and things is invested. Though Sterne seems to have left no opinion of Richardson on record, he must be indebted to the epistolary novelist's change of scale, his report "written to the moment," his emphasis on the domestic foreground of ordinary life, and his restriction of significant action to family and household. No doubt Sterne, as Cross says, had no use for the "caution and discretion" of Richardson's moral code, but we should not overlook the flexibility of the Richardsonian letter and its concern with minutiae. Both Sterne and Richardson are concerned with the circumstances that envelop things and actions. We do not find in Sterne formally described interiors, but we have details of costume, furniture, and other *impedimenta* given as never before. Restriction of overt and large-scale action is pushed very far; life in city, church, camp, even in the home parish is presented only indirectly in Sterne's network of references. One would have to know the book pretty well to remember that Walter Shandy had been a Turkey merchant in Coleman Street. Sterne even avoids set pictures and extended descriptive narrative in the manner of his master Cervantes. "Now the chapter I was obliged to tear out, was the description of this cavalcade, in which Corporal *Trim* and *Obadiah*, upon two coach-horses a-breast, led the way as slow as a patrole—whilst my uncle *Toby*,

LAURENCE STERNE   189 in his laced regimentals and tye-wig, kept his rank with my father, in deep roads and dissertations alternately upon the advantage of learning and arms, as each could get the start" (IV, xxv). Somewhat similarly, Sterne does not undertake to cover as systematically as Fielding or Smollett the stock themes of eighteenth century satire. Hostile satire, as of Dr. Slop, Didius, and other stupid pedants, is very limited, even though much attention is paid to pedantry. In Sterne's world, John Cowper Powys remarks, "There is no need for any monstrous villainy nor for any egregious hypocrisy such as we are offered in Fielding and Dickens."[10] It is in the *Sermons of Mr. Yorick* rather than in *Shandy* that we find ourselves established in the world of the eighteenth century didactic novel.

Sterne exuberantly follows the tradition of learned wit, as has been remarked, the tradition found in *A Tale of a Tub* and *The Memoirs of Martinus Scriblerus,* using the *prima facie* content and methods of scholarship for comic purposes. The writer shows exaggerated concern for trifles, displays obscure, minute, and irrelevant erudition with an affected care for accuracy, and sets it forth with an apparatus of formal rhetoric and logic. The curious and studious reader may well be diverted by Sterne's use of Rabelais, Montaigne, Cervantes, Butler, Burton, Bruscambille, Beroalde de Verville, and many others. This has been a fascinating theme for the commentators ever since Ferriar in his *Illustrations of Sterne* (1798) undertook to expose the novelist as a plagiarist. But it is more important to get at the purpose behind all this. The essential step had been taken by Cervantes; all this lore is attributed in one way or another to a comic pedant. Thus we have Walter Shandy's theories, Uncle Toby's military obsessions, and the elaborate lucubrations of Tristram the narrator himself. Such characters, obsessed with a humor or a hobby, are traditional, and traditional also is the implied or expressed presentation of a rational point of view. This point of view might of course be represented by a reasonable character in the story, but, as we have already noted, Cervantes, Marivaux, and Fielding, to name no

THE EARLY MASTERS OF ENGLISH FICTION

others, had already brought the narrator into the story and made him serve to some extent as the voice of reason.

But the intervention of the narrator may work in different ways: it may be by the rule of good sense, and be dominated by the strong eighteenth century "decent respect for the opinions of mankind," but it may also have the unpredictability of spontaneous response or impulse. Just as Thackeray called one of his important works *The Book of Snobs. By One of Themselves,* so Sterne might have called *Tristram Shandy* "The Book of Humorists. By One of Themselves." The narrator shows varying attitudes: he may say, "When I seem to be arbitrary, you must nevertheless trust me, for I am really working on a rational plan," or else he may say, "I simply obey my impulses." The narrator in *Shandy* plays the game in both these ways. Fielding's narrator asks for belief in the rational plan, and never makes any serious pretense of flouting it; Sterne's narrator asks for sympathetic participation in the game. Fielding's position is close to the conception of the satirist as the man of plain reason and candor; Sterne's position is close to the conception of the satirist as "the *naïf,* the *ingénu,* the simple heart."[11] The imputation of this attitude to a fictitious character appears in the *Quixote* tradition, and also in what we may call the *Gulliver-Candide* tradition. Such a character must always in a certain sense be defeated or frustrated. Yet Sterne's *ingénu* as novelist cannot be completely defeated, for after all he has written his book—here it is before you in print—and from the outset he hopes, not in vain, for the friendly indulgence and approval of the reader:

You must have a little patience. I have undertaken, you see, to write not only my life, but my opinions also; hoping and expecting that your knowledge of my character, and of what kind of a mortal I am, by the one, would give you a better relish for the other: As you proceed further with me, the slight acquaintance which is now beginning betwixt us, will grow into familiarity; and that, unless one of us is in fault, will terminate in friendship—*O diem praeclarum!*—then nothing which has touched me will be thought trifling in its nature, or tedious in its telling. Therefore, my dear friend and companion, if you should think me somewhat sparing of my narrative on my first setting out,—bear with me,— and let me go on, and tell my story my own way:—or if I should seem now and then to trifle upon the road,—or should sometimes put on a fool's cap with a bell to it, for a moment or two as we pass along,—don't fly off,—but rather courteously give me credit for a little more wisdom than appears upon my outside:—and as we jog on, either laugh with me, or at me, or in short, do any thing,—only keep your temper. (I, vi)

Parson Yorick is this same *ingénu* as victim, without full privileges of narration and comment; eventually he takes over as narrator in *A Sentimental Journey*. Though Tristram the narrator has his share of pedantry and ingenuousness, he retains a control that can be described as partly rational and partly social; he remains after all in command of the situations in which the other characters and the reader find themselves, in spite of the fact that he professes to be a victim of impulse, to be so busy that he doesn't know how he is going to get from one chapter to another (VIII, vi).

When we combine the miscellaneous of the "learned wit" tradition with the conception of the novelist as *ingénu* going about his business, we find Sterne moving toward the kind of novel that Edouard in Gide's *Les Faux-Monnayeurs* says he would like to write: "I invent the character of a novelist, whom I make my central figure; and the subject of the book, if you must have one, is just that very struggle between what reality offers him and what he himself desires to make of it."[12] He wants to get everything into the book, and yet he must evolve a style, an artistic mode of treatment. He goes on to say, "It is essentially out of the question for a book of this kind to have a plan." He is keeping a notebook preparatory to the work, and it may be that "if I don't succeed in writing the book, it'll be because the history of the book will have interested me more than the book itself—taken the book's place; and it'll be a very good thing." If these ideas were pushed to the limit, Edouard would be identified with the author of *Les Faux-Monnayeurs*, and the notebook would be fully incorporated in and partly identical with the novel. We do not reach these identities in Gide; there is Edouard and there is also the novelist who writes in the third person about Edouard; we have the separate *Journal des Faux-Monnayeurs* beside the book itself. Sterne moves closer to the identification of the novelist in the book with the novelist writing the book. The prehistory of the novel is given largely in the book itself; he does not publish a *Journal de Shandy* alongside of *Shandy*. Though he may talk about planlessness, that is part of his plan, and he knows that when the novelist proposes getting everything into his book what he really has in mind is the discarding of accepted restraints in his selection of points and details, the substitution of another ideal of artistic unity for the conventional one.

II

In telling a story, reporting how life feels, or trying to find the truth, one must begin with experience, with what is actually nearest at the moment, the content of consciousness. Sterne thus professes to write, like Locke, "a history-book . . . of what passes in a man's own mind" (II, ii). What Sterne says at the beginning of the sermon on a good conscience applies to consciousness also: "In other matters we may be deceived by false appearances. . . . But here the mind has all the evidence and facts within herself" (II, xvii). Like Locke, he believes that one can somehow pass from the data of immediate experience to the construction of an ordered world, but a world strictly bounded by our limited capacities:

Can the deepest enquirers after nature tell us, upon what particular size and motion of parts the various colours and tastes of vegetables depend? . . . Nay, have not the most obvious things that come in our way dark sides, which the quickest sight cannot penetrate into; and do not the clearest and most exalted understandings find themselves puzzled, and at a loss, in every particle of matter?

Go then,—proud man!—and when thy head turns giddy with opinions of thy own wisdom, that thou wouldst correct the measures of the Almighty,—go then,—take a full view of thyself in this glass;—consider thy own faculties,—how narrow and imperfect;—how much they are chequered with truth and falsehood;—how little arrives at thy knowledge, and how darkly and confusedly thou discoverest even that little as in a glass:—consider the beginnings and ends of things, the greatest and the smallest, how they all conspire to baffle thee;—and which way ever thou prosecutest thy enquiries,—what fresh subjects of amazement,—and what fresh reasons to believe there are more yet behind which thou canst never comprehend.—Consider,—these are but part of his ways;—how little a portion is heard of him? Canst thou, by searching, find out God?

—wouldst thou know the Almighty to perfection?—'Tis as high as heaven,
What canst thou do?—'tis deeper than hell, how canst thou know it?[13]

That Sterne considered this traditional doctrine in line with
the findings of Locke is shown by his oft-quoted remark about
Locke's philosophy, reported by Suard: "It is a philosophy
which never attempts to explain the miracle of sensation; but
reverently leaving that miracle in the hands of God, it unfolds
all the secrets of the mind; and shunning the errors to which
other theories of knowledge are exposed, it arrives at all truths
accessible to the understanding."[14] But, since he is a novelist
and not a philosopher, he can enjoy the details as they come; he
has a "negative capability," as Keats calls it, which is denied to
the business-like epistemologist. Here Sterne is more like an
empiricist of the stamp of Bergson or James, and can enjoy a
bath in experience. Whatever comes up has the warrant of immediate experience and the importance of an event in human
history. The arid data of English empiricism are irradiated with
sympathy, and Sterne gives a new reading of the *nihil humani
a me alienum puto* of Terence.

With this approach, the humor of a character, fixed though
it is, is translated from moment to moment into unpredictable
impulses. Every humorist is like Parson Yorick, "as heteroclite
a creature in all his declensions" (I, xi), or like Dryden's Zimri:

> A man so various, that he seem'd to be
> Not one, but all Mankind's Epitome.
> Stiff in Opinions, always in the wrong;
> Was Everything by starts, and Nothing long:
> But, in the course of one revolving Moon,
> Was Chymist, Fidler, States-man, and Buffoon;
> Then all for Women, Painting, Rhiming, Drinking,
> Besides ten thousand Freaks that died in thinking.[15]

The idea applies not only to heteroclites like Yorick and Tristram, but also to Walter Shandy, uniform and systematic though
he was in holding to his favorite ideas (I, xix). "As many pictures as have been given of my father, how like him soever in
different airs and attitudes,—not one, or all of them, can ever
help the reader to any kind of preconception of how my father
would think, speak, or act, upon any untried occasion or occur-

rence of life.—There was that infinitude of oddities in him, and of chances along with it, by which handle he would take a thing, —it baffled, Sir, all calculations" (V, xxiv). As already noted above,[16] the comedy of humors does not necessarily set a fixed character in the midst of a complex and shifting world; it may reverse that situation, and set a complex and shifting character in the midst of a stupid and static world, and it may apply both situations to a single character. The static humorists in the old sense, like Dr. Slop, are comparatively uninteresting; all Sterne's successful characters show in various ways and degrees this interplay between the flux of the mind and the rigidity of fact and convention, or between the bewildering complexity of the facts and the oversimplifications of mind and temperament.

Under these circumstances, how is one to organize the material of experience and attain the fullest practicable knowledge of people and things? Sterne senses the dramatic value of the problem of knowledge, and uses it in his game. "—My good friend, quoth I—as sure as I am I—and you are you—" "—And who are you? said he.—Don't puzzle me; said I" (VII, xxxiii). The humors of Sterne's characters, his own version of the method of "writing to the moment," and the complexities entailed in a close look at the facts make him keenly aware of the great game of cross-purposes called communication. But he is amused and interested; he may profess to be troubled, but he is not really baffled or discouraged by the threat of skepticism or solipsism. Locke had looked with suspicion on the association of ideas or "mental discourse" as a process that worked against the natural and rational relations of things; and he emphasized judgment, the separation or distinction of ideas, as against wit, the ingenious combination of ideas, though he recognized that in relating ideas for the purpose of forming judgments (practical estimates of probability), both agreements and differences among ideas have to be reckoned with, and this calls for what he terms "sagacity."[17] But the fact remains that Locke's "sagacity" is more pedestrian than Sterne's "wit." Sterne is for taking hold of all clues; he enjoys occult agreements and differences. He is not so random or indiscriminate as he appears to be, but Locke would be hard put to it to find order in his "history-book."

Sterne does not get the general out of the particular, or the external world out of the internal, by an orderly Lockean process. He assumes a great scheme in space and time, and no matter what tricks the point and the instant may play upon us the continuum remains secure. Thus the story of the King of Bohemia and his Seven Castles which Trim begins is never told, but remains a point in the expanse of chronology and geography presented by the successive digressions (VIII, xix). Much attention has been paid to the game Sterne plays with time, his awareness of concurrent separate time-systems, the difference between chronological or clock-time and the feeling of time for the individual, the difference between the time it takes for events to happen and the time it takes for the novelist to write about them. Great discrepancies appear: in immediate experience clock-time is indefinitely extended or shortened; as Toby and Walter descend the stair a chapter may be written for each step (IV, x); a day in Tristram's life may take a year in the writing of it (I, xiv). But these apparent discrepancies are then matched up, the minute and the enormous are paired, or correspond. As a novelist Sterne takes advantage of the situation indicated by the mathematician's definition of an infinite series as one in which any part may be put into one-one correspondence with the whole. The system is timeless in the sense that it transcends any given time-scheme. In other words, Sterne's tricks with time become tricks with space.

We may say that Sterne assumes that experience symbolizes or epitomizes reality, as memory epitomizes a span of time, or Hamlet's nutshell includes infinite space. Reality is not simply built up out of single units; it is contained in the given unit. The individual experience somehow images in little and simultaneously a moral order and a cosmic order, the world of conscience and consciousness and the world of microscope and telescope. The early fragment published by Stapfer, the "Meditation on a Plum Tree," shows Sterne's interest in Fontenelle's conception of the plurality of worlds, his idea of a world in a leaf or the blue of a plum. Lehman and Watkins have recently redirected attention to this important fragment, though chiefly with reference to Sterne's treatment of time. Readers of Miss Nicolson's studies will immediately be able to put the following passage into its context:

It's hard to say whether [*sic*] side of ye prospects strikes ye imagination most; whether ye solar system or a drop of pepper water afford a nobler subject of contemplation; in short whether we owe more to ye Telescope or microscope. On one side infinite Power and wisdom appear drawn at *full extent;* on ye other, in *miniature.* The infinitely *strong and bold Strokes there,* ye infinitely *nice and delicate Touches here,* shew equally in both ye divine hand.

By a different conformation of its senses a Creature might be made to apprehend any given Portion of space, as greater, or less in any Proportion, than it appears to us. This we are assured of from Optics. I doubt not also but by a *different conformation* of ye Brain a Creature might be made to apprehend any given portion of time as longer or shorter in any proportion than it appears to us. Glasses can make an *inch* seem a *mile.* I leave it to future ages to invent a method for making a *minute* seem a *year.*[18]

Here Sterne has a vision of a cataclysm, with the imagery of a poem on the Last Judgment, and awakens to find that the wind has merely blown the plums to the ground. We thus have cosmological grounds for the novelist's change of scale; the infinitely great and the infinitely small are interchangeable and equally important. Walter Shandy expounds the importance of the minute in terms of scientific precision: *"Knowledge,* like matter, he would affirm, was divisible *in infinitum;*—that the grains and scruples were as much a part of it, as the gravitation of the whole world.—In a word, he would say, error was error, —no matter where it fell,—whether in a fraction,—or a pound,— 'twas alike fatal to truth, and she was kept down at the bottom of her well as inevitably by a mistake in the dust of a butterfly's wing,—as in the disk of the sun, the moon, and all the stars of heaven put together" (II, xix). Artistic effects too are the results of delicate adjustments and slight touches, the *poco più* and *poco meno* (II, vi). And so Sterne loves miniatures as such; he is fascinated by the idea of the homunculus, or by Uncle

Toby's maps and his fortifications on the bowling green. He can think of his own works as miniatures: "I have lusted earnestly, and endeavoured carefully . . . that these little books, which I here put into thy hands, might stand instead of many bigger books" (IV, xxii). The traffic goes both ways, from the great to the small or from the small to the great. The mind striking in at any point and picking up connections is working with and toward the significant. Once a point is seized on, it is treated with an excess of method. The famous little vignettes or episodes are carefully wrought to scale, subdivided and rounded out with incrementally repeated detail, in order to give us *multum in parvo*. The incident of Uncle Toby and the fly "is to serve for parents and governors instead of a whole volume upon the subject" of philanthropy (II, xii).

The universe is pictured as a great multiple system, in which sense and spirit, macrocosm and microcosm, are linked by analogies and correspondences, and also as a great dynamic system to be studied in terms of cause and effect. Causality lends itself to the same kind of play with great and small, the great cause and the trivial effect, the minute cause and the great effect. "Matters of no more seeming consequence in themselves than, 'Whether my father should have taken off his wig with his right hand or with his left,'—have divided the greatest kingdoms, and made the crowns of the monarchs who governed them, to totter upon their heads" (III, ii). Like Fielding, Sterne loves recondite cause-effect relationships, but Fielding follows out a given sequence to a conclusion, whereas Sterne catches impressionistic glimpses of their operation in the field over which attention ranges. The correspondence and causal connection of great and small are briefly expressed in Sterne's apostrophe in *A Sentimental Journey* to the "great great *Sensorium* of the world! which vibrates, if a hair of our heads but falls upon the ground, in the remotest desert of thy creation."[19] The filaments of sensation, impulse, imagination, and sentiment connect microcosm and macrocosm.

The episode of the reception of the news of Bobby's death

(V, ii-xiv) may be summarized to illustrate the principal features of Sterne's method. Walter Shandy is planning details of Bobby's proposed grand tour, with the map before him; he is interrupted first by the servant Obadiah, who wants to go on an errand but can go neither on horse nor on foot, and then by Uncle Toby's report of the letter telling of Bobby's death. Walter then delivers a pompous speech on mortality, taken out of Burton's *Anatomy of Melancholy;* his discourse is misunderstood in different ways by Toby and Mrs. Shandy. The latter, who just happens to be in the passage, plays her usual part of uncomprehending listener, and is left standing at the door for five minutes and seven chapters. Sterne then diagrams the machinery of the family, and extends the concurrent action:

> Though in one sense, our family was certainly a simple machine, as it consisted of a few wheels; yet there was this much to be said for it, that these wheels were set in motion by so many different springs, and acted one upon the other from such a variety of strange principles and impulses,—that though it was a simple machine, it had all the honour and advantages of a complex one,—and a number of as odd movements within it, as ever were beheld in the inside of a *Dutch* silk-mill.
> Amongst these there was one, I am going to speak of, in which, perhaps, it was not altogether so singular, as in many others; and it was this, that whatever motion, debate, harangue, dialogue, project, or dissertation, was going forwards in the parlour, there was generally another at the same time, and upon the same subject, running parallel along with it in the kitchen. (V, vi)

This sets the stage for Trim's oration on death and for the contrast with Walter's pedantic periods. In the kitchen, Obadiah's announcement of the death makes the maid Susannah think of Mrs. Shandy's green satin nightgown, which may be given to the servant now that the mistress will be going into mourning (and if the mistress herself should die, the whole wardrobe would follow) ; the foolish scullion, thinking of her own case of dropsy, says simply, "So am not I"; Obadiah himself thinks that they will have a terrible task stubbing the Ox-moor (the expense of Bobby's education had postponed that project). The gestures and words of Trim's oration—the stick struck perpendicularly on the floor, the dropping of the hat, the question, "Are we not here now, and gone in a moment?"—acquire by incremental repetition and elaborate commentary a significance that Walter's learning never attains. Sterne restates in humorously solemn style the principle of the tremendous trifle: "Now, as I perceive plainly, that the preservation of our constitution in church and state,—and possibly the preservation of the whole world—or what is the same thing, the distribution and balance of its property and power, may in time to come depend greatly upon the right understanding of this stroke of the corporal's eloquence—I do demand your attention" (V,vii). Yet we still remain in a world of "chamber-maids, green-gowns, and old hats" (V,viii), the world of homely objects and simple thoughts. Thus we have in the space of a few chapters concurrent actions which taken together give the impression of depth or extension, interruption and frustration, futile rhetoric, imperfect communication, surprising cause-effect sequences, unpredictable transitions and associations of ideas, trivial physical symbols for great things, and the basic idea of the machine.

The famous digression on digressions will further illustrate how Sterne plans the presentation of his action in space and time. Walter and Toby have been sitting silently for an hour and a half. Walter asks a question, and Toby begins to answer, but Toby's humorous character impels Sterne at this point to state the theory of the English as a humorous people, Toby knocking the ashes out of his pipe the while. Sterne then applies the theory of humors to the whole family, especially to Aunt Dinah, who had married the coachman, and whose case greatly mortified Uncle Toby's modesty. Walter, on the other hand, was constantly referring to Dinah: "The backslidings of *Venus* in her orbit fortified the *Copernican* system, called so after his name; and the backslidings of my aunt *Dinah* in her orbit, did the same service in establishing my father's system, which, I trust, will for ever hereafter be called the *Shandean System*, after his" (I, xxi). While Walter talked of Dinah, Toby would whistle *Lillibulero;* Sterne calls this the *Argumentum Fistulatorium,* and discusses its classification in logic. Then he pauses to explain and justify his method of "progressive digression":

THE EARLY MASTERS OF ENGLISH FICTION

In this long digression which I was accidentally led into, as in all my digressions (one only excepted) there is a master-stroke of digressive skill, the merit of which has all along, I fear, been overlooked by my reader,—not for want of penetration in him,—but because 'tis an excellence seldom looked for, or expected indeed, in a digression;—and it is this: That though my digressions are all fair, as you observe,—and that I fly off from what I am about, as far, and as often too as any writer in Great Britain; yet I constantly take care to order affairs so, that my main business does not stand still in my absence.

I was just going, for example, to have given you the great outlines of my uncle Toby's most whimsical character;—when my aunt Dinah and the coachman came across us, and led us a vagary some millions of miles into the very heart of the planetary system: Notwithstanding all this, you perceive that the drawing of my uncle Toby's character went on gently all the time;—not the great contours of it,—that was impossible,—but some familiar strokes and faint designations of it, were here and there touched in, as we went along, so that you are much better acquainted with my uncle Toby now than you was before.

By this contrivance the machinery of my work is of a species by itself; two contrary motions are introduced into it, and reconciled, which were thought to be at variance with each other. In a word, my work is digressive, and it is progressive too,—and at the same time.

This, Sir, is a very different story from that of the earth's moving round her axis, in her diurnal rotation, with her progress in her elliptic orbit which brings about the year, and constitutes that variety and vicissitude of seasons we enjoy;—though I own it suggested the thought,—as I believe the greatest of our boasted improvements and discoveries have come from such trifling hints.

Digressions, incontestably, are the sunshine;—they are the life, the soul of reading;—take them out of this book for instance,—you might as well take the book along with them;—one cold eternal winter would reign in every page of it; restore them to the writer;—he steps forth like a bridegroom;—bids All hail; brings in variety, and forbids the appetite to fail.

All the dexterity is in the good cookery and management of them, so as to be not only for the advantage of the reader, but also of the author, whose distress, in this matter, is truly pitiable: For, if he begins a digression,—from that moment, I observe, his whole work stands stock-still;—and if he goes on with his main work,—then there is an end of his digression.

—This is vile work.—For which reason, from the beginning of this, you see, I have constructed the main work and the adventitious parts of it with intersections, and have so complicated and involved the digressive and progressive movements, one wheel within another, that the whole machine, in general, has been kept a-going;—and, what's more, it shall be kept a-going these forty years, if it please the fountain of health to bless me so long with life and good spirits. (I, xxii)

The word "machine" gives the clue here: "machine" points to Tristram's body and life, to the structure of the book, to the structure of the universe. Popular thought might conceive of the world and man as a system operated by a few simple forces and springs providentially planned and running with infallible regularity. But, still under Providence, it might emphasize the complexity of the mechanism, as in the following passage from Shaftesbury:

You have heard it (my Friend!) as a common Saying, that *Interest governs the World.* But, I believe, whoever looks narrowly into the Affairs of it, will find, that *Passion, Humour, Caprice, Zeal, Faction,* and a thousand other Springs, which are counter to *Self-Interest,* have as considerable a part in the Movements of this Machine. There are more Wheels and *Counter-Poises* in this Engine than are easily imagin'd. 'Tis of too complex a kind, to fall under one simple View, or be explain'd thus briefly in a word or two. The Studiers of this *Mechanism* must have a very partial Eye, to overlook all other Motions besides those of the lowest and narrowest compass. 'Tis hard, that in the Plan or Description of this Clock-work, no Wheel or Ballance should be allow'd on the side of the better and more enlarg'd Affections; that nothing should be understood to be done in *Kindness or Generosity;* nothing in *pure Good-Nature* or *Friendship,* or thro any *social* or *natural Affection* of any kind: when, perhaps, the main Springs of this Machine will be found to be either these very *natural Affections* themselves, or a compound kind deriv'd from them, and retaining more than one half of their Nature.[20]

In this optimistic tone, Sterne makes a playful application of the "machine" idea to the structure or "machinery" of his book, and to the events of his story and the actions of his characters. Man is an animal, man is a machine worked by natural forces. The related ideas of animality and mechanism were used for satirical purposes by Swift, for caricature by Smollett, for a brilliant and sympathetic presentation of the human situation by Sterne.[21] All the while, of course, Sterne gets his fun out of the way man is involved in the machinery of the cosmos: "Had Dr. *Slop* beheld *Obadiah* a mile off, posting in a narrow lane directly towards him, at that monstrous rate,—splashing and plunging like a devil through thick and thin, as he approached, would not such a phenomenon, with such a vortex of mud and water moving along with it, round its axis, have been a subject of juster apprehension to Dr. *Slop* in his situation, than the worst of *Whiston's* comets?—To say nothing of the *Nucleus,* that is, of *Obadiah* and the coach-horse.—In my idea, the vortex alone

THE EARLY MASTERS OF ENGLISH FICTION

of 'em was enough to have involved and carried, if not the Doctor, at least the Doctor's pony quite away with it" (II, ix). The astronomical and physiological references are not incidental or arbitrary ornament, but mean that Sterne's book is about the relation of the little to the great world. Whereas the current physico-theology emphasized simplicity and regularity, Sterne professes to find a just representation of the ordered scheme endlessly intricate and perplexing.

"Progressive digression" thus displays human history as it unfolds in space and time, and as the past fuses with the present and the remote with what is close at hand. The art of digression is the art of presenting coexisting aspects of the totality of experience. Sterne achieves such effects on various scales; he has delicate counterpoint within the episode, with incremental repetition of speech and gesture suspending the moment as a tableau and thus giving us a brief conspectus of concurrent action, and then he will proceed suddenly to far wider ranges of reference. One thinks of the use of time in Proust, with multiple memories radiating from a single impression, but a difference is that the wider reference in Sterne is constructed on a framework of quasi-learned and quasi-scientific matter, instead of being minutely compounded of personal reminiscence. Such a cosmic scheme is recognized in Proust also, but Proust maintains a higher degree of subjectivity and relativity: "When a man is asleep, he has in a circle round him the chain of the hours, the sequence of the years, the order of the heavenly host. Instinctively, when he awakes, he looks to these, and in an instant reads off his own position on the earth's surface and the amount of time that has elapsed during his slumbers; but this ordered procession is apt to grow confused, and to break its ranks."[22] Tristram the narrator and the other characters hark back to the past, and conversely the story may get ahead of itself, but past and present are on the same level; the past is not invested with pathos, and Tristram does not long for his lost childhood, or the old soldiers for their early prime. Another comparison which might help to bring out the scholastic and cosmological side of Sterne would be the program of James Joyce—the Odyssean journey in Dublin, or the all-encompassing dream of H. C. Earwicker. But for Sterne man is not swamped or lost in this universe; the past does not crush him, the future does not threaten, and the infinite spaces do not affright. In this connection it is important to remember that the work of the narrator, the telling of the story, is itself one of the concurrent actions; the writing of the novel is an important part of the action of the novel, and therefore may be taken to be an important event in the history of the world, so that man remains the measure of all things.

At the same time Sterne is so keenly aware of the limitations of formal organization that he identifies systematic thought and scholarship with mere scholasticism and pedantry. It is the great Slawkenbergius who exhausts subjects and offers complete explanations (III, xxxviii). Although Slawkenbergius is Walter Shandy's treasury of universal knowledge, Tristram says (III, xlii) that he thinks the best parts of this learned author are the interpolated tales. In Sterne's own practice the incidental tale, episode, or tableau is as good a clue as one can get. But when the great frame of reference is approached in this way, there remains a disparity between the situation at a given time and the conclusion toward which it points or the full meaning which it may convey. Complete realization is never attained on the discursive or rational level. We have what we may call the asymptotic approach, or to borrow a phrase from Aldous Huxley, an everlasting "obstacle race."

In the simplest undertakings there appear insuperable obstacles to getting things done. The author and his characters are constantly being interrupted or distracted by circumstances, accidents, unhappy coincidences, physical conditions, imperfect communications, or the curious workings of their own minds, particularly the strange way in which associations of ideas cut across country. An example may be drawn from the episode of Bobby's death, which has been discussed and analyzed above. Walter Shandy just before he gets the news has been planning the details of Bobby's proposed grand tour.

'Twas a most inauspicious journey; my father having had every foot of it to travel over again, and his calculation to begin afresh, when he had almost got to the end of it, by *Obadiah's* opening the door to acquaint him the family was out of yeast—and to ask whether he might not take the great coach-horse early in the morning and ride in search of some.—With all my heart, *Obadiah,* said my father (pursuing his journey)—take the coach-horse, and welcome.—But he wants a shoe, poor creature! said *Obadiah.*—Poor creature! said my uncle *Toby,* vibrating the note back again, like a string in unison. Then ride the *Scotch* horse, quoth my father hastily.—He cannot bear a saddle upon his back, quoth *Obadiah,* for the whole world.—The devil's in that horse; then take *Patriot,* cried my father, and shut the door.—*Patriot* is sold, said *Obadiah.* —Here's for you! cried my father, making a pause, and looking in my uncle *Toby's* face, as if the thing had not been a matter of fact.—Your worship ordered me to sell him last *April,* said *Obadiah.*—Then go on foot for your pains, cried my father.—I had much rather walk than ride, said *Obadiah,* shutting the door.

What plagues! cried my father, going on with his calculation.—But the waters are out, said *Obadiah,*—opening the door again.

Till that moment, my father, who had a map of *Sanson's,* and a book of the post roads before him, had kept his hand upon the head of his compasses, with one foot of them fixed upon *Nevers,* the last stage he had paid for—purposing to go on from that point with his journey and calculation, as soon as *Obadiah* quitted the room; but this second attack of *Obadiah's,* in opening the door and laying the whole country under water, was too much.—He let go his compasses—or rather with a mixed motion between accident and anger, he threw them upon the table; and then there was nothing for him to do, but to return back to *Calais* (like many others) as wise as he had set out. (V, ii)

In this little study in frustration, as often in his scenes and episodes, Sterne reverses the scheme by which we get confused detail set in the simple framework of a great plan or divinely ordained scheme of things. Instead we get clarity and order in detail, confusion in the total situation. The details are ordered with the clarity and precision of a piece of choreography; the interchange between Walter and Obadiah proceeds by incremental repetition, and we come to a climax in the casting down of the compasses. But in a larger view, the calculation with map and road book is never completed, Obadiah never goes on his errand, and of course Bobby never takes the grand tour. We need hardly be reminded that Walter's plans for Tristram are thwarted at every point. We learn just how it was, according to Walter's theories, that the universe conspired against little Tristram—begotten at the wrong time and subject to unfavorable prenatal influences, his very birth a violation of Walter's obstetrical theories, christened Tristram instead of Trismegistus in direct contradiction of Walter's theories about Christian names, circumcised or worse by the fall of a window-sash (Corporal Trim had taken the weights out to use as field pieces in the game of fortifications).

In spite of overriding obsessions, human ends are infinitely various, but we may say that in *Shandy* the ends are sexual satisfaction, the riding of hobbyhorses, and the full expression of ideas and sentiments. All these entail endless perplexities and an infinity of unfinished business. It is characteristic of Sterne that he is constantly reading sexual meanings into equivocal utterances, and thus attesting man's insistent and unsatisfied interest in the theme. As Professor Work remarks, sexual impotence "hovers like a dubious halo over the head of every Shandy male, including the bull."[23] The most obvious and elaborate though not the best treatment of sex as unfinished business is of course the courtship of Uncle Toby and the Widow Wadman. But other perplexities of the brothers Shandy are more engaging. Uncle Toby is involved in endless intricacies as he tries to tell how he got his wound at the siege of Namur; his simple purpose and good intentions are entangled in the whole terminology of military engineering. Language interposes itself between a man and his own good intentions, and between man and man. The brothers never reach an understanding on intellectual terms. Walter derides Toby's hobbyhorse with great eloquence and a battery of technicalities (III, xxiv); and at the same time he is always trying to impose his own ideas; on this level the brothers can never get together, whether Walter is using Latin or English (III, xxxix). Yet they can meet on the plane of human sympathy, with gesture and physical circumstance effecting what words cannot:

My uncle *Toby* would never attempt any defence against the force of this ridicule, but that of redoubling the vehemence of smoking his pipe; in doing which, he raised so dense a vapour one night after supper, that it set my father, who was a little phthisical, into a suffocating fit of violent coughing; my uncle Toby leaped up without feeling the pain upon his groin,—and, with infinite pity, stood beside his brother's chair, tapping his back with one hand, and holding his head with the other, and from time to time, wiping his eyes with a clean cambric hankerchief, which he pulled out of his pocket.—The affectionate and endearing manner in which my uncle *Toby* did these little offices,—cut my father through his reins, for the pain he had just been giving him.—May my brains be knocked out with a battering ram or a catapulta, I care not which, quoth my father to himself,—if ever I insult this worthy soul more! (III, xxiv)

A given situation in Sterne is a deadlock which may be broken or resolved in various ways, by an emphatic gesture, an interruption of some kind, a flash of intuition or sympathy. Sometimes the resolution may run through a dialogue, as when Trim and Toby communicate, not by exchange of ideas, but by what we may call the antiphonal expression of feeling; they have only to confirm and echo one another (IV, iv; IV, xviii).

Since this is the way "life and opinions" go, this is the way a book which reproduces the movement of "life and opinions" must go. Perhaps this is the answer to the question whether *Tristram Shandy* has a plot, whether the book is finished or not. Certainly there is no single dramatic resolution of a central situation, as in *Clarissa* or *Tom Jones;* on the contrary, to the very end there is a postponement or frustration which illustrates Emerson's remark that comedy is "a non-performance of what is pretended to be performed, at the same time that one is giving loud pledges of performance."[24] And yet, though the ostensible or professed end is not realized, the novelist attains his own end; he builds and presents his world. A basic plot device is that unattained possibilities recede; comedy makes a game of this, even extends it to the procedure of the dramatist or novelist himself, perhaps contents itself with a "happy ending," some form of *de facto* arrangement. It is only by strict limitation to the procedure of the novel of manners, as in *Tom Jones* and *Humphry Clinker,* that the novel can avoid being heavily involved in unfinished business. Tragedy, we may say, accepts neither the *de facto* arrangement nor the indefinite postponement of unattained possibilities; it insists on finishing the business by an ultimate adjustment of personality to unattained possibility. Thus the proposed marriage of Lovelace and Clarissa, in its varying degrees of approach to actuality, is on an entirely different level from the troubled courtship and happy wedding of Tom and Sophia, and the voyage of the *Pequod* would have been no ordinary voyage even if the vessel had got back to its home port. The distinction is not always clear-cut, and it sometimes remains uncertain how far we get an ultimate showdown. Does the deathbed repentance of Don Quixote go any deeper than the final discomfiture of Tartuffe? Can we have conventional serious endings as well as conventional happy endings? It is not merely by way of perpetrating a practical joke that Sterne refuses to round things off in the usual way, or if it is a joke, it is too big a one to be merely funny. His frustrations and approximations produce comedy, dramatize the problem of knowledge and communication, show the limitations of formal rhetoric, traditional learning, and scholarship, and even of the new science and of language itself, and thus set forth the general human situation. In some such way as this it seems possible to correlate the form, the purpose, and the content of *Tristram Shandy*. Perhaps we may say that Cervantes had taken the essential step in the construction of Sterne's world when he set up the partnership of Don Quixote and Sancho Panza; these two make their way as best they can in a world of hard discordant fact and persistent illusion, and their working partnership and the only attainable solution of their problems must be on the basis of loyalty, sympathy, and love.

A comparison as to underlying plan with Joyce's *Ulysses* has already been suggested. If, however, we think of Joyce's use of the *Odyssey,* in Eliot's words, as "simply a way of controlling, of ordering, of giving a shape and a significance to the immense panorama of futility and anarchy which is contemporary history,"[25] the important difference appears that Sterne is lost in no such chaos or wasteland. His disorder gives delight and hurts not, and leads to an inner coherence of vision which does not depend on the arbitrary imposition of a scheme, or on the erection of a great mass of apparatus in the manner of Slawkenbergius. Unlike Joyce, Sterne is never completely carried away

THE EARLY MASTERS OF ENGLISH FICTION

by the scheme to which he appears to be playfully committing himself. He did not live in an age when critics were discussing the aesthetic necessity of such a scheme, however arbitrary. Like Cervantes again, he believed that such schemes were made for man, that man as reader should not be completely subjugated or overawed by literary apparatus, flaunt the apparatus as one may while one is playing the game. There is an elaborate centrifugal and complicating movement in Sterne, but there is also a countermovement toward concentration and simplification. This double movement may be illustrated from the opening of the story. There are so many bypasses and divagations that the life of little Tristram starts before birth and never gets told—it is very difficult to get fairly started away from the *terminus a quo;* but here at the outset there is the converse case of Parson Yorick, so that we begin with a character sketch, a death scene, and an epitaph—a *terminus ad quem.*

It is hard to say whether unity is imposed on *Tristram Shandy* by the function of the narrator, or discovered by the narrator in the great scheme of things. We are here confronted with the problem of knowledge: How much does the knower contribute to what is known? Sterne, as an artist and not a philosopher, is not obliged to answer this question. The narrator is coping with a great system, like Fielding's narrator, but he also enjoys what on the surface appears to be complete liberty. Theoretically he claims the right to start from anything that catches his attention and proceed in any direction. This right, like the convention by which the novelist may claim omniscience and take any point of view, cannot be fully exercised. No artist can use "unchartered freedom"; he must issue himself a charter, if no one else does. The basic assumption in Sterne is that immediate experience, subtle and elusive though it is, can be firmly placed in a general scheme. He would not accept Hume's denial of causal necessity and uniformity, though he is keenly conscious of the difficulty of attaining true knowledge; we have seen that he is close to Locke's position that man can have valid knowledge of a world which is after all much like

Newton's. Tristram the narrator is not identical with young Tristram; as narrator he does not keep to the point of view of the child, or write straight "stream of consciousness"; he is the efficient agent of the far-reaching references in time and space; he is both inside and outside the moment; he is not only the knower of English empirical philosophy, but the philosopher who writes with confidence about that knower—a somewhat different matter. The German exponents of romantic irony who imitated Sterne moved beyond him in the direction of pure subjectivity. At the same time Sterne undertakes to relate the individual to his world by the short cut of sympathy and love, the bonds by which society is held together, and here he is close to the ethics of Hume and Adam Smith.

III

While *Shandy* obviously does not have a plot in the same sense as *Tom Jones,* the fact remains, as Professor Work has pointed out, that we find a coherent time-scheme, two overlapping main actions—the story of the Shandy household and the story of Uncle Toby,—and numerous clues planted early in the story, significant to the initiated, pointing forward to themes which are elaborately developed in the later books.[26] In fact, Sterne substitutes for the unilinear cause-effect sequence often called "plot" a very elaborate set of patterns, themes, and symbols which invite comparison with devices used by later novelists, particularly those who practise the kind of psychological notation called "stream of consciousness" writing. As far as technique is concerned, Sterne and the moderns are much alike: there is an attempt to present or suggest firm order behind or alongside of the apparent chaos of the psychological flux.[27] The ultimate views about the dignity of man may be different, but we can still say of *Tristram Shandy* as of *Ulysses* that it is a book in which design is carried to excess.

All this goes with a high degree of flexibility: in our enthusiasm for the discovery of hidden principles of structure or occult balance we must not deny Sterne the pleasure of experimenta-

THE EARLY MASTERS OF ENGLISH FICTION

tion or the exercise of numerous options as he goes along. He did not spend all his energy devising a code. The eighteenth century did not think of the novelist as one who wrote for fit audience though few, nor did it want its writers to be cryptic. As it was, Sterne's innovations gave him the reputation of being an incorrigible eccentric. But when an eighteenth century writer speaks of appealing to choice souls or to the elite, he has in mind not a coterie but an audience relatively large in proportion to the whole reading public. James Joyce is said to have remarked that any one who wishes to understand his works must give all his time to the study of the subject; the age of Sterne could take such a remark only as a monstrous joke, wilder than any Shandean foible, and only the lack of a sense of humor and proportion in contemporary criticism keeps us from taking it in that way too.

The varying reception of successive installments of the story no doubt influenced Sterne's plans. Of Volumes V and VI he wrote while they were in progress: "These two volumes are, I think, the best—I shall write as long as I live, 'tis, in fact, my hobby-horse: and so much am I delighted with my uncle Toby's imaginary character, that I am become an enthusiast."[28] This is the familiar situation in which a fruitful and self-developing interaction is set up between humorous character and episode. Cervantes, Fielding, and Sterne might all have reported the experience as Scott did later: "When I light on such a character as Bailie Jarvie, or Dalgetty, my imagination brightens, and my conception becomes clearer at every step which I take in his company, although it leads me many a weary mile away from the regular road, and forces me to leap hedge and ditch to get back into the route again. If I resist the temptation, as you advise me, my thoughts become prosy, flat, and dull; I write painfully to myself, and under a consciousness of flagging which makes me flag still more; the sunshine with which fancy had invested the incidents departs from them, and leaves everything dull and gloomy."[29] Volumes V and VI, with the "Bobby's death" sequence in the former, and the story of Le Fever in the latter (skilfully introduced in V, x), come to lay more stress on delicacy of sentiment, less on learned wit. Sterne evidently thought highly of the Le Fever story, and when he tells us Parson Yorick preached a sermon on the subject, writing "Bravo" in the margin and then crossing it out (VI, xi), we virtually hear the novelist remarking, "A good episode, if I do say it myself." In VI, xx, we have what may perhaps be interpreted as a transition to Toby as the principal character, and certainly in VI, xxix, a formal presentation of Toby in a new role. There may be in VI, xxv, an intimated intention to carry the story through to Toby's death. Since he has from the beginning been a major character, this is not a violent shift, and of course the themes of the Shandy family and Uncle Toby can run concurrently, yet we get the impression of free modulation and some degree of improvisation. The fact is, when Sterne says he has things planned to the last iota, he is improvising, and when he says he is completely deranged, he is not deranged at all.

The period of Sterne's residence on the Continent from 1762 to 1764 furnishes copy for Book VII, "a laughing good tempered Satyr against Traveling."[30] With death knocking at the door, Tristram, who is here clearly Laurence Sterne, sets out for the Continent. The motto for this book, "Non enim excursus hic ejus, sed opus ipsum est," boldly attempts to justify the new venture by the doctrine of relevant digression. We may speculate about the prehistory of the travel plan. Sterne, it appears, had originally thought of sending Tristram on a tour with Lord Noddy's son—a burlesque of the stock account of the grand tour that would lend itself to satire in the Rabelaisian and Scriblerian tradition,[31] and was transformed in true Shandean style. This journey of Tristram's is interwoven with memories of an earlier journey taken by the Shandy group (VII, xxvii), in which the humors of Walter, Trim, and Toby were elaborately displayed. The plan for the travels of such a group as a device for presenting "occurrences or scrapes" illustrating diverse humors points to something like the plan of Smollett's *Humphry Clinker*. Sterne's experiments with travel narrative offered two possibilities: the account could stand by itself, as eventually in *A Sentimental Journey,* or it could furnish more books for *Tristram Shandy.* As to Book VII, what probably happened was, as Cross suggests, that Sterne had not succeeded in completing the full account of the Uncle Toby-Widow Wadman affair, which, according to the promises made at the end of Book VI, was to occupy the following books; he therefore fell back on a travel narrative already composed in whole or in part as a separate work or loose continuation, used this material as Book VII, and offered what he had written on the Toby-Wadman affair as Book VIII.[32] In order to make the transition from the travels back to Uncle Toby he represents Tristram as writing Books VIII and IX of *Shandy* on a tour through France (VIII, i; IX, xxiv).

Up to the end of 1766 Sterne seems to have thought of continuing *Tristram* indefinitely. On July 23, 1766, he wrote: "At present I am in my peaceful retreat, writing the ninth volume of Tristram—I shall publish but one this year, and the next I shall begin a new work of four volumes, which when finish'd, I shall continue Tristram with fresh spirit."[33] The four volumes, of course, would be the projected independent travel narrative, two volumes of which were completed as *A Sentimental Journey.* Nevertheless Professor Booth has recently shown that Book IX of *Tristram* bears unmistakable marks of having been composed as the last.[34] This is not quite the same thing as saying, as Professor Booth does, "that the book which he had completed represented the completion of a plan, however rough, which was present in his mind from the beginning." This plan, according to Booth's very able analysis, was to contradict the promise of *The Life and Opinions of Tristram Shandy* made on the title-page by the specific device of substituting Uncle Toby's campaigns and amours. But of course there are innumerable other ways of *not* telling of Tristram's life and opinions—telling Walter Shandy's, for example, or citing Slawkenbergius. And how, Tristram might ask, can I tell of my life and opinions without tracing the cosmic network, without considering the various systems, domestic, educational, and psychological, of which the homunculus is the focal point? But this playfully philosophical view could be used to justify the introduction of almost anything, including the Uncle Toby story and miscellaneous travel material. The situation was very flexible; in July, 1776, Sterne was not thinking of Volume IX as his last, though it seems that he came to do so within the next few weeks, and he could easily have put more travel material into *Shandy* instead of detaching it as *A Sentimental Journey*.

We are to think of Sterne as writing with his eye on the public, and as eager to find out how his readers would take more travel narrative in the vein of Book VII. The *Journey* depends largely on obvious sentiment and pathos, rather than on the learned wit, grotesque ribaldry, and humor which dominate the Walter Shandy story and figure to some extent in the Uncle Toby story. The *Journey* is less abstruse and at the same time less rich and dense than *Shandy;* it does not undertake so much cross reference to an elaborate scheme, and does not play so many tricks with time, space, and memory. It gives us Sterne's familiar themes, as when he says of his characteristic use of detail in "The Wig": "I think I can see the precise and distinguishing marks of national characters more in these nonsensical *minutiae,* than in the most important matters of state." Even the more complex episodes follow easily traceable lines of association: the fear of the Bastille is associated with the starling's repeated cry, "I can't get out," and the sequence ends with a well-planned but conventional apostrophe to the Goddess of Liberty. Then Yorick visualizes a captive in a cell, and bursts into tears. And as he drives to Versailles he fills in the gap with the history of the starling, even to a picture of his own coat of arms with the starling as crest. The famous sentimental episodes in the *Journey* are part of a program to popularize Sterne's methods, to give easy lessons in the Yorick-Shandy vein. Mechanical methods for getting effects, the underlying technical weakness of the Gothic and sentimental tendencies in late eighteenth century fiction, come to the fore. As Yorick visits the grave of the monk of Calais, looks at the snuffbox the monk has given him, and plucks a nettle from the grave, we witness the mechanization of sentiment, the establishment of the sentimental cliché, the side of Sterne that Henry Mackenzie was to imitate in *The Man of Feeling* (1771). In the snuffbox we see a fetish which is to elicit an automatic response, like the ring which Le Fever and his son kiss (*Tristram Shandy,* VI, vii). Geoffrey Tillotson has aptly cited in illustration of this phase of sentimentalism Shenstone's remark that "inanimates, toys, utensils, seem to merit a kind of affection from us, when they have been our companions through various vicissitudes. I have often viewed my watch, standish, snuffbox, with this kind of regard, allotting them a degree of friendship which there are some men who do not deserve."[35] Physical objects and details, as we have seen, play a livelier and more complex role in *Shandy;* they have of course this sentimental and *gemütlich* aspect, but they are also incitements in a comedy of humors, mock-heroic *impedimenta,* symbols of the macrocosm.

How far was this change a deliberate bid for the continuation of public favor? How far does it correspond to changes in Sterne's own feelings and attitudes? These questions have been asked recently; obviously they do not admit of simple answers. Since sentimentalism involves a highly self-conscious and even self-critical attitude toward feeling, it can never be called "sincere" if by that word we mean "simple" or "direct." Concurrently with the *Journey* Sterne wrote the surviving second part of the *Journey to Eliza,* a record of his characteristic literary amour or flirtation with Mrs. Draper in Bombay, the "Bramine." The *Journal* incorporates sections of his correspondence, and manipulates facts and feelings in such a way that it may be considered another exercise in Yorickan fiction; he evidently played with the idea of making literary capital of his amour as he was making literary capital of his travels. He exploits the pathos of his situation in a relatively direct way in the *Journal,* whereas he still operates with his symbols and tableaux in the *Journey.*

Surely Cross was essentially correct in connecting these last phases of Sterne's work with the state of his health.[36] His tuberculosis was not a pose. Professor Putney has recently argued for a complete separation of the *Journey* from Sterne's private life: "Yorick's sentimental pose was adopted in response, not to Sterne's feelings but to popular demand for the pathos at which Sterne excelled."[37] His demonstration that the *Journey* plays up the pathetic vein in *Shandy* is conclusive, but hardly justifies our pronouncing the *Journey* a "hoax." In another important article Putney treats the *Journey* as a subtle exposé of the errors of sentiment, as expounding a gospel of laughter rather than tears.[38] But we are here dealing with a situation that cannot be resolved simply by setting laughter over against tears, or sincerity over against insincerity. The sentimental traveler Yorick, who is indeed different from the Yorick of *Shandy*, is not a rounded portrait of Sterne, but a comic figure representing at the same time sentimentalism and the ultimate refinement or attenuation of the comedy of humors. This is not to say that the portrayal of such a character intends a mere burlesque of sentiment; the comedy of humors had long been moving toward sympathetic presentation, and Sterne caps the climax by sympathizing with the humorous aspects of his own personality.

Extreme sentiment has this in common with the humors, that it may be taken as a mechanical force getting out of control, and so has its ridiculous side. Sterne realizes this principle, and uses it throughout his work for comic effect, but this does not mean that true sentiment is merely mechanical. He discusses the point in his sermon on the Good Samaritan:

In benevolent natures, the impulse to pity is so sudden, that, like instruments of music, which obey the touch—the objects which are fitted to excite such impressions work so instantaneous an effect, that you would think the will was scarce concerned, and that the mind was altogether passive in the sympathy which her own goodness has excited. The truth is,—the soul is generally in such cases so busily taken up, and wholly engrossed by the object of pity, that she does not attend to her own operations, or take leisure to examine the principles upon which she acts. So that the Samaritan, though the moment he saw him he had compassion on him, yet sudden as the emotion is represented, you are not to imagine that it was mechanical, but that there was a settled principle of humanity and goodness which operated within him; and influenced not only the first impulse of kindness, but the continuation of it throughout the rest of so engaging a behaviour.[39]

As has already been suggested in our discussion of Richardson, we may say that if sentimentalism means the proclamation of the absolute validity of spontaneous feeling, then no one, not even Henry Mackenzie, is a sentimentalist. Richardson and Sterne may be called sentimental in the sense that they seek by more and more refined analysis to bring out affiliations, connections, harmonies, and identities between feeling and reason, or between the true, the good, and the beautiful. They assume a settled system, not a mere chaos or anarchy of feeling. The sentimentalist who goes in for pure feeling is an unhistorical abstraction, like the mythical neo-classicist who is completely subjugated by "reason." The relations between feeling and comedy or tragedy are complex, and we cannot rest content with a classification of "laughing" and "weeping" novelists, or of partisans of sentiment and anti-sentiment.

While it is pleasant to enjoy Sterne as a rare bird or a *lusus naturae,* we may learn something more of him and his contemporaries by considering his position in relation to the general enterprise of the eighteenth century novelists. One way of understanding that enterprise is to consider the extent to which they claim adequacy for their interpretation of life as lived by the men about them. Such a claim, we feel, should have its limits. The novel of manners must interpret life by using codes, current ethics, and socially approved or disapproved types; and yet such an interpretation must be accompanied by a sense of the intractable and the insoluble. The novelist must admit such a sense without shattering his frame of reference. The frame is solid in Defoe, though the obscure compulsions of the human will beat against it with the persistence of a buzzing fly at a window pane, so that Defoe attains a dogged iteration of remarkable power. Fielding moves into a more complicated social scene, and modestly and rationally but firmly claims the adequacy of the comic point of view, this point of view involving a large tolerance which includes the normal workings of human nature and extreme variations which may be accepted and enjoyed when accompanied with good intentions. But the comedy of manners does not necessarily carry the novelist beyond the established preference for a good sense at once benevolent and rational. Richardson's studies of the divided mind carry him closer to the ultimate mysteries of personality; sometimes he seems to stumble upon such mysteries rather than to seek them; but it should be noted that the fact that he always assigns his commentary to characters writing letters in his story helps to save him from being forced to claim complete adequacy of interpretation at all points, and gives him in *Clarissa* a saving residue of the insoluble that lies at the heart of tragedy. In comparison with Fielding and Richardson, Smollett's claim to adequacy is perfunctory; he gives us, and it is a great achievement, an intensely recorded and heartily realized but not thoroughly examined life. He is at his best when he takes short views. In relation to this whole situation, Sterne's position appears to be highly original and even unique; he shifts to a comic level the claim of interpretive adequacy; by "a sharper specification of the signs of life" and a shift of scale which follows out Richardson's technique, he carries things to a point of complexity which raises anew the question, "What is truth?" In a telling phrase Professor Crane, as we have noted, describes Fielding's treatment of Tom Jones as involving a "comic analogue of fear." The phrase "comic analogue of the quest for truth" could perhaps be used as a description of the effect Sterne attains by undertaking to give us a picture of the human situation crosshatched with sensation, impulse, and obsession. German criticism, which has made a serious study of Sterne in its own special idiom, long ago set up a contrast between Jean Paul Richter's profound consciousness of the gap between the ideal and the real and the ensuing development of his cosmic irony, and on the other hand Sterne's cheerful acceptance of man's lot.[40] Sterne brilliantly maintains his comic equilibrium; man's predicament is presented along with redoubled assurance that he still "superior walks amid the glad creation," and thus Sterne in his own way continues and elaborates the affirmations of his great contemporaries in prose fiction.

The Parsonage, Coxwold, Yorkshire, the residence of Laurence Sterne. From an old engraving reproduced in Walter Sichel's *Sterne: A Study* (1910).

Notes

Place of publication, if not indicated, is London. The following abbreviations are used for periodicals:

HLQ—*Huntington Library Quarterly*
JEGP—*Journal of English and Germanic Philology*
MLN—*Modern Language Notes*
MP—*Modern Philology*
PMLA—*Publications of the Modern Language Association*
PQ—*Philological Quarterly*
SP—*Studies in Philology*
TLS—(London) *Times Literary Supplement*

I

1. Daniel Defoe, *Romances and Narratives*, ed. G. A. Aitken (16 vols.; 1895), I, 3-4. References below are to this edition, unless indication to the contrary is given. With this passage from *Crusoe* compare the praise of the delightful security of a tradesman's life in *The Complete English Tradesman*, II (1727), i, 106-7.
2. *Twenty Sermons* (1755), pp. 307-8. Sermon xv.
3. *Complete English Tradesman*, II (1727), i, 73.
4. *Complete English Tradesman*, II (1727), i, 174, 184.
5. *Ibid.*, p. 185.
6. See Hans H. Andersen, "The Paradox of Trade and Morality in Defoe," *MP*, XXXIX (1941), 23-46. Cf. *Mist's Journal*, February 7, 1719, repr. William Lee, *Life and Recently Discovered Writings* (1869), II, 100-4.
7. *A New Family Instructor* (1727), pp. 51-53.
8. *The Storm* (1704), sigs. A3v-4r.
9. *Review*, VIII, No. 61, August 14, 1711.
10. *Review*, V; No. 7, April 13, 1708.
11. *Compleat English Gentleman*, ed. K. D. Bülbring (1890), p. 226.
12. *An Essay on Projects*, in *Earlier Life and Chief Earlier Works*, ed. Morley (1889), p. 164.
13. *Review*, I (1704), Preface, sig. A3.
14. *Serious Reflections of Robinson Crusoe*, III, 23.
15. *Complete English Tradesman*, I (1726), 33.
16. William P. Trent, *Daniel Defoe: How to Know Him* (Indianapolis, 1916), p. 175.
17. "Scott and Defoe," *PMLA*, LVI (1941), 716.
18. *Read's Journal*, November 1, 1718, repr. Lee, *Life and Recently Discovered Writings*, I, 282-83.
19. *Defoe in the Pillory and Other Studies* (Bloomington, 1939), pp. 40-41. Indiana University Publications: Humanistic Series, No. 1.
20. "Defoe's Workshop," *More Books*, 6th Ser., XXIII (1948), 323-30.
21. A. W. Secord, *Studies in the Narrative Method of Defoe* (Urbana, 1924), p. 234. University of Illinois Studies in Language and Literature, IX, No. 1.
22. *Cambridge History of English Literature*, IX, 21.
23. Coleman O. Parsons, "Phantom into Fiction," summarized in *PMLA*, LXVII (1952), 144.
24. See Kenneth B. Murdock, *Increase Mather* (Cambridge, U.S.A., 1925), pp. 167-77.
25. *Cambridge History of English Literature*, IX, 20.
26. *Earlier Life and Chief Earlier Works of Daniel Defoe*, ed. Morley (1889), p. 152.
27. Oxford, 1841, I, 2.
28. Preface to *Religious Courtship* (5th ed.; 1737), sig. A2r.
29. William M. Sale, Jr., *Samuel Richardson: Master Printer* (Ithaca, 1950), pp. 162-63. A possible connection between Defoe's domestic conduct-books and Richardson's fiction was suggested by Mrs. Barbauld (*Correspondence of Samuel Richardson* [1804], I, xx), and also by Charlotte E. Morgan (*The Rise of the Novel of Manners* [New York, 1911], pp. 134-35. The theme has been elaborated by L. L. Schücking ("Die Grundlagen des Richardson'schen Romans," *Germanisch-romanische Monatsschrift*, XII [1924], 21-42, 88-110; *Die Familie im Puritanismus* [Leipzig, 1929]).
30. See *A Journal of the Plague Year and Other Pieces*, ed. Arthur W. Secord (New York, 1935), and references there given.

31. *Serious Reflections of Robinson Crusoe*, III, 35.
32. *Complete English Tradesman*, II (1727), i, 79.
33. *A Vision of the Angelic World*, III, 280. Cf. also *Review*, VIII, No. 23, May 17, 1711, the *locus classicus* for this idea.
34. W. P. Ker, *Epic and Romance* (2d ed.; 1922), pp. 5-6.
35. See Benjamin Boyce, "The Question of Emotion in Defoe," *SP*, L (1953), 45-58.
36. I, 209. Cf. also the long description of the "thousand extravagancies" by which the people in the French merchant ship express their joy at being rescued (II, 17-21).
37. *Englishman*, No. 26, December 3, 1713.
38. A. A. Mendilow, *Time and the Novel* (1952), pp. 90-92.
39. In order to appreciate the effect which Defoe obtains by connecting episode and character, compare exactly the same incident presented as a dream or apparition of the Devil to a distressed man, in *An Essay on the History and Reality of Apparitions* (1727), pp. 207-9.
40. For a close study of the legal aspects, see Spiro Peterson, "The Matrimonial Theme of Defoe's *Roxana*," *PMLA*, LXX (1955), 166-91.
41. The subject has been thoroughly studied by Spiro Peterson, "Defoe's *Roxana* and Its Eighteenth Century Sequels," MS Dissertation in Harvard College Library.
42. In the continuation of *Crusoe* events on the island in the hero's absence are reported at length, but this is really interpolated narrative. At the beginning of *Colonel Jacque* there is also an account of an adventure at which the hero is not present.
43. I, lxvii. The passage becomes more intelligible if we accept the reading in all editions after the second, "because all such things are disputed."
44. Samuel Richardson to William Warburton, April 19, 1748, printed in Catalogue of American Art Association, sale of March 18-19, 1925.
45. *Tom Jones*, VIII, i.
46. *Weekly Oracle; or, Universal Library* (1737), p. 161.
47. [William Rufus Chetwood], *The Voyages of Capt. Rich. Falconer* (2nd ed.; 1724), Preface. Chetwood was a bookseller dealing in prose fiction, and one of his associates, Thomas Edlin, includes *Moll Flanders* and *Roxana* in an advertisement appended to *Falconer;* the passage quoted may therefore be taken as advertising for the stories it names, but its point for our purpose remains the same.
48. [James Arbuckle], *A Collection of Letters and Essays . . . Lately Publish'd in the Dublin Journal* (1729), I, 71. Essay dated May 29, 1725.
49. *A Letter to the Society of Booksellers* (1738), p. 31.
50. *Daily Post*, June 22, 1736.
51. See *The Adventures of Lindamira*, ed. Benjamin Boyce (Minneapolis, 1949). First published 1702.

II

1. From a copy in my possession made by Richardson's daughter Martha, afterwards Mrs. Bridgen. Mrs. Barbauld incorporated the first part of the letter, as far as the "Tommy Potts" passage, in her biographical sketch, omitting a few phrases and sentences (*Correspondence of Samuel Richardson* [1804], I, xxix-xliii); this part is reprinted from the Bridgen copy in A. D. McKillop, *Samuel Richardson: Printer and Novelist* (Chapel Hill, 1936), pp. 4-7. The second half of the letter was first printed by Iolo A. Williams, *London Mercury*, VII (1923), 382-84.
2. McKillop, *op. cit.*, especially pp. 284-320; William M. Sale, Jr., *Samuel Richardson: A Bibliographical Record of His Literary Career* (New Haven, 1936), and *Samuel Richardson: Master Printer* (Ithaca, 1951). The last work is an extremely thorough and accurate study of Richardson's printing business, and identifies many of the books which he printed.
3. See A. D. McKillop, "Samuel Richardson's *Advice to an Apprentice*," *JEGP*, XLII (1943), 40-54.
4. A. D. McKillop, "Richardson's Early Writings—Another Pamphlet," *JEGP*, LIII (1954), 72-75.
5. See Katherine Gee Hornbeak, *The Complete Letter-Writer in English* (Northampton, 1934), Smith College Studies in Modern Languages, XV, No. 3-4, and review by W. L. Ustick, *MLN*, LII (1937), 595-96; also Miss Hornbeak, *Richardson's Familiar Letters and the Domestic Conduct Books* (Northampton, 1938), Smith College Studies in Modern Languages, XIX, No. 2; Jean Robertson, *The Art of Letter Writing* (Liver-

pool, 1942); Sister Mary Humiliata, "Standards of Taste Advocated for Feminine Letter-Writing," *HLQ*, XIII (1950), 261-77.

6. Hornbeak, *The Complete Letter-Writer in English*, p. 103.

7. *Correspondence*, I, lxxiii-lxxiv.

8. See Helen S. Hughes, "English Epistolary Fiction before *Pamela*," *Manly Anniversary Studies* (Chicago, 1923), pp. 156-69.

9. Edward W. Hughes, *North Country Life in the Eighteenth Century* (1952), p. 375.

10. *Letters of a Grandmother*, 1732-1735, ed. Gladys Scott Thomson (1943), pp. 84-85.

11. *Diary of the Earl of Egmont*, III (1923), 307-8. *Hist. MSS Comm.*

12. *Correspondence*, I, lxix-lxxiii.

13. *Ibid.*, I, lxxiv-lxxv. Richardson probably got the reference to Molière's "Old Woman" from *Spectator* No. 70.

14. See below, pp. 193-96.

15. *Don Quixote*, II, xl. Trans. I. M. Cohen (Penguin Classics), p. 721.

16. *The Brothers Karamazov*, IV, xii, 1. Trans. Constance Garnett (Modern Library), p. 803.

17. *The Charterhouse of Parma*, chap. vii. Trans. C. K. Scott-Moncrieff (New York, n.d.), p. 171.

18. *Pamela* (Shakespeare Head Edition), II, 67-68. All references below to Richardson's novels are to this edition, unless otherwise indicated.

19. For further discussion of Richardson's use of the letter form see Ernest A. Baker, *The History of the English Novel* (1924-31), IV, 22-24; Godfrey F. Singer, *The Epistolary Novel* (Philadelphia, 1933); Frank G. Black, *The Epistolary Novel in the Late Eighteenth Century* (Eugene, 1940), University of Oregon Monographs: Studies in Literature and Philology, No. 2; Alan D. McKillop, "Epistolary Technique in Richardson's Novels," *Rice Institute Pamphlet*, XXXVIII (1951), 36-54.

20. British Museum Addit. MS 32,557, f. 47. Richard Hurd to Cox Macro, November 7, 1742.

21. William M. Sale, Jr., "From *Pamela* to *Clarissa*," in *The Age of Johnson: Essays Presented to Chauncey Brewster Tinker* (New Haven, 1949), p. 134.

22. Quoted from Forster MS in McKillop, *Richardson*, p. 127.

23. Anthony Trollope, *Can You Forgive Her?* (1864-65), chap. xxii.

24. McKillop, *Richardson*, p. 141; A. D. Culler, *PMLA*, LXIII (1948), 871.

25. See also Charlotte Grandison on Otway's *Orphan* (*Grandison*, IV, 253), and Richardson's elaborate discussion of Whitehead's *Roman Father* (McKillop, *Richardson*, pp. 185-86).

26. John Harrington Smith, *The Gay Couple in Restoration Comedy* (Cambridge, U.S.A., 1948), pp. 198 ff.

27. *The Age of Johnson*, pp. 137-38.

28. *Johnsonian Miscellanies*, ed. G. B. Hill (Oxford, 1897), I, 297.

29. Cf. Postscript to *Clarissa; Tom Jones*, XV, i.

30. See the brilliant discussion by Dorothy Van Ghent, *The English Novel: Form and Function* (New York, 1953), pp. 45-63.

31. See Charles S. Singleton, *An Essay on the Vita Nuova* (Cambridge, U.S.A., 1949), especially chap. III; Francis Fergusson, *Dante's Drama of the Mind* (Princeton, 1953), pp. 153-60.

32. "A Gossip on Romance."

33. *Johnsonian Miscellanies*, ed. G. B. Hill, I, 282.

34. E. L. McAdam, Jr., "A New Letter from Fielding," *Yale Review*, XXXVIII (1948), 304-5. For the record of this letter in the manuscript index to Richardson's correspondence, see McKillop, *Richardson*, p. 170. As McAdam infers, there were other letters between the two novelists. On November 7, 1748, Richardson wrote to Hill that Lyttelton, Thomson, Cibber, and Fielding were among those who had urged him "to make what is called a Happy Ending" for *Clarissa*.

35. *An Analytical Inquiry into the Principles of Taste* (2nd ed.; 1805), p. 289.

36. W. B. Yeats, *The Cutting of an Agate* (New York, 1912), pp. 199-200.

37. The best and most thorough analysis of Sir Charles in the light of his social background is that of Phyllis Patricia Smith, "The Eighteenth-Century Gentleman: Contributing Themes and Their Realization in Sir Charles Grandison," MS Dissertation in Radcliffe College Library.

38. See Brian W. Downs, *Richardson* (1928), p. 191.

39. *Tom Jones*, VI, iii.

40. *Tatler*, No. 182. For the probable connection of this passage with early plans for *The Conscious Lovers*, see John Loftis, "The Genesis of Steele's 'The Conscious

Lovers,' " *Essays Dedicated to Lily B. Campbell* (Berkeley and Los Angeles, 1950), pp. 176-77.

41. James Foster, *Sermons* (3rd ed.; 1736), I, 29-31.

42. British Museum Addit. MS. 35,397, f. 299ᵛ. Dr. Thomas Birch to Philip Yorke, later Lord Hardwicke, September 29, 1750.

43. Maggs Brothers, Catalogue 411 (1921), No. 2215.

44. John Scott, "An Essay on Painting," in Robert Anderson, *The Works of the British Poets*, XI, 767.

45. *Boston Public Library Quarterly*, IV (1952), 219-20. To Lady Echlin, May 17, 1754. The "beloved Sister" is Lady Bradshaigh, one of Richardson's most important correspondents.

46. *Spectator*, No. 588.

47. To Miss Westcomb, no date. From the original in the Huntington Library. See *Correspondence*, ed. Mrs. Barbauld (1804), III, 252-53.

48. VI, 255-56. For Meredith's interest in *Grandison*, see the original version of *The Ordeal of Richard Feverel*, and consider the significant parallels between *Grandison* and *The Egoist*. For a comparison of the feminism of the two writers, see an anonymous article, "Samuel Richardson and George Meredith," *Macmillan's Magazine*, LXXXV (1902), 356-61.

49. S. B. Liljegren, *The English Sources of Goethe's Gretchen Tragedy* (Lund, 1937).

50. *Each Sex in Their Humour* (1764), II, 145-46.

51. Dedication to *The Daughter: or the History of Miss Emilia Royston, and Miss Harriet Ayres* (Dublin, 1775), a revision of *Letters between Emilia and Harriet* (1762).

52. *The Woman of Honour* (1768), I, 139-40.

53. *The School for Wives* (1763), pp. 35-36.

54. E. A. Baker, *The History of the English Novel*, IV (1930), pp. 18-19.

III

1. In addition to the extensive discussions in W. L. Cross, *The History of Henry Fielding* (New Haven, 1918), and F. Homes Dudden, *Henry Fielding* (Oxford, 1952), see W. H. Rogers, "Fielding's Early Aesthetic and Technique," *SP*, XL (1943), 529-51; L. P. Goggin, "Development of Techniques in Fielding's Comedies," *PMLA*, LXVII (1952), 769-81. For supplementary references on Fielding as a dramatist, see Sherburn's note in *A Literary History of England*, ed. A. C. Baugh (New York, 1948), p. 889.

2. For the question of authorship, and the direction and method of the satire, see Cross, I, 303-9; McKillop, *Richardson*, pp. 73-74; Charles B. Woods, "Fielding and the Authorship of *Shamela*," *PQ*, XXV (1946), 248-72; Dudden, I, 319-26; *Shamela*, ed. S. W. Baker, Jr., (Berkeley and Los Angeles, 1953), Introduction.

3. *Champion*, June 10, 1740, repr. 1743, II, 317-18.

4. *Universal Spectator*, March 16, 1734, repr. *London Magazine*, III (1734), 122-23.

5. See Edward N. Hooker's valuable article, "Humour in the Age of Pope," *HLQ*, XI (1948), 361-85. For a somewhat similar distinction between humor as basic temperament, and pseudo-humors of affectation and eccentricity, see Henry L. Snuggs, "The Comic Humours: A New Interpretation," *PMLA*, LXII (1947), 114-22.

6. See William Empson, *The Structure of Complex Words* (1951), pp. 85-86.

7. [Corbyn Morris], *An Essay towards Fixing the True Standards of Wit, Humour, Raillery, Satire, and Ridicule* (1744), repr. Augustan Reprint Society (1947), p. 15. See also Stuart M. Tave, "Corbyn Morris: Falstaff, Humor, and Comic Theory in the Eighteenth Century," *MP*, L (1952), 102-15.

8. Morris, p. 24.

9. *Free Briton*, October 4, 1733, repr. *London Magazine*, II (1733), 494.

10. See Tave, as cited in note 7 above, pp. 105-7.

11. *Covent-Garden Journal*, No. 55, July 18, 1752.

12. Lionel Trilling, "Manners, Morals, and the Novel," in *The Liberal Imagination* (New York, 1950), p. 211.

13. Hugh Dalziel Duncan, *Language and Literature in Society* (Chicago, 1953), p. 53.

14. *The Clergy-Man's Vade Mecum* (2nd ed.; 1707), pp. 163-64. This passage covers exactly the same ground as the discussion between Lady Booby and Parson Adams in IV, ii-iv, except that Joseph could claim a settlement in the parish.

15. Wayne C. Booth, "The Self-Conscious Narrator in Comic Fiction before Tristram

Shandy," *PMLA*, LXVII (1952), 163-85, especially 175 ff. For a less favorable view of the intrusive narrator, see Irma Z. Sherwood, "The Novelists as Commentators," in *The Age of Johnson* (New Haven), 1949), pp. 113-25.

16. See the important essays by Maynard Mack, "The Muse of Satire," and Ricardo Quintana, "Situational Satire: A Commentary on the Method of Swift," reprinted respectively from the *Yale Review* and the *University of Toronto Quarterly* in the *Case Memorial Volume, Studies in the Literature of the Augustan Age* (Ann Arbor, 1952), pp. 219-31, 259-65. See also John M. Bullitt, *Jonathan Swift and the Anatomy of Satire* (Cambridge, U.S.A., 1953), pp. 57-60, and W. B. Ewald, *The Masks of Jonathan Swift* (Oxford, 1954).

17. Byron, *Letters*, ed. Prothero, V, 592, quoted by Dudden, II, 692.

18. The significance of this passage is well brought out by Leo M. Hughes, "The Influence of Fielding's Milieu upon His Humor," *University of Texas Studies in English 1944* (Austin, 1945), p. 284.

19. Carl Moritz, *Travels in England . . . in 1782*, quoted by Rosamond Bayne-Powell. *Eighteenth-Century London Life* (1937), p. 134.

20. The point is well made by Mark Spilka, "Comic Resolution in Fielding's 'Joseph Andrews'," *College English*, XV (1953), 11-19, though I do not accept all his interpretations in detail.

21. *Museum*, III (1747), 7.

22. For a detailed study of the revisions, see Aurélien Digeon, *Le texte des romans de Fielding* (Paris, 1923), pp. 9-58.

23. See W. R. Irwin, *The Making of 'Jonathan Wild'* (New York, 1941).

24. *Clarissa*, IV, 137-38, 276.

25. Ronald S. Crane, "The Plot of *Tom Jones*," *Journal of General Education*, IV (1950), 112-30, reprinted as "The Concept of Plot and the Plot of *Tom Jones*" in *Critics and Criticism: Ancient and Modern* (Chicago, 1952), pp. 616-47.

26. See the list of mock-heroic passages, not quite complete, in Dudden, p. 697 n.

27. For other examples of this device, varying somewhat in detail, see XIII, ii, iv, vii, ix; XIV, ii; XVI, ii, iii; XVIII, ii, x, xi.

28. Preface to *The Princess Casamassima*.

29. *Critics and Criticism: Ancient and Modern*, p. 637.

30. Richard and Elizabeth Griffith, *A Series of Genuine Letters between Henry and Frances*, quoted by E. F. Carritt, *A Calendar of British Taste* (1948), p. 258.

31. A. O. Aldridge, "Shaftesbury and the Deist Manifesto," *Transactions of the American Philosophical Society*, XLI, Part 2 (1951), 303.

32. *Purgatorio*, XVI, 73-75, 103-5, trans. Thomas G. Bergin (Crofts Classics), p. 52.

33. *David Simple* (1744), I, 156.

34. See especially F. T. Blanchard, *Fielding the Novelist* (New Haven, 1925). Dudden concurs with Cross and Blanchard—*Henry Fielding*, chap. xxv.

35. Joseph Spence to William B. Massingberd, printed by Austin Wright, *Joseph Spence* (Chicago, 1950), p. 232. This letter supplements and explains some of the details of publication given by Cross, II, 117. We can now understand why the bookseller Andrew Millar, after announcing publication for February 10, did not actually advertise the book as published until February 28.

36. *Letters of William Shenstone*, ed. Duncan Mallam (Minneapolis, 1939), p. 140. To Lady Luxborough, April 7, 1749.

37. [John Heriot], *The Half-Pay Officer* (1788), I, vi-vii.

38. "A Catalogue of the Most Celebrated Writers of the Present Age," in *Letters Concerning the Present State of England* (1772), pp. 357-58.

39. *Have at You All: Or, The Drury-Lane Journal*, No. 5, February 13, 1752. For the protests against the *chroniques scandaleuses*, see McKillop, *Richardson*, pp. 178-80.

40. *Magazine of Magazines*, I (April, 1751), 289.

41. *A Journey through the Head of a Modern Poet, Being the Substance of a Dream, Occasioned by Reading the Sixth Book of Virgil* (1750), p. 19. Fielding's predecessor at Bow Street was Sir Thomas de Veil.

42. Cross, II, 304-5.

43. *The Cry* (1754), III, 124. Quoted in this connection by Dudden, p. 883 n.

44. Sotheby & Co., Sale Catalogue, July 31-August 1, 1928, p. 86.

45. See George Sherburn, "Fielding's *Amelia*: An Interpretation," *ELH*, III (1936), 1-14, especially 2-3.

46. *Works*, ed. W. E. Henley, *Miscellaneous Writings*, III (1903), 182.

47. *Clarissa*, VI, 3. *An Essay on Man*, II, 129-48, might lend itself to this interpre-

tation, though this is not Pope's final position. For a full and admirable discussion, see Maynard Mack's Introduction, Twickenham Edition, III, i (1950), xxxvi ff.
48. See above, pp. 88-89.
49. G. H. Gerould, *Patterns of English and American Fiction* (Boston, 1942), p. 90.

IV

1. The subject has been closely studied. See Louis M. Martz, "Smollett and the Expedition to Carthagena," *PMLA*, LVI (1941), 428-46; Claude E. Jones, "Smollett and the Navy," *Univ. of California Publications in English*, IX (1942), 31-75; George M. Kahrl, *Tobias Smollett: Traveler-Novelist* (Chicago, 1945), chaps. i and ii; Lewis M. Knapp, *Tobias Smollett: Doctor of Men and Manners* (Princeton, 1949), chap. ii.
2. See H. W. Troyer, *Ned Ward of Grubstreet* (Cambridge, U.S.A., 1946), pp. 141-47, 274-75. For a survey of the material see Charles N. Robinson, *The British Tar in Fact and Fiction* (1909); Harold F. Watson, *The Sailor in English Fiction and Drama, 1550-1800* (New York, 1931).
3. *Letters*, ed. Noyes (Cambridge, U.S.A., 1926), p. 80. To Richard Smith, May 8, 1763.
4. Complete text first printed by H. W. Meikle, "New Smollett Letters," *TLS*, July 24, 1943, p. 360. Letter of June 7, 1748. Love was Smollett's master at Dumbarton Grammar School
5. Transcript in the Forster Collection, Victoria and Albert Museum, 48. E. 4. James Thomson to William Cranstoun, July 20, 1725.
6. British Museum, Sloane MS. 4314, f. 47r. Andrew Millar to Thomas Birch, June 26, 1741.
7. The ironical comments on the conduct of the Carthagena campaign (chaps. xxxi, xxxiii) are exceptional.
8. Herbert Read, *Collected Essays in Literary Criticism* (1938), pp. 243-44.
9. See L. M. Ellison, "Elizabethan Drama and the Works of Smollett," *PMLA*, XLIV (1929), 842-62.
10. *Daily Advertiser*, February 20, 1749.
11. J. H. Plumb, *England in the Eighteenth Century* (Penguin Books, 1950), p. 95.
12. Kahrl, chap. iii.
13. Rufus Putney, "The Plan of *Peregrine Pickle*," *PMLA*, LX (1945), 1051-65.
14. Kahrl, pp. 44-48.
15. *TLS*, July 31, 1943, p. 372. Letter to Alexander Carlyle, October 1, 1749.
16. *Travels through France and Italy* (1766), Letter xxvii.
17. Cf. *Tom Jones*, VII, vii, xiv. Of particular interest is a passage in one of Clarissa's letters in which we see Richardson preparing a Gothic setting for the scene of her impending escape, and then belittling the superstitious fears connected with such a spot (*Clarissa*, II, 303 n.).
18. *Monthly Review*, VIII (1753), 203-14.
19. Cf. also the description of a Sunday dinner of authors, with Smollett as host, in *Humphry Clinker*, Jery's letter of June 10.
20. Laing MSS, University of Edinburgh, II, 263. Cf. *MLN*, XLII (1927), 231-35.
21. For helpful comment on these points, see Kahrl, pp. 59-60.
22. Since the letters form a single series from April 2 to November 20 of an unspecified year, references to *Humphry Clinker* can readily be identified by the writer and date of a given letter.
23. But the device of a comic version of a journey given by one member of a party of travelers is used briefly in Jolter's Journal, *Pickle*, chap. lxvi.
24. *The Adventures of Miss Beverley* (1768), I, 111-12. Cf. Jery, April 30.
25. Lewis M. Knapp, "Smollett's Self-portrait in *The Expedition of Humphry Clinker*," in *The Age of Johnson* (New Haven, 1949), p. 151.
26. *Letters*, ed. Noyes, pp. 108-9.
27. *Citizen of the World*, Letter xxvi.
28. Moncure D. Conway, *Thomas Carlyle* (New York, 1881), pp. 31-32.
29. See V. S. Pritchett, *The Living Novel* (New York, 1947), pp. 36-37.
30. Martz, *Later Career*, pp. 170-71.
31. For the whole subject, see the excellent study by Fred W. Boege, *Smollett's Reputation as a Novelist* (Princeton, 1947).
32. *David Copperfield*, chap. iv; *Uncommercial Traveller*, chap. xii.

V

1. See L. P. Curtis, *The Politicks of Laurence Sterne* (Oxford, 1929).
2. L. P. Curtis, "The First Printer of *Tristram Shandy*," *PMLA*, XLVII (1932), 777-89; J. M. Yoklavich, "Notes on the Early Editions of *Tristram Shandy*," *ibid.*, LXIII (1948), 508-19.
3. See D. W. Jefferson, "*Tristram Shandy* and the Tradition of Learned Wit." *Essays in Criticism*, I (1951), 225-48.
4. *Letters of Laurence Sterne*, ed. L. P. Curtis (Oxford, 1935), p. 77.
5. *Sermons* (1767), II, 221.
6. E. Pons, *Swift: Les années de jeunesse et le 'Conte du Tonneau'* (Strasbourg, 1925), p. 368.
7. *Sermons* (1769), III, 61.
8. IV, ix, x, xiv, xv; V, i, viii.
9. *Letters*, ed. Curtis, p. 11.
10. Introduction to *Tristram Shandy* (Macdonald Illustrated Classics), p. 30.
11. I owe the distinction to Maynard Mack's essay, "The Muse of Satire," repr. *Case Memorial Volume* (Ann Arbor, 1952), p. 228.
12. André Gide, *The Counterfeiters*, trans. Dorothy Bussy (New York, 1927), p. 173. Part II, chap. iii.
13. *Sermons* (1769), III, 268 [so misnumbered for 294]-95. Cf. Pope's *Essay on Man*, II, 19-30.
14. Cross, *The Life and Times of Laurence Sterne* (3rd ed.; 1929), p. 302.
15. *Absalom and Achitophel*, I, 544-52, echoed in *Tristram Shandy*, I, viii.
16. See above, pp. 103-4.
17. John Laird, *Philosophical Incursions into English Literature* (Cambridge, 1946), p. 85.
18. "*Fragment Inédit*," in Paul Stapfer, *Laurence Sterne* (Paris, 1870), pp. xii [so misprinted for xxii]-xxiv. This fragment is in the form of a letter to a certain Mr. Cook. Cross accepts it as genuine, and dates it about 1743. Stapfer, p. 1, refers to *Spectator*, No. 94, and to Locke's *Essay*, II, xv. See B. H. Lehman, "Of Time, Personality, and the Author," in *Studies in the Comic*, University of California Publications in English, VIII, No. 2 (1941), 233-50; W. B. C. Watkins, *Perilous Balance* (Princeton, 1939), p. 134. For the scientific background, see Marjorie Nicolson, *The Microscope and English Imagination* (Northampton, 1935), Smith College Studies in Modern Languages, XVI, No. 4; A. O. Lovejoy, *The Great Chain of Being* (Cambridge, U.S.A., 1936), pp. 236-40.
19. "The Bourbonnois."
20. *Characteristicks* (1737), I, 115-16. "An Essay on the Freedom of Wit and Humour," III, iii.
21. See John M. Bullitt, *Jonathan Swift and the Anatomy of Satire* (Cambridge. U.S.A., 1953), especially chap. iv, "The Mechanical Operation of the Spirit."
22. *Remembrance of Things Past: Swann's Way*, trans. C. K. Scott-Moncrieff (New York, 1934), I, 4.
23. *Tristram Shandy*, ed. James A. Work (New York, 1940), p. lx.
24. Emerson, "The Comic," in *Letters and Social Aims* (Boston, 1893), p. 151. I owe this reference to Bullitt, *Jonathan Swift and the Anatomy of Satire*, p. 104.
25. T. S. Eliot, "*Ulysses*, Order, and Myth," repr. *Critiques and Essays on Modern Fiction*, ed. J. W. Aldridge (New York, 1952), p. 426.
26. *Shandy*, ed. Work, pp. xlvi-li. See also T. Baird, "The Time Scheme of *Tristram Shandy* and a Source," *PMLA*, LI (1936), 803-20; Wayne Booth, "Did Sterne Complete *Tristram Shandy?*", *MP*, XLVIII (1951), 172-83.
27. See Robert Humphrey, *Stream of Consciousness in the Modern Novel* (Berkeley and Los Angeles, 1954), pp. 86 ff.
28. *Letters*, ed. Curtis, p. 143. September 21, 1761.
29. Introductory Epistle to *The Fortunes of Nigel*.
30. *Letters*, ed. Curtis, p. 231. Letter of November 11, 1764.
31. *Shandy*, ed. Work, p. xlvi.
32. Cross, *Life and Times* (3rd ed.; 1929), p. 354.
33. *Letters*, p. 284.
34. *MP*, XLVIII (1951), 172-83.
35. Geoffrey Tillotson, *Essays in Criticism and Research* (Cambridge, 1942), pp. 108-9.

36. *Life and Times* (3rd ed.; 1929), p. 460.

37. Rufus Putney, "The Evolution of *A Sentimental Journey*," *PQ*, XIX (1940), 349-69.

38. Rufus Putney, "Laurence Sterne: Apostle of Laughter," in *The Age of Johnson* (New Haven, 1949), pp. 159-70. A somewhat similar view of Sterne has been presented less judiciously by E. N. Dilworth, *The Unsentimental Journey of Laurence Sterne* (New York, 1948).

39. *Sermons* (1767), I, 60.

40. See Gertrude Joyce Hallamore, *Das Bild Laurence Sternes in Deutschland* (Berlin, 1936), especially pp. 65-66.

Index

Hazlitt, William, 97
Heriot, John, *The Half-Pay Officer*, 135-36
Highland Rogue, The, 40
Hill, Aaron, 52, 54, 56
Hill, John, *Secretary's Guide*, 53
Hoadly, Benjamin, 2
Hogarth, William, 32-33, 51, 55, 101-2, 135, 151, 154, 169
Hooker, E. N., 103
Horace, 78, 119, 151
Hornbeak, Katherine G., 53
Hughes, Edward W., *North Country Life*, 55
Hume, David, 209, 210
Humors, theory of, 103-5, 152-55, 175-76, 183-84, 194-95, 211
Hunter, Dr. John, 175
Hurd, Richard, on *Pamela*, 63
Hutcheson, Francis, 88

Impersonation as a literary device, 9-10, 16, 19, 108

James, Henry, on *Tom Jones*, 127
Johnson Samuel, 80, 118, 183, on *Clarissa*, 73, 77
Jonson, Ben, 104, 152-53, 157-58, 161
Journey through the Head of a Modern Poet, 137
Joyce, James, 102, 179; compared with Sterne, 183, 204, 208-9, 210, 211
Juvenal, 151

Kafka, Franz, 183
Kahrl, George, 149, 157, 160
Ker, W. P., 23
Kipling, Rudyard, 25
Knapp, Lewis M., 166, 174
Knight, Richard Payne, 80
Knox, Robert, 27

Lamb, Charles, 26, 38
Lamotte, Charles, *Essay upon Poetry and Painting*, 102
Le Sage, Alain René, 46, 150-51, 164
Letter to the Society of Booksellers, 44
Letter-writing, manuals of, 53; as educational exercise, 55, 62
Letters of a Grandmother, 56
Lillo, George, *The London Merchant*, 52-53
Locke, John, 44; Sterne's relation to, 57, 193-94, 195-96, 209-10
Lyttelton, George Lord, 129, 162

Mackenzie, Henry, 135; *The Man of Feeling*, 215, 217
Mackercher, Daniel, 162
Magazine of Magazines, 137
Mandeville, Bernard, 4-5
Marivaux, Pierre, 46, 99; *Paysan Parvenu*, 101; *Pharsamon*, 108, 110
Martz, Louis, 166, 167, 172, 179
Mather, Increase, *Remarkable Providences*, 12
Mendilov, A. A., 31

Merchants, social standing of, 3, 66
Meredith, George, in relation to *Grandison*, 91-92
Methodism, in *Humphry Clinker*, 177
Middleton, Conyers, 100
Millar, Andrew, 137
Milton, John, 92
Molière, 57, 99, 177, 208
Montagu, Mary Wortley, 138
Monthly Review, 166
Moore, Dr. John, 167-68
Moore, John Robert, 8, 9
Moritz, Carl, 113
Morris, Corbyn, 103-4
Museum, 114

Original London Post, 25

Parsons, Coleman O., 10-11
Plumb, J. H., 156
Pons, Émile, 186
Pope, Alexander, 102, 162
Powys, John Cowper, 190
Prévost, Abbé, 46
Prior, Matthew, 131
Prison scenes in fiction, 29, 142, 154-55, 162
Proust, Marcel, 183, 203
Putney, Rufus, 160, 216

Quin, James, 162

Rabelais, François, 188
Read, Herbert, 153
Read's Journal, 9
Recognition, as a plot device, 105, 109, 111
Richardson, Samuel, autobiographical letter, 47-51; parents, 47; early interest in letters and stories, 48-49; private correspondence, 48, 50-51; career as printer, 47-48, 52; early writings, 50, 52-53; relation to Defoe, 13-15, 37, 41, 43, 52, 53, 62; use of letter-form, 51, 53-55, 84-85, 90, 92; narrative method, 58-60; role of editor in his novels, 42; use of detail, 59-60; use of gesture, 85, 187; ideals of benevolence and natural goodness, 88-89; relation to sentimentalism, 88, 93-94; characters considered as people in real life, 92-93; influence and reputation, 92-97

works: *Æsop's Fables*, 50; *Apprentice's Vade Mecum*, 52-53; *Clarissa*, 64-81; comparison with *Pamela*, 64, 67; social background, 64-67, 69; the Harlowe family, 64-65, 67-68; dramatic conflict in, 67-68; as tragedy, 71, 74-75, 80-81; elements from comedy, 71-72; development of plot, 70, 72-74, 76-77, 119; love theme in, 75-76; epistolary technique in, 51, 61, 68-69, 70, 77; character of the heroine, 67-68, 69-70, 73, 79, 94; Lovelace, 65, 67-68, 71-74, 75, 76, 79, 94, 115, 128, 140-141; Anna Howe, 68, 70-72; Belford, 68, 76; Solmes, 66, 73; contemporary reception of, 94; other references, 14, 42, 218; *Letters Written to and for*